Student Solutions Manual
for Keller and Warrack's

Statistics

for Management and Economics

Sixth Edition

Gerald Keller
Wilfrid Laurier University

THOMSON
★
BROOKS/COLE

Australia • Canada • Mexico • Singapore • Spain • United Kingdom • United States

0-534-39191-5

Printed by Webcom

For more information about our products, contact us at:
Thomson Learning Academic Resource Center
1-800-423-0563

For permission to use material from this text, contact us by:
Phone: 1-800-730-2214
Fax: 1-800-731-2215
Web: www.thomsonrights.com

Asia
Thomson Learning
5 Shenton Way #01-01
UIC Building
Singapore 068808

Australia
Nelson Thomson Learning
102 Dodds Street
South Street
South Melbourne, Victoria 3205
Australia

Canada
Nelson Thomson Learning
1120 Birchmount Road
Toronto, Ontario M1K 5G4
Canada

Europe/Middle East/South Africa
Thomson Learning
High Holborn House
50-51 Bedford Row
London WC1R 4LR
United Kingdom

Latin America
Thomson Learning
Seneca, 53
Colonia Polanco
11560 Mexico D.F.
Mexico

Spain
Paraninfo Thomson Learning
Calle/Magallanes, 25
28015 Madrid, Spain

TABLE OF CONTENTS

How we produced the Solutions

How We Produced the Solutions

Chapter 2

Excel was employed to draw the histograms, bar charts, pie charts, line charts, and scatter diagrams.

Chapter 4

Excel was used to draw box plots and compute the descriptive statistics for exercises with data sets.

Chapters 6 through 9

Probabilities were computed manually. Probability trees were used where possible.

Chapters 10 through 20

Calculations for exercises that provided statistics either in the exercise itself or in Appendix A were completed manually. Confidence interval estimates used critical values obtained from the tables in Appendix B. In some cases we were required to use approximations. As a consequence some confidence interval estimates will differ slightly from those produced by computer. In tests of hypothesis where the sampling distribution is normal, p-values were computed manually using Table 3. Excel was employed to calculate the p-value for all other tests.

Appendix A does not contain statistics for the chapter review exercises in Chapters 12 and 13 and the exercises in the two review chapters (14 and 24). Excel produced these solutions.

Chapters 13, 14, and 24

We employed the F-test of two variances at the 5% significance level to decide which one of the equal-variances or unequal-variances t-test and estimator of the difference between two means to use to solve the problem. Additionally, for exercises that compare two populations and are accompanied by data files, our answers were derived by defining the sample from population 1 as the data stored in the first column (often column A in Excel and column 1 in Minitab). The data stored in the second column represent the sample from population 2. Paired differences were defined as the difference between the variable in the first column minus the variable in the second column.

Chapters 17 and 24

In the exercises whose datasets contained interval data we used a nonparametric technique after examining the relevant histograms and subjectively judging the variable to be "extremely nonnormal."

Chapters 19 and 20

Excel produced all the solutions to these exercises.

Chapter 21

Most solutions were produced manually. Excel solved the more time-consuming exercises.

Chapter 22

All control charts were produced by Excel.

Chapter 23

Solutions to these exercises were completed manually.

All answers have been-double-checked for accuracy. However, we cannot be absolutely certain that there are no errors. Students should not automatically assume that solutions that don't match ours are wrong. When and if we discover mistakes we will post corrected answers on our

web page. (See page 16 in the textbook for the address.) If you find any errors, please email the author (address on web page). We will be happy to acknowledge you with the discovery.

Chapter 1

1.2 Descriptive statistics summarizes a set of data. Inferential statistics makes inferences about populations from samples.

1.4a The complete production run

b 1000 chips

c Proportion of the production run that is defective

d Proportion of sample chips that are defective (7.5%)

e Parameter

f Statistic

g Because the sample proportion is less than 10%, we can conclude that the claim is true.

1.6a Flip the coin 100 times and count the number of heads and tails

b Outcomes of flips

c Outcomes of the 100 flips

d Proportion of heads

e Proportion of heads in the 100 flips

1.8a The population consists of the fuel mileage of all the taxis in the fleet.

b The owner would like to know the mean mileage.

c The sample consists of the 50 observations.

d The statistic the owner would use is the mean of the 50 observations.

e The statistic would be used to estimate the parameter from which the owner can calculate total costs. We computed the sample mean to be 19.8 mpg.

Chapter 2

2.2 a Interval

b Interval

c Nominal

d Ordinal

2.4 a Nominal

b Interval

c Nominal

d Interval

e Ordinal

2.6 a Interval

b Interval

c Nominal

d Ordinal

e Interval

2.8 a Interval

b Ordinal

c Nominal

d Ordinal

2.10 a Ordinal

b Ordinal

c Ordinal

2.12 10 or 11

2.14 a 7 to 9

b Interval width $\approx \dfrac{6.1 - 5.2}{7} = .13$ (rounded to .15); upper limits: 5.25, 5.40, 5.55, 5.70, 5.85, 6.00, 6.15

2.16 a

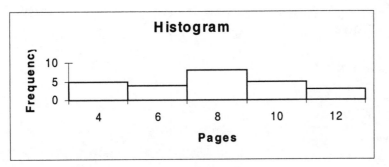

b

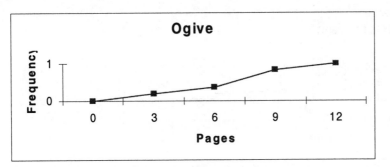

2.18

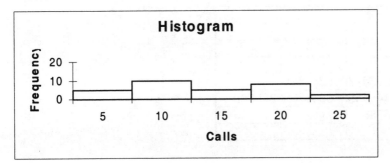

2.20 a

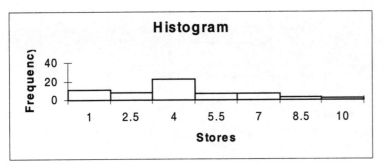

b

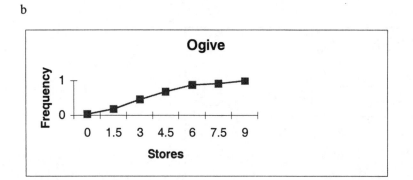

2.22 a

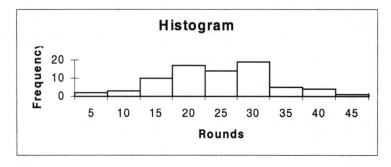

b

Stem & Leaf Display				
Stems	**Leaves**			
0	->359			
1	->0023334445556677888888899			
2	->000012233344444555566667888889999			
3	->00000112556668			
4	->2			

c

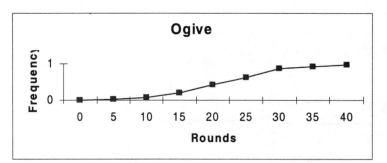

2.24 a The number of bins should be 7, 8, or 9. We chose 7.

b

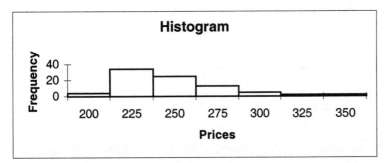

c The histogram is positively skewed, unimodal, and not bell-shaped.

d We learn that most prices lie between 200 and 275 thousand dollars with a small number of houses selling for more than $275,000.

2.26 a The histogram should contain 9 or 10 bins. We chose 10.

b

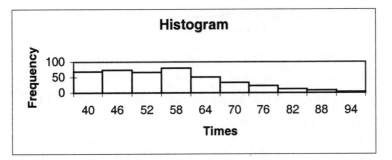

c The histogram is positively skewed.

d There is more than one modal class.

e The histogram is not bell-shaped.

2.28

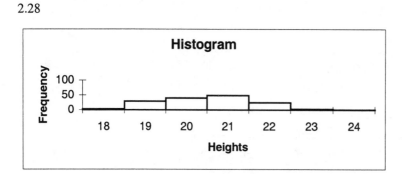

The histogram is unimodal, bell-shaped and roughly symmetric. Most of the heights lie between 18 and 23 inches.

2.30

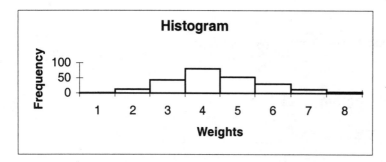

The histogram is unimodal, symmetric and bell-shaped. Most tomatoes weigh between 2 and 7 ounces with a small fraction weighing less than 2 ounces or more than 7 ounces.

2.32

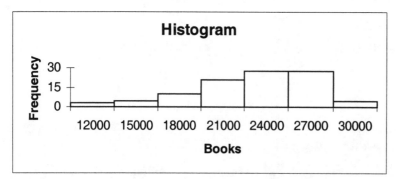

The histogram of the number of books shipped daily is negatively skewed, It appears that there is a maximum number that the company can ship.

2.34 a

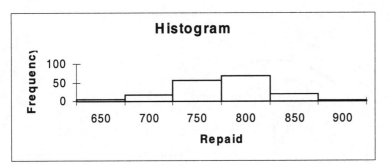

b

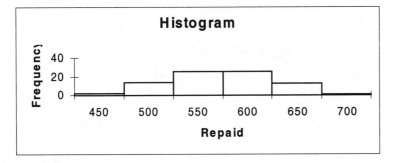

d This scorecard is a much better predictor.

2.36 a

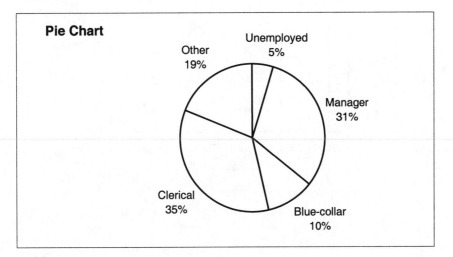

2.38

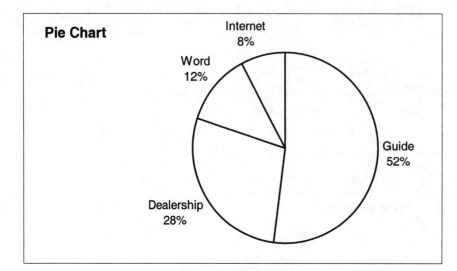

2.40

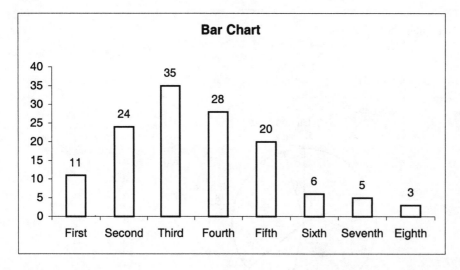

2.42a A bar chart is suitable for these results. A pie chart is incorrect.

b

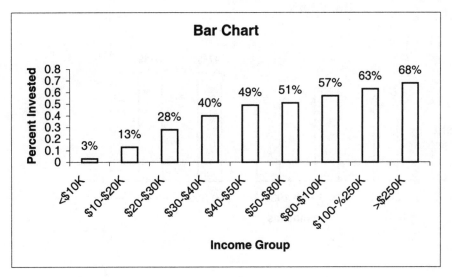

2.44

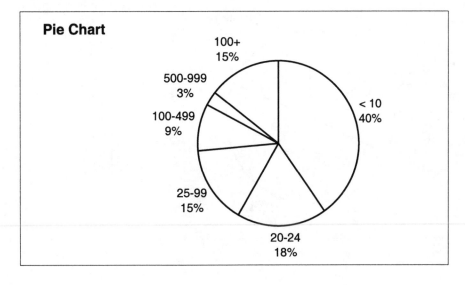

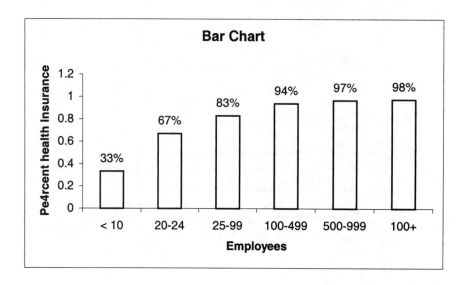

2.46

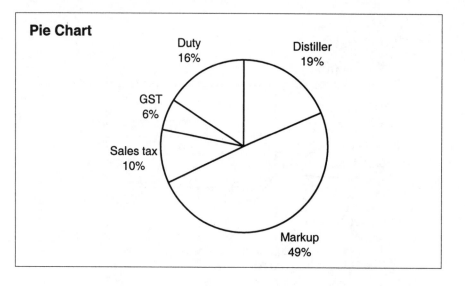

2.48

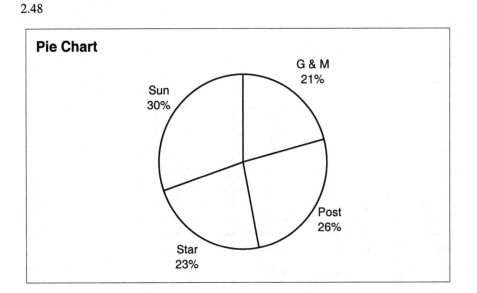

The four newspapers each have a market share of subway riders of approximately 25%.

2.50

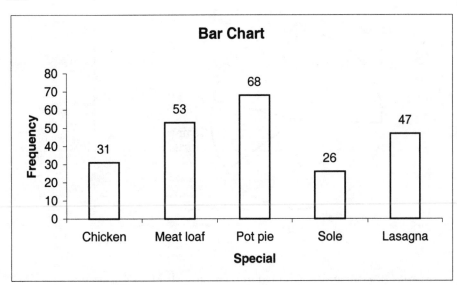

The two most popular specials are turkey pot pie and meat loaf.

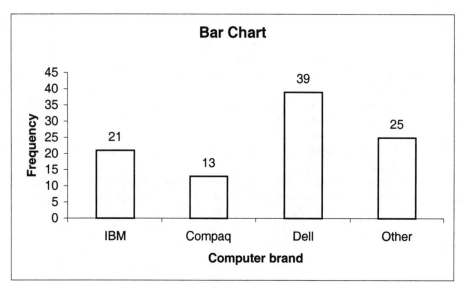

b

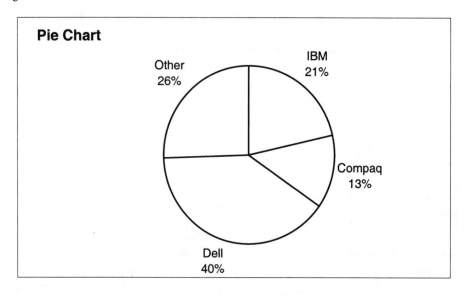

c Dell is most popular with 40% proportion, followed by other, 26%, IBM, 21% and Compaq, 13%.

2.54

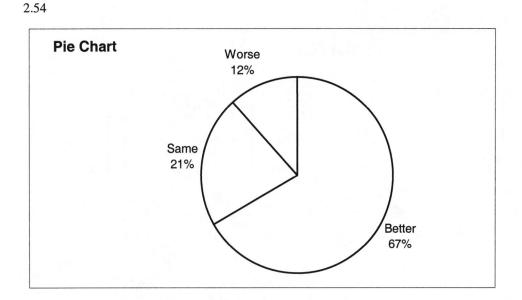

67% said the economy would get better, 21% said the same, and the rest stated that the economy would worsen.

2.56 Males

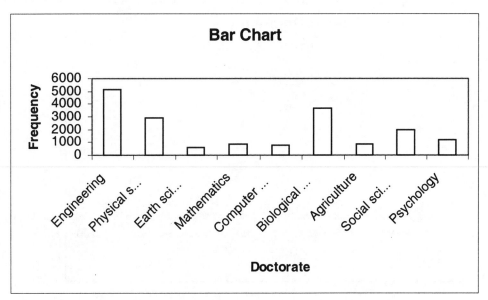

Females

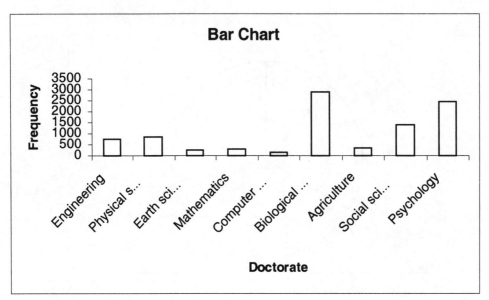

The two bar charts are somewhat similar.

2.58

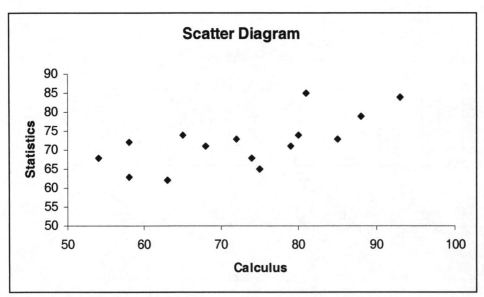

There is a moderately strong positive relationship between calculus and statistics marks.

2.60

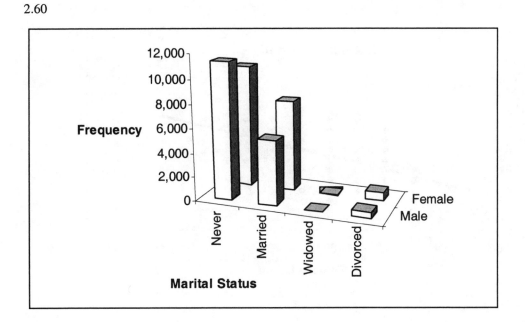

Gender and marital status are unrelated.

2.62 a

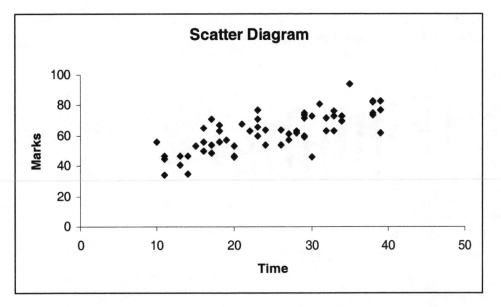

b There is a strong positive linear relationship between time spent studying and marks.

2.64a

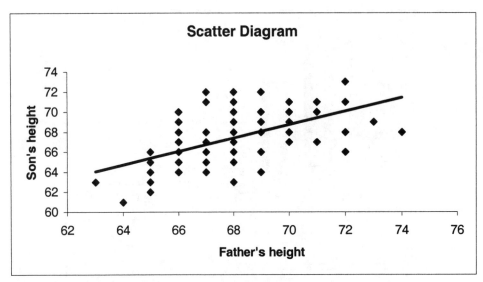

b The direction is positive.

c There does appear to be a linear relationship.

2.66a

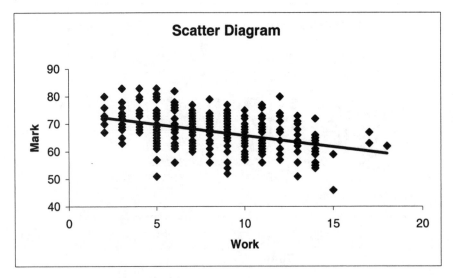

b There is apparently a weak negative linear relationship.

2.68

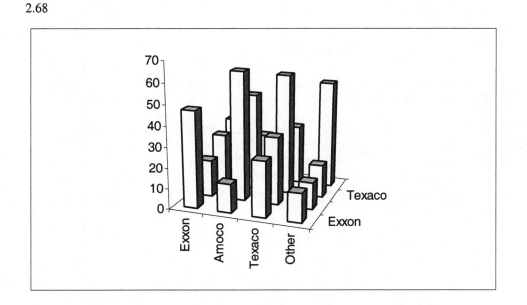

There is a relationship between the last two purchases. There is some brand loyalty.

2.70a

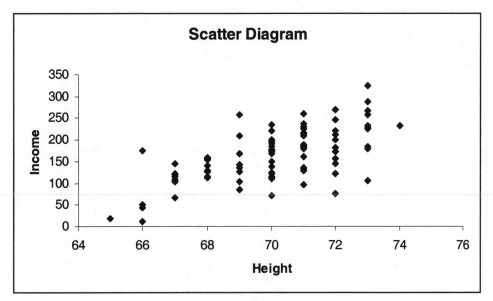

b There is a moderately strong linear relationship between the two variables. Taller MBA graduates earn more on average than shorter ones.

2.72

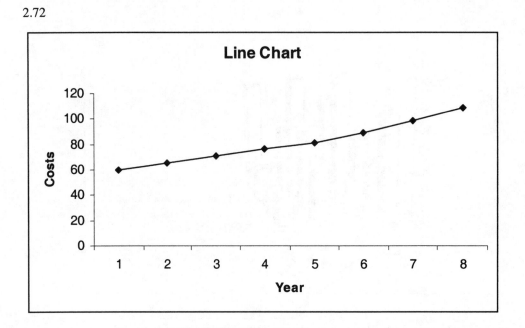

2.74

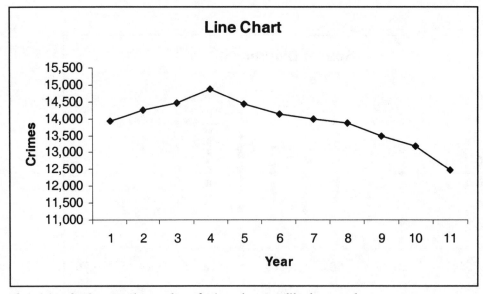

After rising for 3 years, the number of crimes has steadily decreased.

2.76

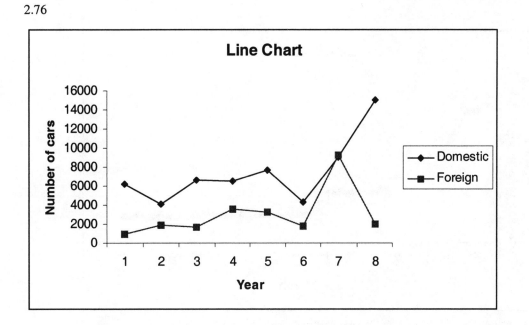

The number of recalls of domestic cars was increasing whereas the number of recalls of foreign cars remains flat.

2.78a

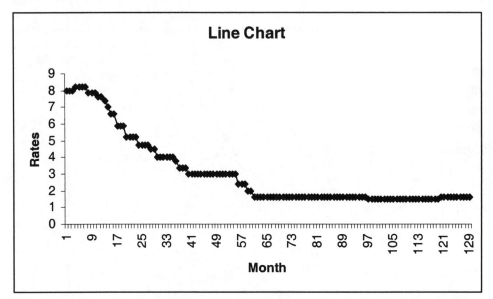

b There was a large decrease over the first half of the period, but has leveled since.

2.80a

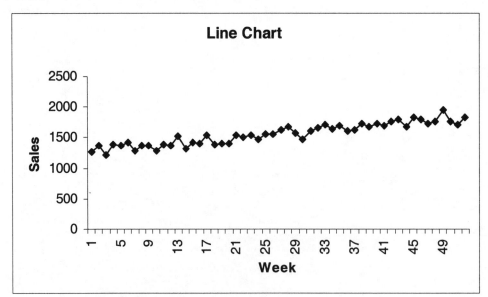

b There has been a gradual weekly increase in sales.

2.82

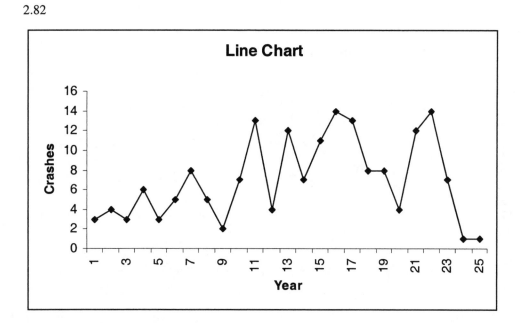

After an erratic increase over the first 20 years the number has fallen in the past 4 years.

2.84

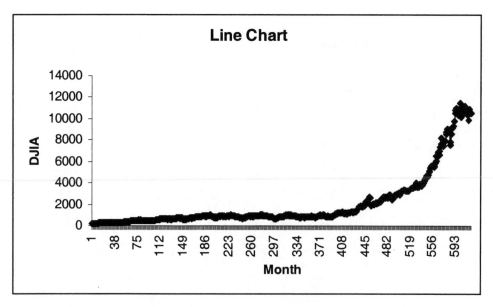

The trend until month 408 was slow but steady. Since then the index has grown exponentially.

2.86

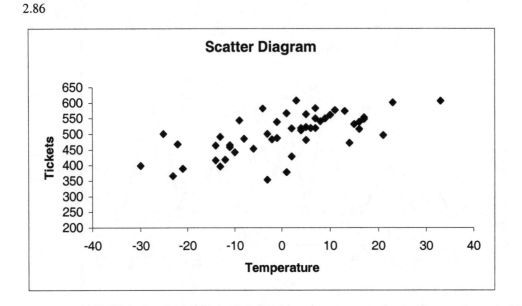

There is a moderately strong positive linear relationship between temperature and the number of tickets.

2.88

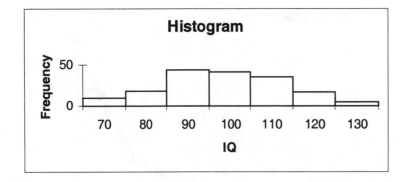

Most of the IQs are distributed between 70 and 120. The center of the distribution is about 90.

2.90

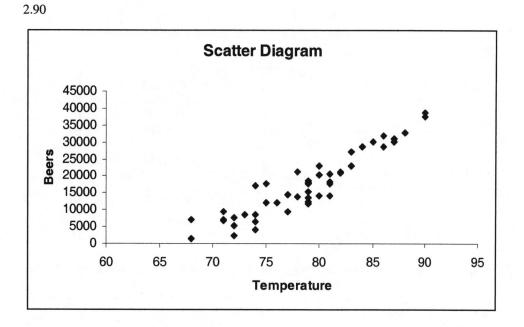

There is a strong positive linear relationship between temperature and the number of beers sold.

2.92

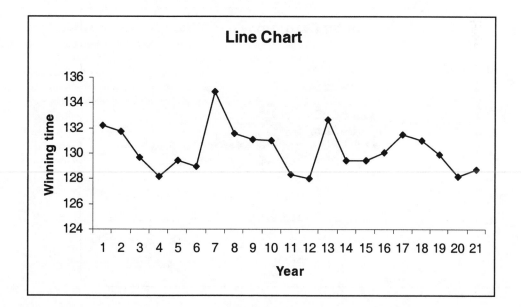

Although there are year-to-year fluctuations the winning time appears to be constant.

2.94

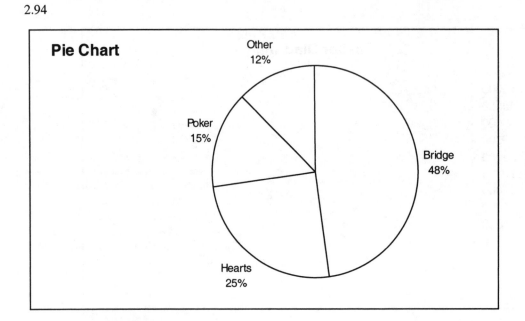

Most students play bridge.

2.96

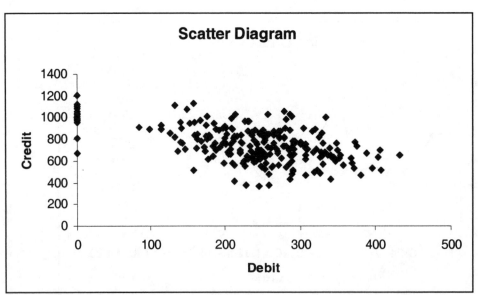

There is a moderately strong negative linear relationship.

2.98

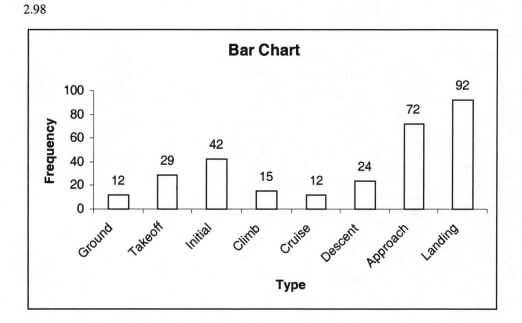

Approach and landing appear to be the most common.

2.100

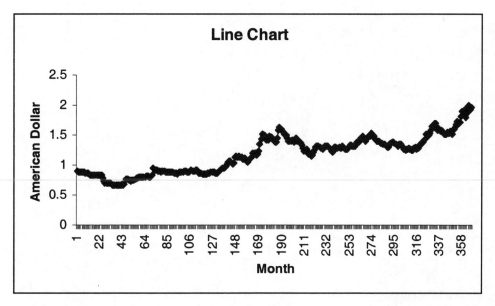

The value of the American dollar has risen over the years.

2.102

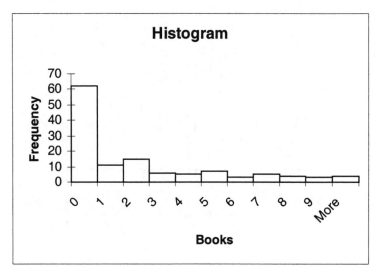

Most students borrowed no books.

2.104

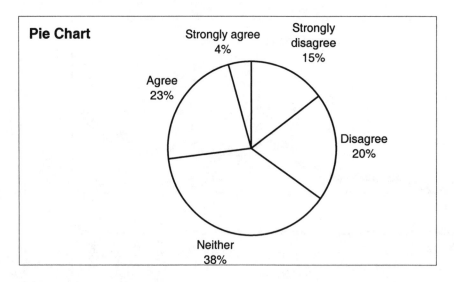

Most students would not agree.

2.106

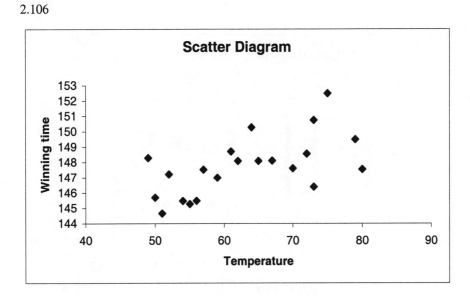

There is a moderately strong positive linear relationship between temperature and winning time.

2.108a

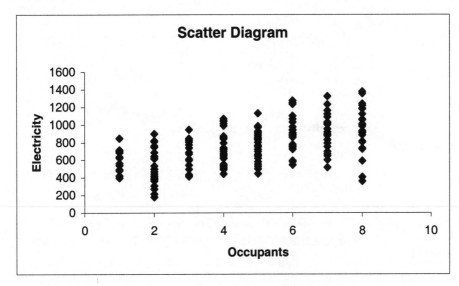

b There is moderately strong positive linear relationship between the number of occupants and electricity use.

2.110

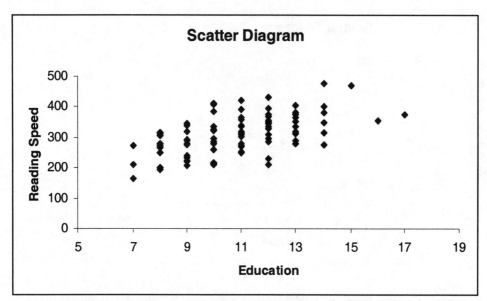

There is a moderately strong linear relationship between years of education and reading speed.

2.112

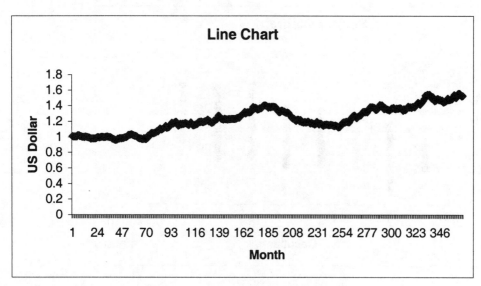

The US dollar has steadily increased in value compared to the Canadian dollar.

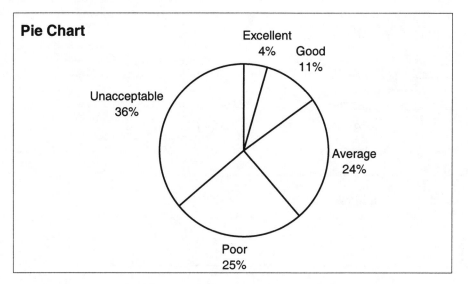

The overall impression is poor.

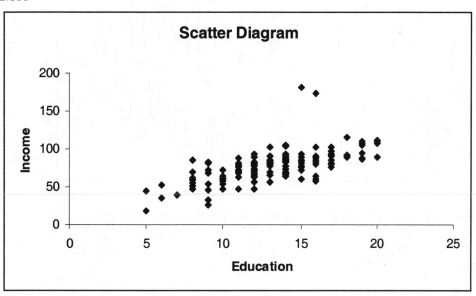

There is a moderately strong positive linear relationship between education and income.

2.118

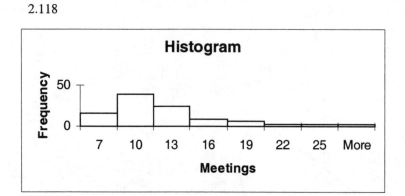

Most directors attended less than 13 meetings.

2.120

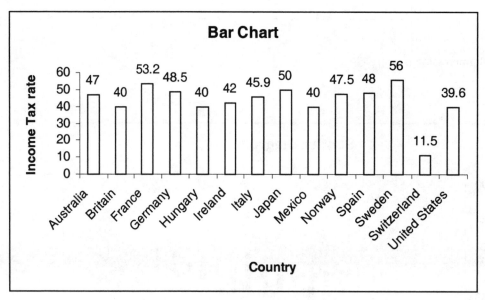

All countries, except Switzerland set their highest income tax rate at about 40% or higher.

Chapter 3

3.2 Grade D, at best. Because the chart is cluttered and not organized for clarity, the reader cannot quickly grasp the information being conveyed. The pictures of the workers add nothing of value.

3.4 Interest rates were increased throughout 1994, following a sharp increase in GDP growth at the end of 1993. The inflation rate remained fairly stable throughout 1994, providing at least some justification for the increase in interest rates.

3.6 This graph should receive at least a grade of B. This graph allows the reader to easily compare the trends in the employment growth rates for the four different education groups. During the early 1990's, growth in employment increased significantly for the most educated group, but declined sharply for the least educated group.

3.8

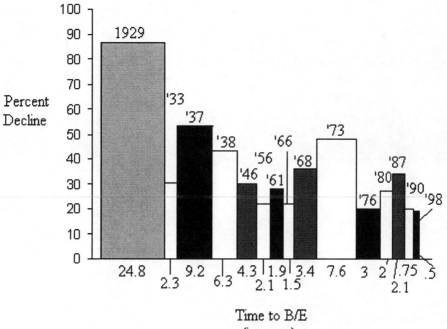

3.10 To make the comparison clear we cg=hanged the units of income to tens of thousands.

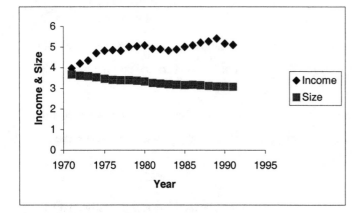

Another way to distort the graphs is to omit the data for years 1990 and 1992.

3.12a

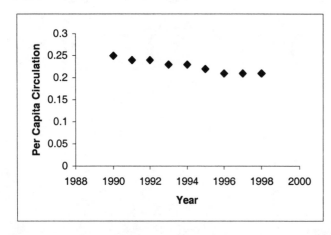

b

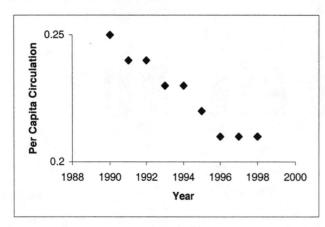

Chapter 4

4.2 a $\bar{x} = \dfrac{\sum x_i}{n} = \dfrac{5+7+0+3+15+6+5+9+3+8+10+5+2+0+12}{15} = \dfrac{90}{15} = 6.0$

Ordered data: 0, 0, 2, 3, 3, 5, 5, 5, 6, 7, 8, 9, 10, 12, 15; Median = 5

Mode = 5

b The mean number of sick days is 6, the median is 5, and the most frequent number of sick days is 5.

4.4 a $\bar{x} = \dfrac{\sum x_i}{n} = \dfrac{33+29+45+60+42+19+52+38+36}{9} = \dfrac{354}{9} = 39.3$

Ordered data: 19, 29, 33, 36, 38, 42, 45, 52, 60; Median = 38

Mode: all

b The mean amount of time is 39.3 minutes. Half the group took less than 38 minutes.

4.6 $R_g = \sqrt[3]{(1+R_1)(1+R_2)(1+R_3)} - 1 = \sqrt[3]{(1+.25)(1-.10)(1+.50)} - 1 = .19$

4.8 a $\bar{x} = \dfrac{\sum x_i}{n} = \dfrac{.10+.22+.06-.05+.20}{5} = \dfrac{.53}{5} = .106$

Ordered data: -.05, .06, .10, .20, .22; Median = .10

b $R_g = \sqrt[5]{(1+R_1)(1+R_2)(1+R_3)(1+R_4)(1+R_5)} - 1 = \sqrt[5]{(1+.10)(1+.22)(1+.06)(1-.05)(1+.20)} - 1 = $

.102

c The geometric mean

4.10 a Year 1 rate of return = $\dfrac{1200-1000}{1000} = .20$

Year 2 rate of return = $\dfrac{1200-1200}{1200} = 0$

Year 3 rate of return = $\dfrac{1500-1200}{1200} = .25$

Year 4 rate of return = $\dfrac{2000-1500}{1500} = .33$

b $\bar{x} = \dfrac{\sum x_i}{n} = \dfrac{.20 + 0 + .25 + .33}{4} = \dfrac{.78}{4} = .195$

Ordered data: 0, .20, .25, .33; Median = .225

c $R_g = \sqrt[4]{(1 + R_1)(1 + R_2)(1 + R_3)(1 + R_4)} - 1 = \sqrt[4]{(1 + .20)(1 + 0)(1 + .25)(1 + .33)} - 1 = .188$

d The geometric mean is because $1000(1.188)^4 = 2000$

4.12 a $\bar{x} = 24{,}329$; median = 24,461

b The mean starting salary is $24,329. Half the sample earned less than $24,461.

4.14a $\bar{x} = 152.02$; median = 158

b The mean expenditure is $152.02 and half the sample spent less than $158

4.16a $\bar{x} = 30.53$; median = 31; mode = 32

b The mean training time is 30.53. Half the sample trained for less than 31 hours.

4.18 $\bar{x} = 472.35$; median = 472.5

b The mean expenditure is $472.35. Half the sample spent less than $472.50

4.20 $\bar{x} = \dfrac{\sum x_i}{n} = \dfrac{4 + 5 + 3 + 6 + 5 + 6 + 5 + 6}{8} = \dfrac{40}{8} = 5$

$s^2 = \dfrac{\sum (x_i - \bar{x})^2}{n - 1} = \dfrac{[(4 - 5)^2 + (5 - 5)^2 + \ldots + (6 - 5)^2]}{8 - 1} = \dfrac{8}{7} = 1.14$

4.22 $\bar{x} = \dfrac{\sum x_i}{n} = \dfrac{0 + (-5) + (-3) + 6 + 4 + (-4) + 1 + (-5) + 0 + 3}{10} = \dfrac{-3}{10} = -.3$

$s^2 = \dfrac{\sum (x_i - \bar{x})^2}{n - 1} = \dfrac{[(0 - (-.3))^2 + ((-5) - (-.3))^2 + \ldots + (3 - (-.3))^2]}{10 - 1} = \dfrac{136.1}{9} = 15.12$

$s = \sqrt{s^2} = \sqrt{15.12} = 3.89$

4.24 a: $s^2 = 51.5$

b: $s^2 = 6.5$

c: $s^2 = 174.5$

4.26 6, 6, 6, 6, 6

4.28 a From the empirical rule we know that approximately 68% of the observations fall between 46 and 54. Thus 16% are less than 46 (the other 16% are above 54).

b Approximately 95% of the observations are between 42 and 58. Thus, only 2.5% are above 58 and all the rest, 97.5% are below 58.

c See (a) above; 16% are above 54.

4.30 a Nothing

b At least 75% lie between 60 and 180.

c At least 88.9% lie between 30 and 210.

4.32 $s^2 = 40.73$ mph^2 , and s = 6.38 mph; at least 75% of the speeds lie within 12.76 mph of the mean;

at least 88.9% of the speeds lie within 16.29 mph of the mean

4.34 $s^2 = .0858$ cm^2 , and s = .2929cm; at least 75% of the lengths lie within .5858 of the mean; at least 88.9% of the rods will lie within .8787 cm of the mean.

4.36a s = 15.01

b In approximately 68% of the days the number of arrivals falls between 83 (rounded from 83.04) and 113; on approximately 95% of the hours the number of arrivals fall between 68 and 128; on approximately 99.7% of the hours the number of arrivals fall between 53 and 143.

4.38 30th percentile: $L_{30} = (10 + 1)\dfrac{30}{100} = (11)(.30) = 3.3$; the 30th percentile is 22.3.

80th percentile: $L_{80} = (10 + 1)\dfrac{80}{100} = (11)(.80) = 8.8$; the 80th percentile 30.8.

4.40 First quartile: $L_{25} = (13+1)\dfrac{25}{100} = (14)(.25) = 3.5$; the first quartile 13.05.

Second quartile: $L_{50} = (13+1)\dfrac{50}{100} = (14)(.5) = 7$; the second quartile is 14.7.

Third quartile: $L_{75} = (13+1)\dfrac{75}{100} = (14)(.75) = 10.5$; the third quartile is 15.6.

4.42 Interquartile range = 15.6 −13.05 = 2.55

4.44 First quartile = 5.75, third quartile = 15; interquartile range = 15 − 5.75 = 9.25

4.46

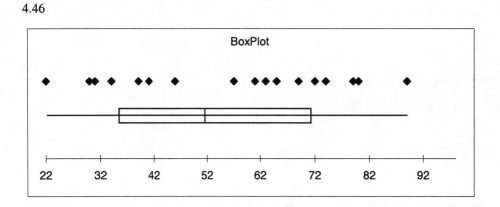

4.48 Dogs

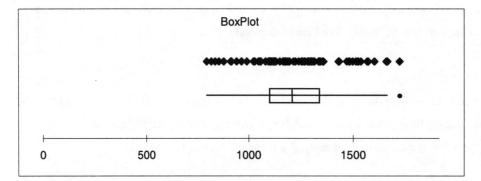

Cats

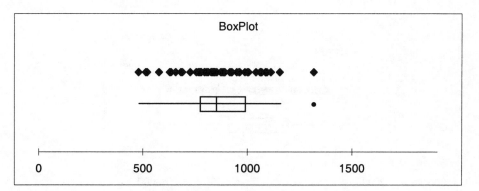

Dogs cost more money than cats. Both sets of expenses are positively skewed.

4.50 BA

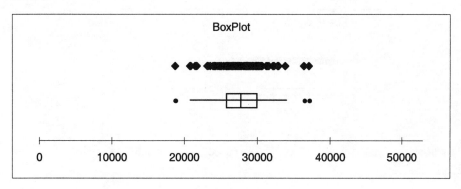

BSc

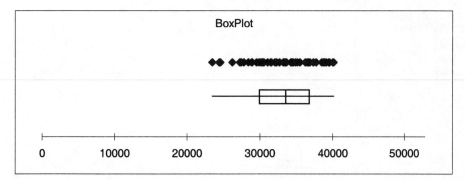

BBA

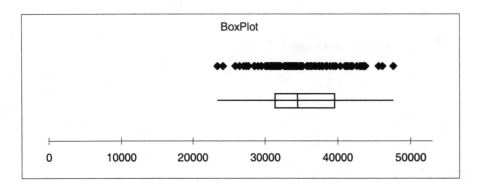

Other

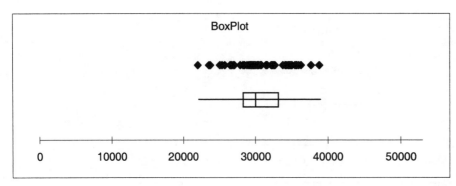

The starting salaries of BA and other are the lowest and least variable. Starting salaries for BBA and BSc are higher.

4.52a

Private course:

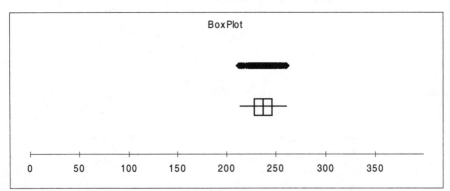

Public course:

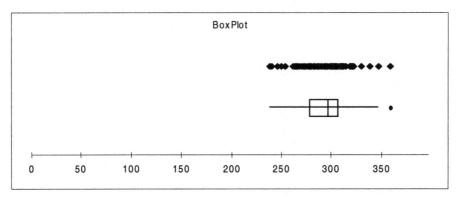

b The amount of time taken to complete rounds on the public course are larger and more variable than those played on private courses.

4.54 The quartiles are 697.19, 804.90, and 909.38. One-quarter of mortgage payments are less than $607.19 and one quarter exceed $909.38.

4.56

x_i	y_i	$(x_i - \bar{x})(y_i - \bar{y})$
45	77	182.03
22	31	354.53
16	28	584.63
50	49	-179.67
44	63	26.73
31	84	-73.47
48	40	-282.17
27	92	-225.07
30	72	-47.97
28	67	-40.87
$\bar{x} = 34.1$	$\bar{y} = 60.3$	298.7

$$\text{cov}(x,y) = \frac{298.7}{9} = 33.19$$

$$r = \frac{\text{cov}(x, y)}{s_x s_y} = \frac{33.19}{(11.79)(22.30)} = .1262$$

39

4.58

x_i	y_i	$(x_i - \bar{x})(y_i - \bar{y})$
23	9.6	69.51
46	11.3	3.94
60	12.8	6.46
54	9.8	-6.64
28	8.9	73.29
33	12.5	-7.69
25	12.0	1.96
31	11.4	13.56
36	12.6	-7.92
88	13.7	59.99
90	14.4	90.48
99	15.9	183.28
$\bar{x} = 51.08$	$\bar{y} = 12.08$	480.23

a $\text{cov}(x,y) = \dfrac{480.23}{11} = 43.66$

b $r = \dfrac{\text{cov}(x, y)}{s_x s_y} = \dfrac{43.66}{(27.38)(2.05)} = .7788$

c There is a moderately strong positive linear relationship.

4.60 $r = \dfrac{\text{cov}(x, y)}{s_x s_y} = \dfrac{-150}{(16)(12)} = -.7813$

There is a moderately strong negative linear relationship.

4.62 a

	Cigarettes	Days
Cigarettes	107.81	
Days	20.46	19.72

$\text{cov}(x,y) = 20.46(231/230) = 20.55$

b

	Cigarettes	Days
Cigarettes	1	
Days	0.4437	1

r = .4437

c The coefficient of correlation tells us that there is a weak positive linear relationship between smoking and the duration of colds.

4.64 a r = -.7501

b There is a strong negative linear relationship between age and Internet use.

4.66

	Height	Income
Height	1	
Income	0.6460	1

r = .6460. There is a moderately strong positive linear relationship.

4.68

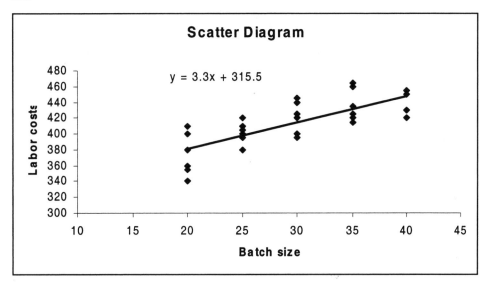

$\hat{y}$ = 315.5 + 3.3x; Fixed costs = $315.50, variable costs = $3.30

4.70

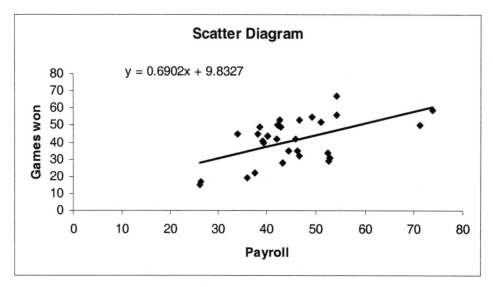

$\hat{y}$ = 9.8327 + .6902x; Cost to win one more game = 1million/.6902 = $1,448,855

4.72 $\bar{x}$ = 7.08, s = 2.93

4.74

Stores	
Mean	3.75
Standard Error	0.29
Median	4
Mode	4
Standard Deviation	2.23
Sample Variance	4.97
Kurtosis	-0.23
Skewness	0.51
Range	9
Minimum	0
Maximum	9
Sum	225
Count	60

$\bar{x}$ = 3.75, median = 4, s = 2.23

4.76a s = 12.93

b At least 75% of the times lie within 25.86 minutes of the mean; at least 88.9% of the times lie within 38.79 minutes of the mean.

c It is more precise.

4.78 $\bar{x} = 3.90$, median = 3.81, s = 1.32

4.80

Coffees	
Mean	29913
Standard Error	1722
Median	30660
Mode	#N/A
Standard Deviation	12174
Sample Variance	148213791
Kurtosis	0.12
Skewness	0.22
Range	59082
Minimum	3647
Maximum	62729
Sum	1495639
Count	50

a $\bar{x} = 29{,}913$, median = 30,660

b $s^2 = 148{,}213{,}791$; s = 12,174

c

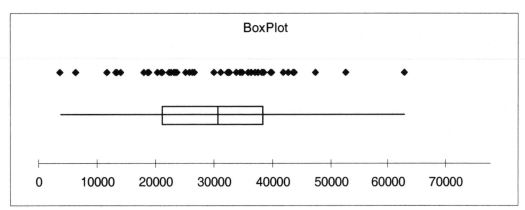

d The number of coffees sold varies considerably.

4.82a

	Temperature	Coffees
Temperature	260	
Coffees	-144003	145249515

cov(x,y) = -144,003(50/49) = -146,942

	Temperature	Coffees
Temperature	1	
Coffees	-0.7409	1

r = -.7409

b $\hat{y} = 49,337 - 554x$

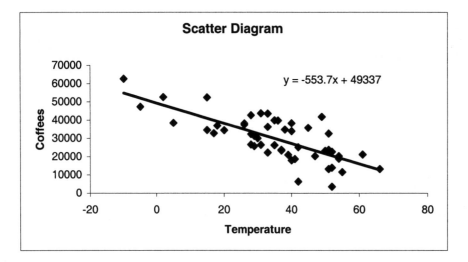

c There is a moderately strong negative linear relationship. For each additional degree of temperature the number of coffees sold decreases on average by 554 cups.

d In this exercise we determined that the number of cups of coffee sold is related to temperature, which may explain the variability in coffee sales. .

4.84

Internet	
Mean	26.32
Standard Error	0.60
Median	26
Mode	21
Standard Deviation	9.41
Sample Variance	88.57
Kurtosis	-0.071
Skewness	0.15
Range	52
Minimum	2
Maximum	54
Sum	6579
Count	250

a $\bar{x} = 26.32$ and median = 26

b $s^2 = 88.57$, s = 9.41

c

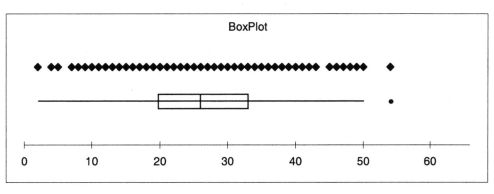

d The times are positively skewed. Half the times are above 26 hours.

4.86a

	Education	Internet
Education	3.67	
Internet	11.55	88.22

cov(x,y) = 11.55(250/249) = 11.60

	Education	Internet
Education	1	
Internet	0.6418	1

r = .6418

b

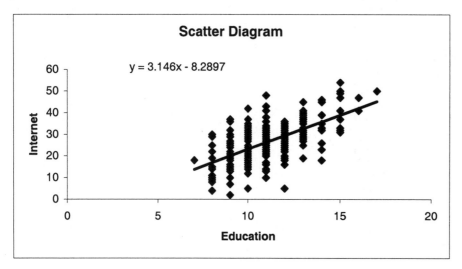

Scatter Diagram

y = 3.146x - 8.2897

c There is a moderately strong positive linear relationship between Internet use and education. For each additional year of education Internet use increases on average by 3.15 hours per month.

d This exercise helps explain the variation in Internet use.

4.88a

	Corn	Rainfall
Corn	387.78	
Rainfall	1118.57	8738.66

cov(x,y) = 1118.575(150/149) = 1126.07

	Corn	Rainfall
Corn	1	
Rainfall	0.6076	1

r = .6076

b

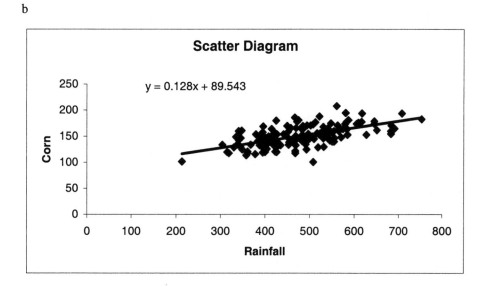

c There is a moderately strong positive linear relationship between yield and rainfall. For each additional inch of rainfall yield increases on average by .13 bushels.

d In this exercise we determined that yield is related to rainfall, which helps explain the variability in corn yield.

4.90a, b, and c

Vocabulary	
Mean	226.49
Standard Error	3.11
Median	223
Mode	215
Standard Deviation	43.99
Sample Variance	1934.8
Kurtosis	-0.27
Skewness	0.089
Range	240
Minimum	114
Maximum	354
Sum	45297
Count	200
Largest(50)	259
Smallest(50)	193

a The mean vocabulary is 226.49 words. The median is 223, which tells us that half the children had vocabularies greater than 223 words and half had less.

b The variance is 1934.8 and the standard deviation is 43.99. Both indicate a great deal of variation between children.

c The quartiles are 193, 223, and 259.

4.92a

	Temperature	Winning times
Temperature	1	
Winning times	0.5984	1

r = .5984

b There is a moderately strong positive linear relationship between the winning times of women and temperatures.

c They appear to provide the same type of information.

4.94a

Debts	
Mean	12067
Standard Error	179.9
Median	12047
Mode	11621
Standard Deviation	2632
Sample Variance	6929745
Kurtosis	-0.41
Skewness	-0.21
Range	12499
Minimum	4626
Maximum	17125
Sum	2582254
Count	214

$\bar{x}$ = 12,067, median = 12,047, mode = 11,621

b The mean debt is $12,067. Half the sample incurred debts below $12,047 and half incurred debts above. The mode is $11,621.

Chapter 5

5.2a The study is observational. The statistics practitioner did not randomly assign stores to buy cans or bottles.

b Randomly assign some stores to receive only cans and others to receive only bottles.

5.4a A survey can be conducted by means of a personal interview, a telephone interview, or a self-administered questionnaire.

b A personal interview has a high response rate relative to other survey methods, but is expensive because of the need to hire well-trained interviewers and possibly pay travel-related costs if the survey is conducted over a large geographical area. A personal interview also will likely result in fewer incorrect responses that arise when respondents misunderstand some questions. A telephone interview is less expensive, but will likely result in a lower response rate. A self-administered questionnaire is least expensive, but suffers from lower response rates and accuracy than interviews.

5.6a The sampled population will exclude those who avoid large department stores in favor or smaller shops, as well as those who consider their time too valuable to spend participating in a survey. The sampled population will therefore differ from the target population of all customers who regularly shop at the mall.

b The sampled population will contain a disproportionate number of thick books, because of the manner in which the sample is selected.

c The sampled population consists of those eligible voters who are at home in the afternoon, thereby excluding most of those with full-time jobs (or at school).

5.8a A self-selected sample is a sample formed primarily on the basis of voluntary inclusion, with little control by the designer of the survey.

b Choose any recent radio or television poll based on responses of listeners who phone in on a volunteer basis.

c Self-selected samples are usually biased, because those who participate are more interested in the issue than those who don't, and therefore probably have a different opinion.

5.10 No, because the sampled population consists of the responses about the professor's course. We cannot make draw inferences about all courses.

5.12 We used Excel to generate 30 six-digit random numbers. Because we will ignore any duplicate numbers generated, we generated 30 six-digit random numbers and will use the first 20 unique random numbers to select our sample. The 30 numbers generated are shown below.

169,470	744,530	22,554	918,730	320,262	503,129
318,858	698,203	822,383	938,262	800,806	56,643
836,116	123,936	80,539	154,211	391,278	940,154
110,630	856,380	222,145	692,313	949,828	561,511
909,269	811,274	288,553	749,627	858,944	39,308

5.14 Use cluster sampling, letting each city block represent a cluster.

5.18 Three types of nonsampling errors:

    (1) Error due to incorrect responses

    (2)Nonresponse error, which refers to error introduced when responses are not obtained from some members of the sample. This may result in the sample being unrepresentative of the target population.

    (3)Error due to selection bias, which arises when the sampling plan is such that some members of the target population cannot possibly be selected for inclusion in the sample.

Chapter 6

6.2 a Subjective approach

b If all the teams in major league baseball have exactly the same players the New York Yankees will win 25% of all World Series.

6.4 a Subjective approach

b The Dow Jones Industrial Index will increase on 60% of the days if economic conditions remain unchanged.

6.6 {Adams wins. Brown wins, Collins wins, Dalton wins}

6.8 a {0, 1, 2, 3, 4, 5}

b {4, 5}

c $P(5) = .10$

d $P(2, 3, \text{ or } 4) = P(2) + P(3) + P(4) = .26 + .21 + .18 = .65$

e $P(6) = 0$

6.10 P(Contractor 1 wins) = 2/6, P(Contractor 2 wins) = 3/6, P(Contractor 3 wins) = 1/6

6.12 a P(shopper does not use credit card) = P(shopper pays cash) + P(shopper pays by debit card)

   $= .30 + .10 = .40$

b P(shopper pays cash or uses a credit card) = P(shopper pays cash) + P(shopper pays by credit card)

   $= .30 + .60 = .90$

6.14 a P(single) = .15, P(married) = .50, P(divorced) = .25, P(widowed) = .10

b Relative frequency approach

6.16 $P(A_1) = .1 + .2 = .3$, $P(A_2) = .3 + .1 = .4$, $P(A_3) = .2 + .1 = .3$.

$P(B_1) = .1 + .3 + .2 = .6$, $P(B_2) = .2 + .1 + .1 = .4$.

6.18 a $P(A_1 | B_1) = \dfrac{P(A_1 \text{ and } B_1)}{P(B_1)} = \dfrac{.4}{.7} = .5714$

b $P(A_2 | B_1) = \dfrac{P(A \text{ and } B_1)}{P(B_1)} = \dfrac{3}{.7} = .4286$

c Yes. It is not a coincidence. Given B_1 the events A_1 and A_2 constitute the entire sample space.

6.20 The events are not independent because $P(A_1 | B_2) \neq P(A_1)$.

6.22 $P(A_1 | B_1) = \dfrac{P(A_1 \text{ and } B_1)}{P(B_1)} = \dfrac{.20}{.20 + .60} = .25$; $P(A_1) = .20 + .05 = .25$; the events are independent.

6.24 $P(A_1) = .15 + .25 = .40$, $P(A_2) = .20 + .25 = .45$, $P(A_3) = .10 + .05 = .15$.

$P(B_1) = .15 + 20 + .10 = .45$, $P(B_2) = .25 + .25 + .05 = .55$.

6.26 a $P(A_1 \text{ or } A_2) = P(A_1) + P(A_2) = .40 + .45 = .85$.

b $P(A_2 \text{ or } B_2) = P(A_2) + P(B_2) - P(A_2 \text{ and } B_2) = .45 + .55 - .25 = .75$

c $P(A_3 \text{ or } B_1) = P(A_3) + P(B_1) - P(A_3 \text{ and } B_1) = .15 + .45 - .10 = .50$

6.28 a P(debit card) $= .04 + .18 + .14 = .36$

b P(over \$100 | credit card) $= \dfrac{P(\text{credit card and over } \$100)}{P(\text{credit card})} = \dfrac{.23}{.03 + .21 + .23} = .4894$

c P(credit card or debit card) = P(credit card) + P(debit card) = $.47 + .36 = .83$

6.30 a P(He is a smoker) $= .12 + .19 = .31$

b P(He does not have lung disease) $= .19 + .66 = .85$

c P(He has lung disease | he is a smoker) $= \dfrac{P(\text{he has lung disease and he is a smoker})}{P(\text{he is a smoker})} = \dfrac{.12}{.31} = .3871$

d P(He has lung disease | he does not smoke) =

$$\frac{P(\text{he has lung disease and he does not smoke})}{P(\text{he does not smoke})} = \frac{.03}{.69} = .0435$$

6.32 a P(manual | math-stats) = .23/(.23 + .36) = .23/.59 = .3898

b P(computer) = .36 + .30 = .66

c No, because P(manual) = .23 + .11 = .34, which is not equal to P(manual | math-stats).

6.34 a P(ulcer) = .01 + .03 + .03 + .04 = .11

b P(ulcer | none) = .01/(.01 + .22) = .01/.23 = .0435

c P(none | ulcer) = .01/(.01 + .03 + .03 + .04) = .01/.11 = .0909

d No, because P(ulcer) = .11 and P(ulcer | none) = .0435

6.36 a P(remember) = .15 + .18 = .33

b P(remember | violent) = .15/(.15 + .35) = .15/.50 = .30

c Yes, the events are dependent.

6.38 a P(uses a spreadsheet) = .298 + .209 = .507

b P(uses a spreadsheet | male) = .209/(.209 + .265) = .441

c b P(female | spreadsheet user) = .298/(.298 + .209) = .588

6.40 a P(provided by employer) = .166 + .195 + .230 = .591

b P(provided by employer | professional/technical) = .166/(.166 + .094) = .638

c Yes, because P(provided by employer) ≠ P(provided by employer | professional/technical)

6.42 a P(under 20) = .2307 + .0993 + .5009 = .8309

b P(retail) = .5009 + .0876 + .0113 = .5998

c P(20 to 99 | construction) = .0189/(.2307 + .0189 + .0019) = .0751

6.44 P(purchase | see ad) = .18/(.18 + .42) = .30; P(purchase | do not see ad) = .12/(.12 + .28) = .30; the ads are not effective.

6.46 a P(bachelor's degree | west) = .0418/(.0359 + .0608 + .0456 + .0181 + .0418 + .0180) = .1898

b P(northwest | high school graduate) = .0711/(.0711 + .0843 + .1174 + .0608) = .2131 c P(south) = .0683 + .1174 + .0605 + .0248 + .0559 + .0269 = .3538

d No because P(bachelor's degree) = .0350 + .0368 + .0559 + .0418 = .1695 ≠ P(bachelor's degree | west)

6.48

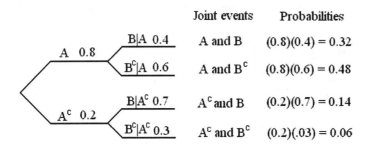

6.50

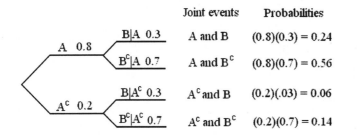

6.52

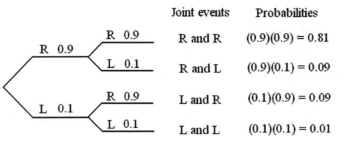

a P(R and R) = .81

b P(L and L) = .01

c P(R and L) + P(L and R) = .09 + .09 = .18

d P(Rand L) + P(L and R) + P(R and R) = .09 + .09 + .81 = .99

6.54a

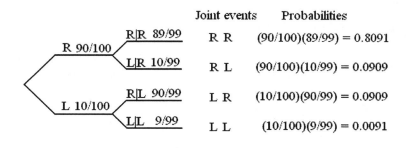

	Joint events	Probabilities
	R R	(90/100)(89/99) = 0.8091
	R L	(90/100)(10/99) = 0.0909
	L R	(10/100)(90/99) = 0.0909
	L L	(10/100)(9/99) = 0.0091

b P(RR) = .8091

c P(LL) = .0091

d P(RL) + P(LR) = .0909 + .0909 = .1818

e P(RL) + P(LR) + P(RR) = .0909 + .0909 + .8091 = .9909

6.56

First contract	Second contract	Joint events	Probabilities
		win and win	(0.4)(0.7) = 0.28
		win and lose	(0.4)(0.3) = 0.12
		lose and win	(0.6)(0.5) = 0.3
		lose and lose	(0.6)(0.5) = 0.3

a P(win both) = .28

b P(lose both) = .30

c P(win only one) = .12 + .30 = .42

6.58

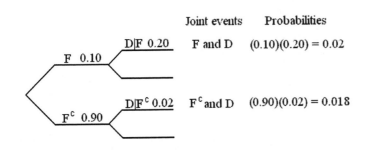

$P(D) = .02 + .018 = .038$

6.60

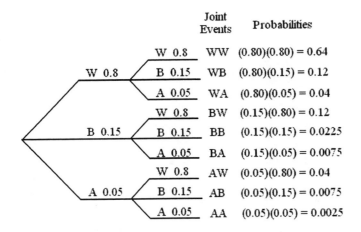

Diversity index $= .12 + .04 + .12 + .0075 + .04 + .0075 = .335$

6.62

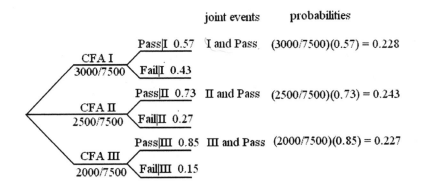

joint events · probabilities

I and Pass $(3000/7500)(0.57) = 0.228$

II and Pass $(2500/7500)(0.73) = 0.243$

III and Pass $(2000/7500)(0.85) = 0.227$

P(pass) = .228 + .243 + .227 = .698

6.64

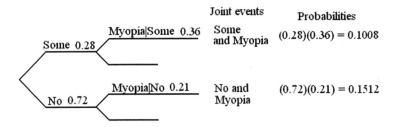

Joint events   Probabilities

Some and Myopia $(0.28)(0.36) = 0.1008$

No and Myopia $(0.72)(0.21) = 0.1512$

P(myopic) = .1008 + .1512 = .2520

6.66 Let A = mutual fund outperforms the market in the first year

B = mutual outperforms the market in the second year

$P(A \text{ and } B) = P(A)P(B \mid A) = (.15)(.22) = .033$

6.68 Define the events:

M: The main control will fail.

B_1: The first backup will fail.

B_2: The second backup will fail

The probability that the plane will crash is

$P(M \text{ and } B_1 \text{ and } B_2) = [P(M)][\, P(B_1)][\, P(B_2)]$

$= (.0001) (.01) (.01) = .00000001$

We have assumed that the 3 systems will fail independently of one another.

6.70

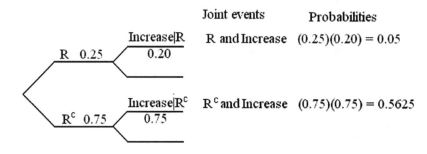

	Joint events	Probabilities
Increase|R	R and Increase	(0.25)(0.20) = 0.05
Increase|R^c	R^c and Increase	(0.75)(0.75) = 0.5625

R   0.25 / 0.20

R^c 0.75 / 0.75

P(Increase) = .05 + .5625 = .6125

6.72 P(A and B) = .32, P(A^C and B) = .14, P(B) = .46, P(B^C) = .54

a P(A | B) = P(A and B)/P(B) = .32/.46 = .696

b P(A^C | B) = P(A^C and B)/P(B) = .14/.46 = .304

c P(A and B^C) = .48; P(A | B^C) = P(A and B^C)/ P(B^C) = .48/.54 =.889

d P(A^C and B^C) = .06; P(A^C | B^C) = P(A^C and B^C)/ P(B^C) = .06/.54 = .111

6.74 P(F | D) = P(F and D)/P(D) = .020/.038 = .526

6.76 P(CFA I | passed) = P(CFA I and passed)/P(Passed) = .228/.698 = .327

6.78 P(A) = .40, P(B | A) = .85, P(B | A^C) = .29

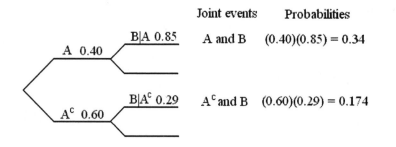

	Joint events	Probabilities
B|A 0.85	A and B	(0.40)(0.85) = 0.34
B|A^c 0.29	A^c and B	(0.60)(0.29) = 0.174

A 0.40

A^c 0.60

P(B) = .34 + .174 = .514

P(A | B) = P(A and B)/P(B) = .34/.514 = .661

58

6.80 Define events: A = smoke, B_1 = did not finish high school, B_2 = high school graduate, B_3 = some college, no degree, B_4 = completed a degree

$P(A \mid B_1) = .40, P(A \mid B_2) = .34, P(A \mid B_3) = .24, P(A \mid B_4) = .14$

From Exercise 6.45: $P(B_1) = .1055, P(B_2) = .3236, P(B_3) = .1847, P(B_4) = .3862$

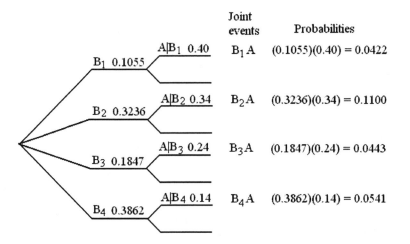

$P(A) = .0422 + .1100 + .0443 + .0541 = .2506$

$P(B_4 \mid A) = .0541/.2506 = .2159$

6.82 Define events: A = win series, B = win first game

$P(A) = .60, P(B \mid A) = .70, P(B \mid A^C) = .25$

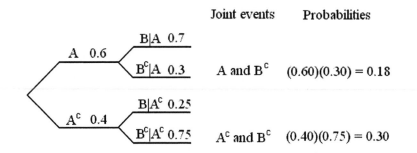

$P(B^C) = .18 + .30 = .48$

$P(A \mid B^C) = P(A \text{ and } B^C)/P(B^C) = .18/.48 = .375$

6.84 Define events: A = win contract A and B = win contract B

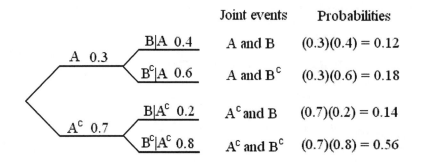

	Joint events	Probabilities
B|A 0.4	A and B	$(0.3)(0.4) = 0.12$
B^C|A 0.6	A and B^C	$(0.3)(0.6) = 0.18$
B|A^C 0.2	A^C and B	$(0.7)(0.2) = 0.14$
B^C|A^C 0.8	A^C and B^C	$(0.7)(0.8) = 0.56$

$P(B^C) = P(A \text{ and } B^C) + P(A^C \text{ and } B^C) = .18 + .56 = .74$

$P(A^C|B^C) = P(A^C \text{ and } B^C)/P(B^C) = .56/.74 = .757$

6.86 Define events: A = woman, B = drug is effective

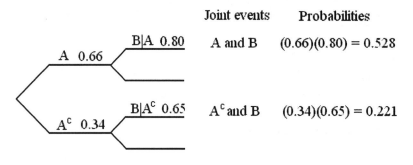

	Joint events	Probabilities
B|A 0.80	A and B	$(0.66)(0.80) = 0.528$
B|A^C 0.65	A^C and B	$(0.34)(0.65) = 0.221$

$P(B) = .528 + .221 = .749$

6.88 P(Idle roughly)

= P(at least one spark plug malfunctions) = 1- P(all function) = $1 - (.90^4) = 1-.6561 = .3439$

6.90 a P(pass) = .86 + .03 = .89

b P(pass | miss 5 or more classes) = .03/(.09 + .03) = .250

c P(pass | miss less than 5 classes) = .86/(.86 + .02) = .977

d No since P(pass) ≠ P(pass | miss 5 or more classes)

6.92 a P(excellent) = .27 + .22 = .49

b P(excellent | man) = .22/(.22 + .10 + .12 + .06) = .44

c P(man | excellent) = .22/(.27 + .22) = .449

d No, since P(excellent) ≠ P(excellent | man)

6.94 Define events: A_1 = Low-income earner, A_2 = medium-income earner, A_3 = high-income earner, B = die of a heart attack

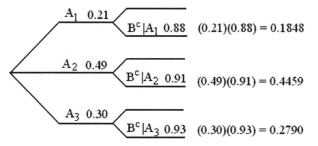

probabilities

A_1 0.21

$B^c|A_1$ 0.88   (0.21)(0.88) = 0.1848

A_2 0.49

$B^c|A_2$ 0.91   (0.49)(0.91) = 0.4459

A_3 0.30

$B^c|A_3$ 0.93   (0.30)(0.93) = 0.2790

$P(B^C)$ = .1848 + .4459 + .2790 = .9097

$P(A_1 | B^C)$ = .1848/.9097 = .2031

6.96 Define events: A = purchase extended warranty, B = regular price

a P(A | B) = P(A and B)/P(B) = .21/(.21 + .57) = .2692

b P(A) = .21 + .14 = .35

c No, because P(A) ≠ P(A | B)

6.98 Define events: A = job security is an important issue, B = pension benefits is an important issue

P(A) = .74, P(B) = .65, P(A | B) = .60

a P(A and B) = P((B)P(A | B) = (.65)(.60) = .39

b P(A or B) = .74 + .65 -.39 = 1

6.100 P(T) = .5

Chapter 7

7.2 a any value between 0 and several hundred miles

b No, because we cannot identify the second value or any other value larger than 0.

c No, uncountable means infinite.

d The variable is continuous.

7.4 a 0, 1, 2, …, 100

b Yes.

c Yes, there are 101 values.

d The variable is discrete because it is countable.

7.6 p(x) = 1/6 for x = 1, 2 ,3 ,4 ,5, and 6

7.8 a P(2 ≤ X ≤ 5) = p(2) + p(3) + p(4) + p(5) = .310 + .340 + .220 + .080 = .950

b P(X > 5) = p(6) + p(7) = .019 + .001 = .020

c P(X < 4) = p(0) + p(1) + p(2) + p(3) = .005 + .025 + .310 + .340 = .680

7.10 a P(X > 0) = p(2) + p(6) + p(8) = .3 + .4 + .1 = .8

b P(X ≥ 1) = p(2) + p(6) + p(8) = .3 + .4 + .1 = .8

c P(X ≥ 2) = p(2) + p(6) + p(8) = .3 + .4 + .1 = .8

d P(2 ≤ X ≤ 5) = p(2) = .3

7.12 a P(X < 2) = p(0) + p(1) = .05 + ..43 = .48

b P(X > 1) = p(2) + p(3) = .31 + .21 = .52

7.14 a P(0 heads) = P(TT) = 1/4

b P(1 head) = P(HT) + P(TH) = 1/4 + 1/4 = 1/2

c P(2 heads) = P(HH) = 1/4

d P(at least 1 head) = P(1 head) + P(2 heads) = 1/2 + 1/4 = 3/4

7.16 a P(2 heads) = P(HHT) + P(HTH) + P(THH) = 1/8 + 1/8 + 1/8 = 3/8

b P(1 heads) = P(HTT) + P(THT) = P(TTH) = 1/8 + 1/8 + 1/8 = 3/8

c P(at least 1 head) = P(1 head) + P(2 heads) + P(3 heads) = 3/8 + 3/8 + P(HHH)

    = 3/8 + 3/8 + 1/8 = 7/8

d P(at least 2 heads) = P(2 heads) + P(3 heads) = 3/8 + 1/8 = 4/8 = 1/2

7.18 a P(4 books) = p(4) = .06

b P(8 books) = p(8) = 0

c P(no books) = p(0) = .35

d P(at least 1 book) = 1 – p(0) = 1 - .35 = .65

7.20 a P(X = 3) = p(3) = .21

b b P(X ≥ 5) = p(5) + p(6) + p(7) + p(8) = .12 + .08 + .06 + .05 = .31

c P(5 ≤ X ≤ 7) = p(5) + p(6) + p(7) = .12 + .08 + .06 = .26

7.22 $\mu = E(X) = \sum xp(x)$ = -2(.59) +5(.15) + 7(.25) +8(.01) = 1.4

$\sigma^2 = V(X) = \sum (x-\mu)^2 p(x)$ = (-2-1.4)^2 (.59) + (5-1.4)^2 (.15) + (7-1.4)^2 (.25) + (8-1.4)^2 (.01)

      = 17.04

$\sigma = \sqrt{\sigma^2} = \sqrt{17.04}$ = 4.13

7.24

x	0	1	2	3
y = 3x + 2	2	5	8	11
Probability	.4	.3	.2	.1

7.26 E(Y) = E(3X + 2) = 3E(X) + 2 = 3(1.0) + 2 = 5.0

V(Y) = V(3X + 2) = 3^2 V(X) = 9(1.0) = 9.0

$\sigma = \sqrt{\sigma^2} = \sqrt{9.0}$ = 3.0

7.28 $\mu = E(X) = \sum xp(x)$ = 0(.1) + 1(.3) + 2(.4) + 3(.2) = 1.7

$$\sigma^2 = V(X) = \sum (x-\mu)^2 p(x) = (0\text{-}1.7)^2(.1) + (1\text{-}1.7)^2(.3) + (2\text{-}1.7)^2(.4) + (3\text{-}1.7)^2(.2) = .81$$

$$\sigma = \sqrt{\sigma^2} = \sqrt{.81} = .9$$

7.30

x	1	2	3	4	5	6	7
y	.25	.50	.75	1.00	1.25	1.50	1.75
p(y)	.05	.15	.15	.25	.20	.10	.10

7.32 $\mu = E(X) = \sum xp(x) = 1(.05) + + 2(.15) + 3(.15) + 4(.25) + 5(.20) + 6(.10) + 7(.10) = 4.1$

$\sigma^2 = V(X) = \sum (x-\mu)^2 p(x) = (1\text{-}4.1)^2(.05) + (2\text{-}4.1)^2(.15) + (3\text{-}4,1)^2(.15) + (4-4.1)^2(.25)$

$$+ (5\text{-}4.1)^2(.20) + (6\text{-}4.1)^2(.10) + (7\text{-}4.1)^2(.10) = 2.69$$

$\sigma = \sqrt{\sigma^2} = \sqrt{2.69} = 1.64$

$Y = .25, E(Y) = .25E(X) = .25(4.1) = 1.025$

$V(Y) = V(.25X) = .25^2 V(X) = .0625(2.69) = .168$

$\sigma = \sqrt{\sigma^2} = \sqrt{1.68} = .410$

7.34 $Y = 10X$

$E(Y) = E(10X) = 10E(X) = 10(2.76) = 27.6$

$V(Y) = V(10X) = 10^2 V(X) = 100(2.302) = 230.2$

$\sigma = \sqrt{\sigma^2} = \sqrt{230.2} = 15.17$

7.36 $\mu = E(X) = \sum xp(x) = 1(.24) + 2(.18) + 3(.13) + 4(.10) + 5(.07) + 6(.04)$

$$+ 7(.04) + 8(.20) = 3.86$$

$\sigma^2 = V(X) = \sum (x-\mu)^2 p(x) = (1\text{-}3.86)^2(.24) + (2\text{-}3.86)^2(.18) + (3\text{-}3.86)^2(.13)$

$$+ (4\text{-}3.86)^2(.10) + (5\text{-}3.86)^2(.07) + (6\text{-}3.86)^2(.04) + (7\text{-}3.86)^2(.04)$$

$$+ (8\text{-}3.86)^2(.20) = 6.78$$

$\sigma = \sqrt{\sigma^2} = \sqrt{6.78} = 2.60$

7.38 E(Value of coin) = 400(.40) + 900(.30) + 100(.30) = 460. Take the $500.

7.40 Profit = 4(X) ; Expected profit = 4E(X) = 4(1.85) = $7.40

7.42 E(damage costs) = .01(400) + .02(200) + .10(100) + .87(0) = 18. The owner should pay up to $18 for the device.

7.44 a $\displaystyle\sum_{all\ x}\sum_{all\ y} xyp(x, y) = (1)(1)(.5) + (1)(2)(.1) + (2)(1)(.1) + (2)(2)(.3) = 2.1$

$\displaystyle COV(X, Y) = \sum_{all\ x}\sum_{all\ y} xyp(x, y) - \mu_x\mu_y = 2.1 - (1.4)(1.4) = .14$

$\sigma_x = \sqrt{\sigma_x^2} = \sqrt{.24} = .49,\ \sigma_y = \sqrt{\sigma_y^2} = \sqrt{.24} = .49$

$\rho = \dfrac{COV(X,Y)}{\sigma_x\sigma_y} = \dfrac{.14}{(.49)(.49)} = .58$

7.46 a

x + y	p(x + y)
2	.5
3	.2
4	.3

b $\mu_{x+y} = E(X+Y) = \displaystyle\sum (x+y)p(x+y) = 2(.5) + 3(.2) + 4(.3) = 2.8$

$\sigma_{x+y}^2 = V(X+Y) = \displaystyle\sum [(x+y)-\mu_{x+y}]^2 p(x+y) = (2\text{-}2.8)^2 (.5) + (3\text{-}2.8)^2 (.2) + (4\text{-}2.8)^2 (.3) = .76$

c Yes

7.48 a $\displaystyle\sum_{all\ x}\sum_{all\ y} xyp(x, y) = (1)(1)(.28) + (1)(2)(.12) + (2)(1)(.42) + (2)(2)(.18) = 2.08$

$\displaystyle COV(X, Y) = \sum_{all\_x}\sum_{all\_y} xyp(x, y) - \mu_x\mu_y = 2.08 - (1.6)(1.3) = 0$

$\sigma_x = \sqrt{\sigma_x^2} = \sqrt{.24} = .49,\ \sigma_y = \sqrt{\sigma_y^2} = \sqrt{.21} = .46$

$\rho = \dfrac{COV(X,Y)}{\sigma_x\sigma_y} = \dfrac{0}{(.49)(.46)} = 0$

7.50 a

x + y	p(x + y)
2	.28
3	.54
4	.18

b $\mu_{x+y} = E(X+Y) = \sum (x+y)p(x+y) = 2(.28) + 3(.54) + 4(.18) = 2.9$

$\sigma_{x+y}^2 = V(X+Y) = \sum [(x+y)-\mu_{x+y}]^2\, p(x+y) = (2-2.9)^2\,(.28) + (3-2.9)^2\,(.54) + (4-2.9)^2\,(18) = .45$

c Yes

7.52

		x	
y	0	1	2
1	.42	.21	.07
2	.18	.09	.03

7.54 a

Refrigerators, x	p(x)
0	.22
1	.49
2	.29

b

Stoves, y	p(y)
0	.34
1	.39
2	.27

c $\mu_x = E(X) = \sum xp(x) = 0(.22) + 1(.49) + 2(.29) = 1.07$

$\sigma^2 = V(X) = \sum (x-\mu)^2 p(x) = (0-1.07)^2\,(.22) + (1-1.07)^2\,(.49) + (2-1.07)^2\,(.29) = .505$

d $\mu_y = E(Y) = \sum yp(y) = 0(.34) + 1(.39) + 2(.27) = .93$

$\sigma^2 = V(Y) = \sum (y-\mu)^2 p(y) = (0-.93)^2\,(.34) + (1-.93)^2\,(.39) + (2-.93)^2\,(.27) = .605$

e $\displaystyle\sum_{all\ x}\sum_{all\ y} xyp(x, y) = (0)(1)(.08) + (0)(1)(.09) + (0)(2)(.05) + (1)(0)(.14) + (1)(1)(.17)$

$+ (1)(2)(18) + (2)(0)(.12) + (21)(1)(13) + (2)(2)(.04) = .95$

$\displaystyle COV(X, Y) = \sum_{all\ x}\sum_{all\ y} xyp(x, y) - \mu_x\mu_y = .95 - (1.07)(.93) = -.045$

$$\sigma_x = \sqrt{\sigma_x^2} = \sqrt{.505} = .711, \ \sigma_y = \sqrt{\sigma_y^2} = \sqrt{.605} = .778$$

$$\rho = \frac{COV(X,Y)}{\sigma_x \sigma_y} = \frac{-.045}{(.711)(.778)} = -.081$$

7.56 a $P(X = 1 \mid Y = 0) = P(X =1 \text{ and } Y = 0)/P(Y = 0) = .14/.34 = .412$

b $P(Y = 0 \mid X = 1) = P(X =1 \text{ and } Y = 0)/P(X = 1) = .14/.49 = .286$

c $P(X = 2 \mid Y = 2) = P(X =2 \text{ and } Y = 2)/P(Y = 2) = .04/.27 = .148$

7.58 $E\left(\sum X_i\right) = \sum E(X_i) = 35 + 20 + 20 + 50 + 20 = 145$

$V\left(\sum X_i\right) = \sum V(X_i) = 8 + 5 + 4 + 12 + 2 = 31$

$\sigma = \sqrt{31} = 5.57$

7.60 $E\left(\sum X_i\right) = \sum E(X_i) = 10 + 3 + 30 + 5 + 100 + 20 = 168$

$V\left(\sum X_i\right) = \sum V(X_i) = 3^2 + 0^2 + 10^2 + 1^2 + 20^2 + 8^2 = 574$

$\sigma = \sqrt{574} = 24.0$

7.62 $E(R_p) = .211$

$V(R_p) = w_1^2 \sigma_1^2 + w_2^2 \sigma_2^2 + 2w_1 w_2 \rho \sigma_1 \sigma_2$

$\quad = (.30)^2(.02)^2 + (.70)^2(.15^2) + 2(.30)(.70)(.25)(.02)(.15)$

$\quad = .0114$

$\sigma_{R_p} = \sqrt{.0114} = .1067$

7.64 The expected value does not change. The standard deviation decreases.

7.66 $E(R_p) = w_1 E(R_1) + w_2 E(R_2) = (.60)(.09) + (.40)(.13) = .1060$

$V(R_p) = w_1^2 \sigma_1^2 + w_2^2 \sigma_2^2 + 2w_1 w_2 \rho \sigma_1 \sigma_2$

$\quad = (.60)^2(.15)^2 + (.40)^2(.21^2) + 2(.60)(.40)(.4)(.15)(.21)$

$\quad = .0212$

The statistics used in Exercises 7.68 to 7.80 were computed by Excel. The variances were taken from the variance-covariance matrix. As a result they are the population parameters. To convert to statistics multiply the variance of the portfolio returns by $n/(n-1)$.

7.68 a

	Stock		
	1	2	3
Means	.0463	.1293	-.0016
Variances	.0148	.0100	.0039

b Invest all your money in stock 2; it has the largest mean return.

c Invest all your money in stock 3; it has the smallest variance.

7.70 a

Portfolio of 3 Stocks				
		Stock 1	Stock 2	Stock 3
Variance-Covariance Matrix	Stock 1	0.0148		
	Stock 2	0.0037	0.0100	
	Stock 3	0.0015	-0.0012	0.0039
Expected Returns		0.0463	0.1293	-0.0016
Weights		0.5	0.3	0.2
Portfolio Return				
Expected Value	0.0616			
Variance	0.0060			
Standard Deviation	0.0777			

b The mean return on this portfolio is greater than the mean returns on stocks 1 and 3 and the portfolio in Exercise 7.69, but smaller than that of stock 2. The variance of the returns on this portfolio is smaller than that for stocks 1 and 2 and larger than that of stock 3 and the portfolio in Exercise 7.69.

7.72 a

Portfolio of 3 Stocks				
		Stock 1	Stock 2	Stock 3
Variance-Covariance Matrix	Stock 1	0.0957		
	Stock 2	-0.0288	0.2345	
	Stock 3	0.0004	0.0243	0.0515
Expected Returns		0.0232	0.0601	0.0136
Weights		0.3	0.4	0.3
Portfolio Return				
Expected Value	0.0351			
Variance	0.0498			
Standard Deviation	0.2231			

b The mean return on the portfolio is greater than the mean returns on stocks 1 and 3, but smaller than that of stock 2. The variance of the returns on the portfolio is smaller than that for the three stocks.

7.74 a

	Stock			
	1	2	3	4
Means	.0187	-.0176	.0153	.0495
Variances	.0615	.0232	.0228	.0517

b Invest all your money in stock 4; it has the largest mean return.

c Invest all your money in stock 3; it has the smallest variance.

7.76 a

Portfolio of 4 Stocks					
		Stock 1	Stock 2	Stock 3	Stock 4
Variance-Covariance Matrix	Stock 1	0.0615			
	Stock 2	-0.0012	0.0232		
	Stock 3	0.0168	-0.0022	0.0228	
	Stock 4	0.0129	0.0179	-0.0005	0.0517
Expected Returns		0.0187	-0.0176	0.0153	0.0495
Weights		0.20	0.20	0.10	0.50
Portfolio Return					
Expected Value	0.0265				
Variance	0.0231				
Standard Deviation	0.1521				

b The mean return on this portfolio is greater than the mean return on stocks 1, 2, and 3, and the mean return on the portfolio in Exercise 7.75. It is smaller than the mean return on stock 4. The variance of the returns on this portfolio is smaller than that for stocks 1, 2, and 4, but larger than the variance on the returns of stock 3 and the variance of the returns on the portfolio in Exercise 7.75.

7.78 a

	GE	SEAGRAM	COKE	MCDONALDS
GE	0.0019			
SEAGRAM	0.0004	0.0043		
COKE	0.0004	-0.0005	0.0017	
MCDONALDS	0.0004	0.0011	0.0002	0.0025

b Invest in General Electric and Coca-Cola.

7.80 We created a portfolio with the following weights

General Electric	40%
Seagram	10%
Coca-Cola	40%
McDonald's	10%

Portfolio of 4 Stocks			GE	SEAGRAM	COKE	MCDONALDS
Variance-Covariance Matrix	GE		0.0019			
	SEAGRAM		0.0004	0.0043		
	COKE		0.0004	-0.0005	0.0017	
	MCDONALDS		0.0004	0.0011	0.0002	0.0025
Expected Returns			0.0231	0.0148	0.0213	0.0156
Weights			0.40	0.10	0.40	0.10
Portfolio Return						
Expected Value		0.0208				
Variance		0.0008				
Standard Deviation		0.0289				

7.82 a $P(X = 3) = P(X \leq 3) - P(X \leq 2) = .650 - .383 = .267$

b $P(X = 5) = P(X \leq 5) - P(X \leq 4) = .953 - .850 = .103$

c $P(X = 8) = P(X \leq 8) - P(X \leq 7) = 1.000 - .998 = .002$

7.84 $P(X = x) = \dfrac{n!}{x!(n-x)!} \, p^x (1-p)^{n-x}$

a $P(X = 0) = \dfrac{5!}{0!(5-0)!} \, (.4)^0 (1-.4)^{5-0} = .0778$

b a $P(X = 2) = \dfrac{5!}{2!(5-2)!} \, (.4)^2 (1-.4)^{5-2} = .3456$

c $P(X \le 3) = p(0) + p(1) + p(2) + p(3) = .0778 + .2592 + .3456 + .2304 = .9130$

d $P(X \ge 2) = p(2) + p(3) + p(4) + p(5) = .3456 + .2304 + .0768 + .01024 = .6630$

7.86 a .07776

b .34560

c .91296

d .66304

7.88 a .17119

b .09164

c .90953

d .81056

7.90 Binomial distribution with p = .25

a $P(X = 1) = \dfrac{4!}{1!(4-1)!} \, (.25)^1 (1-.25)^{4-1} = .4219$

b Table 1 with n = 8: $p(2) = P(X \le 2) - P(X \le 1) = .679 - .367 = .312$

c Excel: p(10) = .14436

7.92 a $P(X = 2) = \dfrac{5!}{2!(5-2)!} \, (.45)^2 (1-.45)^{5-2} = .3369$

b Excel with n = 25 and p = .45: $P(X \ge 10) = 1 - P(X \le 9) = 1 - .2424 = .7576$

7.94 a $P(X = 2) = \dfrac{5!}{2!(5-2)!} \, (.52)^2 (1-.52)^{5-2} = .2990$

b Excel with n = 25 and p = .52: $P(X \ge 10) = 1 - P(X \le 9) = 1 - .08033 = .91967$

7.96 Table 1 with n = 25 and p = .3: $P(X \leq 10) = .902$

7.98 Table 1 with n = 25 and p = .75: $P(X \geq 15) = 1 - P(X \leq 14) = 1 - .030 = .970$

7.100 $P(X = 0) = \dfrac{4!}{0!!(4-0)!} \, (.7)^0 (1-.7)^{4-0} = .0081$

7.102 Table 1 with n = 25 and p = .10

a $P(X = 0) = P(X \leq 0) = .072$

b $P(X < 5) = P(X \leq 4) = .902$

c $P(X > 2) = P(X \geq 3) = 1 - P(X \leq 2) = 1 - .537 = .463$

7.104 Excel with n = 100 and p = .20: $P(X > 40) = P(X \geq 41) = 1 - P(X \leq 40) = 1 - .999999 = .000001$

7.106 a $P(X = 0) = \dfrac{e^{-\mu}\mu^x}{x!} = \dfrac{e^{-2}2^0}{0!} = .1353$

b $P(X = 3) = \dfrac{e^{-\mu}\mu^x}{x!} = \dfrac{e^{-2}2^3}{3!} = .1804$

c $P(X = 5) = \dfrac{e^{-\mu}\mu^x}{x!} = \dfrac{e^{-2}2^5}{5!} = .0361$

7.108 a .13534

b .18045

c .03609

7.110a $P(X = 0) = P(X \leq 0) = .607$

b $P(X = 1) = P(X \leq 1) - P(X \leq 0) = .910 - .607 = .303$

c $P(X = 2) = P(X \leq 2) - P(X \leq 1) = .986 - .910 = .076$

7.112 a Table 2 with $\mu = 3.5$: $P(X = 0) = P(X \leq 0) = .030$

b Table 2 with $\mu = 3.5$: $P(X \geq 5) = 1 - P(X \leq 4) = 1 - .725 = .275$

c Table 2 with $\mu = 3.5/7$: $P(X = 1) = P(X \leq 1) - P(X \leq 0) = .910 - .607 = .303$

72

7.114 a $P(X = 0$ with $\mu = 2) = \dfrac{e^{-\mu}\mu^x}{x!} = \dfrac{e^{-2}(2)^0}{0!} = .1353$

b $P(X = 10$ with $\mu = 14) = \dfrac{e^{-\mu}\mu^x}{x!} = \dfrac{e^{-14}(14)^{10}}{10!} = .0663$

7.116 $P(X = 0$ with $\mu = 2) = \dfrac{e^{-\mu}\mu^x}{x!} = \dfrac{e^{-2}(2)^0}{0!} = .1353$

7.118 $P(X = 0$ with $\mu = 80/200) = \dfrac{e^{-\mu}\mu^x}{x!} = \dfrac{e^{-.4}(.4)^0}{0!} = .6703$

7.120 a Table 2 with $\mu = 1.5$: $P(X \geq 2) = 1 - P(X \leq 1) = 1 - .558 = .442$

b Table 2 $\mu = 6$: $P(X < 4) = P(X \leq 3) = .151$

7.122 a $P(X = 0$ with $\mu = 1.5) = \dfrac{e^{-\mu}\mu^x}{x!} = \dfrac{e^{-1.5}(1.5)^0}{0!} .2231$

b Table 2 with $\mu = 4.5$: $P(X \leq 5) = .703$

c Table 2 with $\mu = 3.0$: $P(X \geq 3) = 1 - P(X \leq 2 = 1 - .423 = .577$

7.124 a $E(X) = np = 40(.02) = .8$

b $P(X = 0) = \dfrac{40!}{0!(40-0)!} (.02)^0 (1-.02)^{40-0} = .4457$

7.126 a $P(X = 10$ with $\mu = 8) = \dfrac{e^{-\mu}\mu^x}{x!} = \dfrac{e^{-8}(8)^{10}}{10!} = .0993$

b Table 2 with $\mu = 8$: $P(X > 5) = P(X \geq 6) = 1 - P(X \leq 5) = 1 - .191 = .809$

c Table 2 with $\mu = 8$: $P(X < 12) = P(X \leq 11) = .888$

7.128 Table 1 with n = 10 and p = .3: $P(X > 5) = P(X \geq 6) = 1 - P(X \leq 5) = 1 - .953 = .047$

7.130 Table 1 with n = 10 and p = .20: $P(X \geq 6) = 1 - P(X \leq 5) = 1 - .994 = .006$

73

7.132 a Excel with n = 80 and p = .70: P(X > 65) = P(X $\geq$ 66) = 1 – P(X $\leq$ 65) = 1 - .99207 = .00793

b E(X) = np = 80(.70) = 56

c $\sigma = \sqrt{np(1-p)^2} = \sqrt{80(.70)(1-.70)} = 4.10$

7.134 Table 1 with n = 25 and p = .40:

a P(X = 10) = P(X $\leq$ 10) – P(X $\leq$ 9) = .586 - .425 = .161

b P(X < 5) = P(X $\leq$ 4) = .009

c P(X > 15) = P(X $\geq$ 16) = 1 – P(X $\leq$ 15) = 1 - .987 = .013

7.136 a $\mu = E(X) = \sum xp(x) = 0(.36) + 1(.22) + 2(.20) + 3(.09) + 4(.08) + 5(.05) = 1.46$

$\sigma^2 = V(X) = \sum (x-\mu)^2 p(x) = (0-1.46)^2 (.36) + (1-1.46)^2 (.22) + (2-1.46)^2 (.20)$

$\qquad + (3-1.46)^2 (.09) + (4-1.46)^2 (.08) + (5-1.46)^2 (.05) = 2.23$

$\sigma = \sqrt{\sigma^2} = \sqrt{2.23} = 1.49$

b $\mu = E(X) = \sum xp(x) = 0(.15) + 1(.18) + 2(.23) + 3(.26) + 4(.10) + 5(.08) = 2.22$

$\sigma^2 = V(X) = \sum (x-\mu)^2 p(x) = (0-2.22)^2 (.15) + (1-2.22)^2 (.18) + (2-2.22)^2 (.23)$

$\qquad + (3-2.22)^2 (.26) + (4-2.22)^2 (.10) + (5-2.22)^2 (.08) = 2.11$

$\sigma = \sqrt{\sigma^2} = \sqrt{2.11} = 1.45$

c Viewers of nonviolent shows remember more about the product that was advertised.

7.138 p = .08755 because P(X $\geq$ 1) = 1- P(X = 0 with n = 10 and p = .08755) = 1- .40 = .60

7.140 Binomial with n = 5 and p = .01.

x	p(x)
0	.95099
1	.04803
2	.00097
3	.00001
4	0
5	0

Chapter 8

8.2 a $P(X > 45) \approx \dfrac{(60-45) \times 2}{50 \times 15} + \dfrac{(75-60) \times 2}{50 \times 15} = .0800$

b $P(10 < X < 40) \approx \dfrac{(15-10) \times 17}{50 \times 15} + \dfrac{(30-15) \times 7}{50 \times 15} + \dfrac{(40-30) \times 6}{50 \times 15} = .3333$

c $P(X < 25) \approx \dfrac{(-15-[-30]) \times 6}{50 \times 15} + \dfrac{(0-[-15]) \times 10}{50 \times 15} + \dfrac{(15-0) \times 17}{50 \times 15} + \dfrac{(25-15) \times 7}{50 \times 15} = .7533$

d $P(35 < X < 65) \approx \dfrac{(45-35) \times 6}{50 \times 15} + \dfrac{(60-45) \times 2}{50 \times 15} + \dfrac{(65-60) \times 2}{50 \times 15} = .1333$

8.4 a

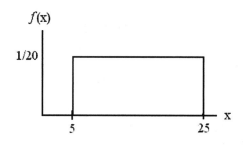

b $P(X > 25) = 0$

c $P(10 < X < 15) = (15-10)\dfrac{1}{20} = .25$

d $P(5.0 < X < 5.1) = (5.1-5)\dfrac{1}{20} = .005$

8.6 $f(x) = \dfrac{1}{(60-30)} = \dfrac{1}{30}$ $\quad 30 < x < 60$

a $P(X > 55) = (60-55)\dfrac{1}{30} = .1667$

b $P(30 < X < 40) = (40-30)\dfrac{1}{30} = .3333$

c $P(X = 37.23) = 0$

8.8 $.10 \times (60 - 30) = 3$; The top decile = 60-3 = 57 minutes

8.10 $.20(175-110) = 13$. Bottom 20% lie below $(110 + 13) = 123$ tons

8.12 a

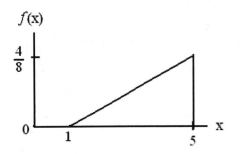

b $P(2.0 < X < 4.0) = P(X < 4) - P(X < 2) = (3)(3/8)(.5) - (1)(1/8)(.5) = .5625 - .0625 = .5$

c $P(X < 3) = (2)(2/8)(.5) = .25$

8.14 a $f(x) = .10 - .005x$ $0 \le x \le 20$

b $P(X > 10) = (10)(.05)(.5) = .25$

c $P(6 < X < 12) = P(X > 6) - PX > 12) = (14)(.07)(.5) - (8)(.04)(.5) = .49 - .16 = .33$

8.16 $P(0 < Z < 1.51) = .4345$

8.18 $P(0 < Z < 1.59) = .4441$

8.20 $P(0 < Z < 2.3) = .4893$

8.22 $P(Z > -1.44) = P(Z < 1.44) = .5 + P(0 < Z < 1.44) = .5 + .4251 = .9251$

8.24 $P(Z > 1.67) = .5 - P(0 < Z < 1.67) = .5 - .4525 = .0475$

8.26 $P(1.14 < Z < 2.43) = P(0 < Z < 2.43) - P(0 < Z < 1.14) = .4925 - .3729 = .1196$

8.28 $P(Z > 3.09) = .5 - P(0 < Z < 3.09) = .5 - .4990 = .0010$

76

8.30 $P(Z > 4.0) = 0$

8.32 $P(0 < Z < z_{.045}) = .5 - .045 = .4550;\ z_{.045} = 1.70$

8.34 $P(X > 145) = P\left(\dfrac{X - \mu}{\sigma} > \dfrac{145 - 100}{20}\right) = P(Z > 2.25) = .5 - P(0 < Z < 2.25)$

$= .5 - .4878 = .0122$

8.36 $P(800 < X < 1100) = P\left(\dfrac{800 - 1000}{250} < \dfrac{X - \mu}{\sigma} < \dfrac{1100 - 1000}{250}\right) = P(-.8 < Z > .4)$

$= P(0 < Z < .4) + P(0 < Z < .8) = .1554 + .2881 = .4435$

8.38 a $P(5 < X < 10) = P\left(\dfrac{5 - 6.3}{2.2} < \dfrac{X - \mu}{\sigma} < \dfrac{10 - 6.3}{2.2}\right) = P(-.59 < Z > 1.68)$

$= P(0 < Z < 1.68) + P(0 < Z < .59 = .4535 + .2224 = .6759$

b $P(X > 7) = P\left(\dfrac{X - \mu}{\sigma} > \dfrac{7 - 6.3}{2.2}\right) = P(Z > .32) = .5 - P(0 < Z < .32)$

$= .5 - .1255 = .3745$

c $P(X < 4) = P\left(\dfrac{X - \mu}{\sigma} < \dfrac{4 - 6.3}{2.2}\right) = P(Z < -1.05) = .5 - P(0 < Z < 1.05)$

$= .5 - .3531 = .1469$

8.40 $P(X > 5000) = P\left(\dfrac{X - \mu}{\sigma} > \dfrac{5000 - 5100}{200}\right) = P(Z > -.5) = .5 + P(0 < Z < .5)$

$= .5 + .1915 = .6915$

8.42 a $P(X > 12000) = P\left(\dfrac{X - \mu}{\sigma} > \dfrac{12000 - 10000}{2400}\right) = P(Z > .83) = .5 - P(0 < Z < .83)$

$= .5 - .2967 = .2033$

b $P(X < 9000) = P\left(\dfrac{X - \mu}{\sigma} < \dfrac{9000 - 10000}{2400}\right) = P(Z < -.42) = .5 - P(0 < Z < .42)$

$= .5 - .1628 = .3372$

8.44 a $P(X > 70) = P\left(\dfrac{X-\mu}{\sigma} > \dfrac{70-65}{4}\right) = P(Z > 1.25) = .5 - P(0 < Z < 1.25)$

$= .5 - .3944 = .1056$

b $P(X < 60) = P\left(\dfrac{X-\mu}{\sigma} < \dfrac{60-65}{4}\right) = P(Z < -1.25) = .5 - P(0 < Z < 1.25)$

$= .5 - .3944 = .1056$

c $P(55 < X < 70) = P\left(\dfrac{55-65}{4} < \dfrac{X-\mu}{\sigma} < \dfrac{70-65}{4}\right) = P(-2.50 < Z < 1.25)$

$= P(0 < Z < 2.50) + P(0 < Z < 1.25) = .4938 + .3944 = .8882$

8.46 Top 5%: $P(0 < Z < z_{.05}) = .5 - .05 = .4500$; $z_{.05} = 1.645$

$z_{.05} = \dfrac{x-\mu}{\sigma}$; $1.645 = \dfrac{x-32}{1.5}$; $x = 34.4675$

Bottom 5%: $P(-z_{.05} < Z < 0) = .5 - .05 = .4500$; $-z_{.05} = -1.645$

$-z_{.05} = \dfrac{x-\mu}{\sigma}$; $-1.645 = \dfrac{x-32}{1.5}$; $x = 29.5325$

8.48 $P(X > 8) = P\left(\dfrac{X-\mu}{\sigma} > \dfrac{8-7.2}{.667}\right) = P\,Z > 1.2) = .5 - P(0 < Z < 1.2)$

$= .5 - .3849 = .1151$

8.50 a $P(X > 10) = P\left(\dfrac{X-\mu}{\sigma} > \dfrac{10-7.5}{2.1}\right) = P\,Z > 1.19) = .5 - P(0 < Z < 1.19)$

$= .5 - .3830 = .1170$

b $P(7 < X < 9) = P\left(\dfrac{7-7.5}{2.1} < \dfrac{X-\mu}{\sigma} < \dfrac{9-7.5}{2.1}\right) = P(-.24 < Z < .71)$

$= P(0 < Z < .24) + P(0 < Z < .71) = .0948 + .2611 = .3559$

c $P(X < 3) = P\left(\dfrac{X-\mu}{\sigma} < \dfrac{3-7.5}{2.1}\right) = P\,Z < -2.14) = .5 - P(0 < Z < 2.14)$

$= .5 - .4838 = .0162$

d $P(-z_{.05} < Z < 0) = .5 - .05 = .4500$; $-z_{.05} = -1.645$;

$$-z_{.05} = \frac{x - \mu}{\sigma}; \quad -1.645 = \frac{x - 7.5}{2.1}; \quad x = 4.05 \text{ hours}$$

8.52 $P(-z_{.01} < Z < 0) = .5 - .01 = .4900; \quad -z_{.01} = -2.33$

$$-z_{.01} = \frac{x - \mu}{\sigma}; \quad -2.33 = \frac{x - 11500}{800}; \quad x = 9{,}636 \text{ pages}$$

8.54 a $P(X > 30) = P\left(\frac{X - \mu}{\sigma} > \frac{30 - 27}{7}\right) = P(Z > .43) = .5 - P(0 < Z < .43)$

$$= .5 - .1664 = .3336$$

b $P(X > 40) = P\left(\frac{X - \mu}{\sigma} > \frac{40 - 27}{7}\right) = P(Z > 1.86) = .5 - P(0 < Z < 1.86)$

$$= .5 - .4686 = .0314$$

c $P(X < 15) = P\left(\frac{X - \mu}{\sigma} < \frac{15 - 27}{7}\right) = P(Z < -1.71) = .5 - P(0 < Z < 1.71)$

$$= .5 - .4564 = .0436$$

d $P(0 < Z < z_{.20}) = .5 - .20 = .3000; \quad z_{.20} = .84$

$$z_{.20} = \frac{x - \mu}{\sigma}; \quad .84 = \frac{x - 27}{7}; \quad x = 32.88$$

8.56 a $P(X < 10) = P\left(\frac{X - \mu}{\sigma} < \frac{10 - 16.40}{2.75}\right) = P(Z < -2.33) = .5 - P(0 < Z < 2.33)$

$$= .5 - .4901 = .0099$$

b $P(-z_{.10} < Z < 0) = .5 - .10 = .4000; \quad -z_{.10} = 1.28$

$$-z_{.10} = \frac{x - \mu}{\sigma}; \quad -1.28 = \frac{x - 16.40}{2.75}; \quad x = 12.88$$

8.58 $P(0 < Z < z_{.02}) = .5 - .02 = .4800; \quad z_{.02} = 2.05$

$$z_{.02} = \frac{x - \mu}{\sigma}; \quad 2.05 = \frac{x - 100}{16}; \quad x = 132.80 \text{ (rounded to 133)}$$

8.60 $P(0 < Z < z_{.06}) = .5 - .06 = .4400; \quad z_{.06} = 1.55$

$$z_{.06} = \frac{x - \mu}{\sigma}; \ 1.55 = \frac{x - 200}{30}; \ x = 246.5 \text{ (rounded to 247)}$$

8.62 $P(0 < Z < z_{.30}) = .5 - .30 = .2000; \ z_{.30} = .52$

$$z_{.30} = \frac{x - \mu}{\sigma}; \ .52 = \frac{x - 850}{90}; \ x = 896.8 \text{ (rounded to 897)}$$

8.64 From Exercise 7.57: $\mu = 65$, $\sigma^2 = 21$, and $\sigma = 4.58$

$$P(X > 60) = P\left(\frac{X - \mu}{\sigma} > \frac{60 - 65}{4.58}\right) = P(Z > -1.09) = .5 + .3621 = .8621$$

8.66 From Exercise 7.59: $\mu = 100$, $\sigma^2 = 30$, and $\sigma = 5.48$

$$P(X < 110) = P\left(\frac{X - \mu}{\sigma} < \frac{110 - 100}{5.48}\right) = P(Z < 1.82) = .5 + .4656 = .9656$$

8.68 a $P(X > 25) = P\left(\frac{X - \mu}{\sigma} > \frac{25 - 14}{18}\right) = P(Z > .61) = .5 - .2291 = .2709$

b $P(X < 0) = P\left(\frac{X - \mu}{\sigma} < \frac{0 - 14}{18}\right) = P(Z < -.78) = .5 - .2823 = .2177$

8.70 a $P(X < 0) = P\left(\frac{X - \mu}{\sigma} < \frac{0 - .12}{02}\right) = P(Z < -6.00) = 0$

b $P(X > .20) = P\left(\frac{X - \mu}{\sigma} > \frac{.20 - .12}{.02}\right) = P(Z > 4.00) = 0$

c $P(X < 0) = P\left(\frac{X - \mu}{\sigma} < \frac{0 - .25}{.15}\right) = P(Z < -1.67) = .5 - .4525 = .0475$

d $P(X > .20) = P\left(\frac{X - \mu}{\sigma} > \frac{.20 - .25}{.15}\right) = P(Z > -.33) = .5 + .1293 = .6293$

8.72 The probability of losing money is greater than that for stock 1 but less than that for stock 2. The probability of returning more that 20% is greater than that for stock 1 but less than that for stock 2.

8.74 a $P(X < 0) = P\left(\dfrac{X - \mu}{\sigma} < \dfrac{0 - .106}{.1456}\right) = P(Z < -.73) = ..5 - .2673 = .2327$

b $P(X > .15) = P\left(\dfrac{X - \mu}{\sigma} > \dfrac{.15 - .106}{.1456}\right) = P(Z > .30) = .5 - .1179 = .3821$

The statistics used in Exercises 7.68 to 7.80 were computed by Excel. The variances were taken from the variance-covariance matrix. As a result they are the population parameters. These values were used in producing the solutions to Exercises 8.76 to 8.79

8.76 a $P(X < 0) = P\left(\dfrac{X - \mu}{\sigma} < \dfrac{0 - .058}{.064}\right) = P(Z < -.91) = .5 - .3186 = .1814$

b $P(X > .20) = P\left(\dfrac{X - \mu}{\sigma} > \dfrac{.20 - .058}{.064}\right) = P(Z > 2.22) = .5 - .4868 = .0132$

8.78 a $P(X < 0) = P\left(\dfrac{X - \mu}{\sigma} < \dfrac{0 - .0351}{.2231}\right) = P(Z < -.16) = .5 - .0636 = .4364$

b $P(X > .40) = P\left(\dfrac{X - \mu}{\sigma} > \dfrac{.40 - .0351}{.2231}\right) = P(Z > 1.64) = .5 - .4495 = .0505$

8.80

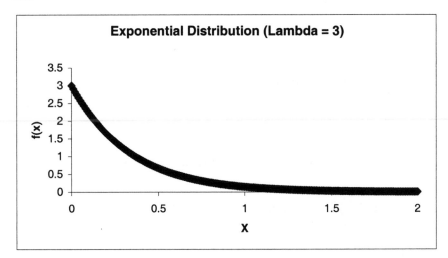

8.82 a $P(X > 1) = e^{-.5(1)} = e^{-.5} = .6065$

a $P(X > .4) = e^{-.5(.4)} = e^{-.2} = .8187$

c $P(X < .5) = 1 - e^{-.5(.5)} = 1 - e^{-.25} = 1 - .7788 = .2212$

d $P(X < 2) = 1 - e^{-.5(2)} = 1 - e^{-1} = 1 - .3679 = .6321$

8.84 a $P(X > 2) = e^{-.3(2)} = e^{-.6} = .5488$

b $P(X < 4) = 1 - e^{-.3(4)} = 1 - e^{-1.2} = 1 - .3012 = .6988$

c $P(1 < X < 2) = e^{-.3(1)} - e^{-.3(2)} = e^{-.3} - e^{-.6} = .7408 - .5488 = .1920$

d $P(X = 3) = 0$

8.86 $\mu = 1/\lambda = 25$ hours; $\lambda = .04$ breakdowns/hour

$P(X > 50) = e^{-.04(50)} = e^{-2} = .1353$

8.88 $\mu = 1/\lambda = 5$ minutes; $\lambda = .2$ customer/minute

$P(X < 10) = 1 - e^{-.2(10)} = 1 - e^{-2} = 1 - .1353 = .8647$

8.90 $\mu = 1/\lambda = 7.5$ minutes; $\lambda = .133$ service/minute

$P(X < 5) = 1 - e^{-.133(5)} = 1 - e^{-.665} = 1 - .5143 = .4857$

8.92 $\mu = 1/\lambda = 6$ minutes; $\lambda = .167$ customers/minute

$P(X > 10) = e^{-.167(10)} = e^{-1.67} = .1889$

8.94	a 2.724	b 1.282	c 2.132	d 2.528
8.96	a 1.6556	b 2.6810	c 1.9600	d 1.6602
8.98	a .1744	b .0231	c .0251	d .0267
8.100	a 17.2919	b 50.8922	c 2.70554	d 53.5400

8.102   a 33.5705   b 866.911   c 24.3976   d 261.058

8.104   a .4881   b .9158   c .9988   d .9077

8.106   a 2.84   b 1.93   c 3.60   d 3.37

8.108   a 1.5204   b 1.5943   c 2.8397   d 1.1670

8.110   a .1050   b .1576   c .0001   d .0044

Chapter 9

9.2 a $P(\overline{X} = 3) = P(1,5) + P(2,4) + P(3,3) + P(4,2) + P(5,1) = 5(1/36) = 5/36$

b $P(\overline{X} = 4) = P(2,6) + P(3,5) + P(4,4) + P(5,3) + P(6,2) = 5(1/36) = 5/36$

c $P(\overline{X} = 1) = P(1,1) = 1/36$

d $P(\overline{X} = 6) = P(6,6) = 1/36$

9.4 a $P(\overline{X} = 1) = (1/6)^5 = .0001286$

b $P(\overline{X} = 6) = (1/6)^5 = .0001286$

9.6 No because of the central limit theorem.

9.8 a $P(\overline{X} > 1050) = P\left(\dfrac{\overline{X} - \mu}{\sigma/\sqrt{n}} > \dfrac{1050 - 1000}{200/\sqrt{25}}\right) = P(Z > 1.25) = .5 - P(0 < Z < 1.25)$

$= .5 - .3944 = .1056$

b $P(\overline{X} < 960) = P\left(\dfrac{\overline{X} - \mu}{\sigma/\sqrt{n}} < \dfrac{960 - 1000}{200/\sqrt{25}}\right) = P(Z < -1.00) = .5 - P(0 < Z < 1.00)$

$= .5 - .3413 = .1587$

c $P(\overline{X} > 1100) = P\left(\dfrac{\overline{X} - \mu}{\sigma/\sqrt{n}} > \dfrac{1100 - 1000}{200/\sqrt{25}}\right) = P(Z > 2.50) = .5 - P(0 < Z < 2.50)$

$= .5 - .4938 = .0062$

9.10 a $P(49 < \overline{X} < 52) = P\left(\dfrac{49 - 50}{5/\sqrt{4}} < \dfrac{\overline{X} - \mu}{\sigma/\sqrt{n}} < \dfrac{52 - 50}{5/\sqrt{4}}\right) = P(-.40 < Z < .80)$

$= P(0 < Z < .40) + P(0 < Z < .80) = .1554 + .2881 = .4435$

b $P(49 < \overline{X} < 52) = P\left(\dfrac{49 - 50}{5/\sqrt{16}} < \dfrac{\overline{X} - \mu}{\sigma/\sqrt{n}} < \dfrac{52 - 50}{5/\sqrt{16}}\right) = P(-.80 < Z < 1.60)$

$= P(0 < Z < .80) + P(0 < Z < 1.60) = .2881 + .4452 = .7333$

c $P(49 < \overline{X} < 52) = P\left(\dfrac{49-50}{5/\sqrt{25}} < \dfrac{\overline{X}-\mu}{\sigma/\sqrt{n}} < \dfrac{52-50}{5/\sqrt{25}}\right) = P(-1.00 < Z < 2.00)$

$$= P(0 < Z < 1.00) + P(0 < Z < 2.00) = .3413 + .4772 = .8185$$

9.12 a $P(49 < \overline{X} < 52) = P\left(\dfrac{49-50}{20/\sqrt{4}} < \dfrac{\overline{X}-\mu}{\sigma/\sqrt{n}} < \dfrac{52-50}{20/\sqrt{4}}\right) = P(-.10 < Z < .20)$

$$= P(0 < Z < .10) + P(0 < Z < .20) = .0398 + .0793 = .1191$$

b $P(49 < \overline{X} < 52) = P\left(\dfrac{49-50}{20/\sqrt{16}} < \dfrac{\overline{X}-\mu}{\sigma/\sqrt{n}} < \dfrac{52-50}{20/\sqrt{16}}\right) = P(-.20 < Z < .40)$

$$= P(0 < Z < .20) + P(0 < Z < .40) = .0793 + .1554 = .2347$$

c $P(49 < \overline{X} < 52) = P\left(\dfrac{49-50}{20/\sqrt{25}} < \dfrac{\overline{X}-\mu}{\sigma/\sqrt{n}} < \dfrac{52-50}{20/\sqrt{25}}\right) = P(-.25 < Z < .50)$

$$= P(0 < Z < .25) + P(0 < Z < .50) = .0987 + .1915 = .2902$$

9.14 We can answer part (c) and possibly part (b) depending on how nonnormal the population is.

9.16 a $P(X > 60) = P\left(\dfrac{X-\mu}{\sigma} > \dfrac{60-52}{6}\right) = P(Z > 1.33) = .5 - P(0 < Z < 1.33)$

$$= .5 - .4082 = .0918$$

b $P(\overline{X} > 60) = P\left(\dfrac{\overline{X}-\mu}{\sigma/\sqrt{n}} > \dfrac{60-52}{6/\sqrt{3}}\right) = P(Z > 2.31) = .5 - P(0 < Z < 2.31)$

$$= .5 - .4896 = .0104$$

c $[P(X > 60)]^{3} = [.0918]^{3} = .00077$

9.18 a $P(X < 75) = P\left(\dfrac{X-\mu}{\sigma} < \dfrac{75-78}{6}\right) = P(Z < -.50) = .5 - P(0 < Z < .50)$

$$= .5 - .1915 = .3085$$

b $P(\overline{X} < 75) = P\left(\dfrac{\overline{X}-\mu}{\sigma/\sqrt{n}} < \dfrac{75-78}{6/\sqrt{50}}\right) = P(Z < -3.54) = .5 - P(0 < Z < 3.54) = .5 - .5 = 0$

9.20 a $P(\overline{X} < 5.97) = P\left(\dfrac{\overline{X} - \mu}{\sigma / \sqrt{n}} < \dfrac{5.97 - 6.05}{.18 / \sqrt{36}}\right) = P(Z < -2.67) = .5 - P(0 < Z < 2.67)$

$= .5 - .4962 = .0038$

b It appears to be false.

9.22 The professor needs to know the mean and standard deviation of the population of the weights of elevator users and that the distribution is not extremely nonnormal.

9.24 P(Total time > 300) = $P(\overline{X} > 300 / 60) = P(\overline{X} > 5) = P\left(\dfrac{\overline{X} - \mu}{\sigma / \sqrt{n}} > \dfrac{5 - 4.8}{1.3 / \sqrt{60}}\right) = P(Z > 1.19)$

$= .5 - P(0 < Z < 1.19) = .5 - .3830 = .1170$

9.26 $P(\overline{X} < 53,000) = P\left(\dfrac{\overline{X} - \mu}{\sigma / \sqrt{n}} < \dfrac{53,000 - 55,000}{4,600 / \sqrt{38}}\right) = P(Z < -2.68)$

$= .5 - P(0 < Z < 2.68) = .5 - .4963 = .0037$

9.28 $P(\hat{P} > .60) = P\left(\dfrac{\hat{P} - p}{\sqrt{p(1 - p) / n}} > \dfrac{.60 - .5}{\sqrt{(.5)(1 - .5) / 300}}\right) = P(Z > 3.46) = 0$

9.30 $P(\hat{P} > .60) = P\left(\dfrac{\hat{P} - p}{\sqrt{p(1 - p) / n}} > \dfrac{.60 - .6}{\sqrt{(.6)(1 - .6) / 300}}\right) = P(Z > 0) = .5$

9.32 $P(\hat{P} < .22) = P\left(\dfrac{\hat{P} - p}{\sqrt{p(1 - p) / n}} > \dfrac{.22 - .25}{\sqrt{(.25)(1 - .25) / 800}}\right) = P(Z < -1.96)$

$= .5 - P(0 < Z < 1.96) = .5 - .4750 = .0250$

9.34 $P(\hat{P} < .49) = P\left(\dfrac{\hat{P} - p}{\sqrt{p(1 - p) / n}} < \dfrac{.49 - .55}{\sqrt{(.55)(1 - .55) / 500}}\right) = P(Z < -2.70)$

$= .5 - P(0 < Z < 2.70) = .5 - .4965 = .0035$

9.36 $P(\hat{P} < .50) = P\left(\dfrac{\hat{P} - p}{\sqrt{p(1-p)/n}} < \dfrac{.50 - .53}{\sqrt{(.53)(1-.53)/400}}\right) = P(Z < -1.20)$

$= .5 - P(0 < Z < 1.20) = .5 - .3849 = .1151$; the claim may be true

9.38 $P(\hat{P} > .10) = P\left(\dfrac{\hat{P} - p}{\sqrt{p(1-p)/n}} > \dfrac{.10 - .05}{\sqrt{(.05)(1-.05)/400}}\right) = P(Z > 4.59) = 0$; the claim appears to be

false

9.40 a $P(\hat{P} < .45) = P\left(\dfrac{\hat{P} - p}{\sqrt{p(1-p)/n}} < \dfrac{.45 - .50}{\sqrt{(.50)(1-.50)/600}}\right) = P(Z < -2.45)$

$= .5 - P(0 < Z < 2.45) = .5 - .4929 = .0071$

b The claim appears to be false.

9.42 $P(\hat{P} < .70) = P\left(\dfrac{\hat{P} - p}{\sqrt{p(1-p)/n}} < \dfrac{.70 - .75}{\sqrt{(.75)(1-.75)/460}}\right) = P(Z < -2.48)$

$= .5 - P(0 < Z < 2.48) = .5 - .4934 = .0066$

9.44 The claim appears to be false.

9.46 $P(\overline{X}_1 - \overline{X}_2 > 25) = P\left(\dfrac{(\overline{X}_1 - \overline{X}_2) - (\mu_1 - \mu_2)}{\sqrt{\dfrac{\sigma_1^2}{n_1} + \dfrac{\sigma_2^2}{n_2}}} > \dfrac{25 - (280 - 270)}{\sqrt{\dfrac{25^2}{50} + \dfrac{30^2}{50}}}\right) = P(Z > 2.72)$

$= .5 - P(0 < Z < 2.72) = .5 - .4967 = .0033$

9.48 $P(\overline{X}_1 - \overline{X}_2 > 0) = P\left(\dfrac{(\overline{X}_1 - \overline{X}_2) - (\mu_1 - \mu_2)}{\sqrt{\dfrac{\sigma_1^2}{n_1} + \dfrac{\sigma_2^2}{n_2}}} > \dfrac{0 - (40 - 38)}{\sqrt{\dfrac{6^2}{25} + \dfrac{8^2}{25}}}\right) = P(Z > -1.00)$

$= .5 + P(0 < Z < 1.00) = .5 + .3413 = .8413$

9.50 $P(\overline{X}_1 - \overline{X}_2 > 0) = P\left(\dfrac{(\overline{X}_1 - \overline{X}_2) - (\mu_1 - \mu_2)}{\sqrt{\dfrac{\sigma_1^2}{n_1} + \dfrac{\sigma_2^2}{n_2}}} > \dfrac{0 - (140 - 138)}{\sqrt{\dfrac{6^2}{25} + \dfrac{8^2}{25}}}\right) = P(Z > -1.00)$

$$= .5 + P(0 < Z < 1.00) = .5 + .3413 = .8413$$

9.52 a $P(X_1 - X_2 > 0) = P\left(\dfrac{(X_1 - X_2) - (\mu_1 - \mu_2)}{\sqrt{\sigma_1^2 + \sigma_2^2}} > \dfrac{0 - (73 - 77)}{\sqrt{12^2 + 10^2}}\right) = P(Z > .26)$

$$= .5 - P(0 < Z < .26) = .5 - .1026 = .3974$$

b $P(\overline{X}_1 - \overline{X}_2 > 0) = P\left(\dfrac{(\overline{X}_1 - \overline{X}_2) - (\mu_1 - \mu_2)}{\sqrt{\dfrac{\sigma_1^2}{n_1} + \dfrac{\sigma_2^2}{n_2}}} > \dfrac{0 - (73 - 77)}{\sqrt{\dfrac{12^2}{4} + \dfrac{10^2}{4}}}\right) = P(Z > .51)$

$$= .5 - P(0 < Z < .51) = .5 - .1950 = .3050$$

9.54 $P(\overline{X}_1 - \overline{X}_2 < 0) = P\left(\dfrac{(\overline{X}_1 - \overline{X}_2) - (\mu_1 - \mu_2)}{\sqrt{\dfrac{\sigma_1^2}{n_1} + \dfrac{\sigma_2^2}{n_2}}} < \dfrac{0 - (10 - 15)}{\sqrt{\dfrac{3^2}{25} + \dfrac{3^2}{25}}}\right) = P(Z < 5.89) = 1$

Chapter 10

10.2

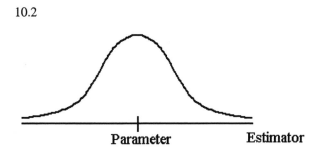

Parameter   Estimator

10.4 An unbiased estimator is consistent if the difference between the estimator and the parameter grows smaller as the sample size grows.

10.6

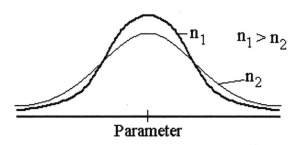

n_1 $n_1 > n_2$

n_2

Parameter

10.8

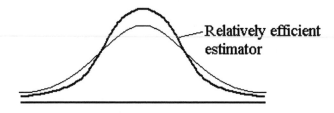

Relatively efficient estimator

10.10 $\bar{x} \pm z_{\alpha/2}\sigma/\sqrt{n} = 100 \pm 1.645(25/\sqrt{50}) = 100 \pm 5.82$; LCL = 94.18, UCL = 105.82

10.12 The interval widens.

10.14 $\bar{x} \pm z_{\alpha/2}\sigma/\sqrt{n} = 100 \pm 1.96(50/\sqrt{50}) = 100 \pm 13.86$; LCL = 86.14, UCL = 113.86

10.16 $\bar{x} \pm z_{\alpha/2}\sigma/\sqrt{n} = 100 \pm 1.96(25/\sqrt{25}) = 100 \pm 9.80$; LCL = 90.20, UCL = 109.80

10.18 The interval narrows.

10.20 $\bar{x} \pm z_{\alpha/2}\sigma/\sqrt{n} = 200 \pm 1.96(25/\sqrt{50}) = 200 \pm 6.93$; LCL = 193.07, UCL = 206.93

10.22 $\bar{x} \pm z_{\alpha/2}\sigma/\sqrt{n} = 500 \pm 1.645(12/\sqrt{50}) = 500 \pm 2.79$; LCL = 497.21, UCL = 502.79

10.24 $\bar{x} \pm z_{\alpha/2}\sigma/\sqrt{n} = 500 \pm 2.575(12/\sqrt{50}) = 500 \pm 4.37$; LCL = 495.63, UCL = 504.37

10.26 $\bar{x} \pm z_{\alpha/2}\sigma/\sqrt{n} = 500 \pm 1.645(10/\sqrt{50} = 500 \pm 2.33$; LCL = 497.67, UCL = 502.33

10.28 The interval narrows.

10.30 $\bar{x} \pm z_{\alpha/2}\sigma/\sqrt{n} = 500 \pm 1.645(12/\sqrt{200}) = 500 \pm 1.40$; LCL = 498.60, UCL = 501.40

10.32 $\bar{x} \pm z_{\alpha/2}\sigma/\sqrt{n} = 100 \pm 1.645(12/\sqrt{50}) = 100 \pm 2.79$; LCL = 97.21, UCL 102.79

10.34 Yes, because the expected value of the sample median is equal to the population mean.

10.36 Because the variance of the sample mean is less than the variance of the sample median, the sample mean is relatively more efficient than the sample median.

10.38 sample median $\pm z_{\alpha/2} \dfrac{1.2533\,\sigma}{\sqrt{n}} = 500 \pm 1.645\dfrac{1.2533\,(12)}{\sqrt{50}} = 500 \pm 3.50$

10.40 The median is calculated by placing all the observations in order. Thus, the median loses the potential information contained in the actual values in the sample. This results in a wider interval estimate.

10.42 $\bar{x} \pm z_{\alpha/2} \sigma / \sqrt{n} = 43.75 \pm 1.96(10/\sqrt{8}) = 43.75 \pm 6.93$; LCL = 36.82, UCL = 50.68

10.44 $\bar{x} \pm z_{\alpha/2} \sigma / \sqrt{n} = 9.85 \pm 1.645(8/\sqrt{20}) = 9.85 \pm 2.94$; LCL = 6.91, UCL = 12.79

10.46 $\bar{x} \pm z_{\alpha/2} \sigma / \sqrt{n} = 22 \pm 2.575(5/\sqrt{100}) = 22 \pm 1.29$; LCL = 20.71, UCL = 23.29

10.48 $\bar{x} \pm z_{\alpha/2} \sigma / \sqrt{n} = 25 \pm 1.645(6/\sqrt{50}) = 25 \pm 1.40$; LCL = 23.60, UCL = 26.40

10.50 $\bar{x} \pm z_{\alpha/2} \sigma / \sqrt{n} = 252.38 \pm 1.96(30/\sqrt{400}) = 252.38 \pm 2.94$; LCL = 249.44, UCL = 255.32

10.52 $\bar{x} \pm z_{\alpha/2} \sigma / \sqrt{n} = 12.10 \pm 1.645(2.1/\sqrt{200}) = 12.10 \pm .24$; LCL = 11.86, UCL = 12.34. We estimate that the mean rate of return on all real estate investments lies between 11.86% and 12.34%. This type of estimate is correct 90% of the time.

10.54 $\bar{x} \pm z_{\alpha/2} \sigma / \sqrt{n} = .510 \pm 2.575(.1/\sqrt{250}) = .510 \pm .16$; LCL = .494, UCL = .526. We estimate that the mean growth rate of this type of grass lies between .494 and .526 inch . This type of estimate is correct 99% of the time.

10.56 $\bar{x} \pm z_{\alpha/2} \sigma / \sqrt{n} = 19.28 \pm 1.645(6/\sqrt{250}) = 19.28 \pm .62$; LCL = 18.66, UCL = 19.90. We estimate that the mean leisure time per week of Japanese middle managers lies between 18.66 and 19.90 hours. This type of estimate is correct 90% of the time.

10.58 $\bar{x} \pm z_{\alpha/2} \sigma / \sqrt{n} = 585,063 \pm 1.645(30,000/\sqrt{80}) = 585,063 \pm 5,518$; LCL = 579,545, UCL = 590,581. We estimate that the mean annual income of all company presidents lies between $579,545 and $590,581. This type of estimate is correct 90% of the time.

10.60 $\bar{x} \pm z_{\alpha/2}\sigma/\sqrt{n} = 27.19 \pm 1.96(8/\sqrt{100}) = 27.19 \pm 1.57; \text{LCL} = 25.62, \text{UCL} = 28.76$

10.62 $n = \left(\frac{z_{\alpha/2}\sigma}{W}\right)^2 = \left(\frac{1.645 \times 100}{10}\right)^2 = 271$

10.64 $n = \left(\frac{z_{\alpha/2}\sigma}{W}\right)^2 = \left(\frac{1.645 \times 50}{20}\right)^2 = 17$

10.66 $n = \left(\frac{z_{\alpha/2}\sigma}{W}\right)^2 = \left(\frac{2.575 \times 250}{50}\right)^2 = 166$

10.68 $n = \left(\frac{z_{\alpha/2}\sigma}{W}\right)^2 = \left(\frac{1.96 \times 250}{50}\right)^2 = 97$

10.70 a The sample size decreases.

b the sample size decreases.

c The sample size increases.

10.72 150 ± 1

10.74 $\bar{x} \pm z_{\alpha/2}\sigma/\sqrt{n} = 150 \pm 1.645(20/\sqrt{271}) = 150 \pm 2$

10.76 $n = \left(\frac{z_{\alpha/2}\sigma}{W}\right)^2 = \left(\frac{1.96 \times 200}{10}\right)^2 = 1537$

10.78 $\bar{x} \pm z_{\alpha/2}\sigma/\sqrt{n} = 500 \pm 1.96(100/\sqrt{1537}) = 500 \pm 5$

10.80 a The width of the confidence interval estimate is equal to what was specified.

b The width of the confidence interval estimate is narrower than what was specified.

c The width of the confidence interval estimate is wider than what was specified.

10.82 $n = \left(\dfrac{z_{\alpha/2}\sigma}{W} \right)^2 = \left(\dfrac{2.575 \times 360}{20} \right)^2 = 2149$

10.84 $n = \left(\dfrac{z_{\alpha/2}\sigma}{W} \right)^2 = \left(\dfrac{1.645 \times 20}{1} \right)^2 = 1083$

10.86 $n = \left(\dfrac{z_{\alpha/2}\sigma}{W} \right)^2 = \left(\dfrac{1.96 \times 15}{2} \right)^2 = 217$

Chapter 11

11.2 H_0 : I will complete the Ph.D.

       H_1 : I will not be able to complete the Ph.D.

11.4 H_0 : Risky investment is more successful

       H_1 : Risky investment is not more successful

11.6 The defendant in both cases was O. J. Simpson. The verdicts were logical because in the criminal trial the amount of evidence to convict is greater than the amount of evidence required in a civil trial. The two juries concluded that there was enough (preponderance of) evidence in the civil trial, but not enough evidence (beyond a reasonable doubt) in the criminal trial.

11.8 Rejection region: $z > z_\alpha = z_{.03} = 1.88$

$$z = \frac{\bar{x} - \mu}{\sigma / \sqrt{n}} = \frac{51 - 50}{5 / \sqrt{9}} = .60$$

p-value = $P(Z > .60) = .5 - .2257 = .2743$

There is not enough evidence to infer that $\mu > 50$.

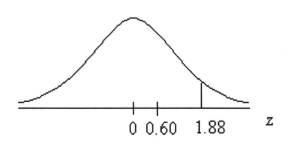

0   0.60   1.88   z

11.10 Rejection region: $z < -z_{\alpha/2} = -z_{.025} = -1.96$ or $z > z_{\alpha/2} = z_{.025} = 1.96$

$$z = \frac{\bar{x} - \mu}{\sigma/\sqrt{n}} = \frac{100 - 100}{10/\sqrt{100}} = 0$$

p-value = 2P(Z > 0) = 2(.5) = 1.00

There is no evidence to infer that $\mu \neq 100$.

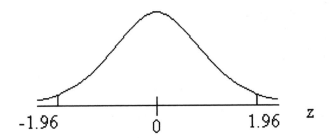

11.12 Rejection region: $z < -z_{\alpha} = -z_{.05} = -1.645$

$$z = \frac{\bar{x} - \mu}{\sigma/\sqrt{n}} = \frac{48 - 50}{15/\sqrt{100}} = -1.33$$

p-value = P(Z < -1.33) = .5 - .4082 = .0918

There is not enough evidence to infer that $\mu < 50$.

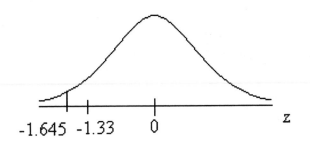

11.14 $z = \dfrac{\overline{x} - \mu}{\sigma / \sqrt{n}} = \dfrac{52 - 50}{5 / \sqrt{25}} = 2.00$ p-value = $P(Z > 2.00) = .5 - .4772 = .0228$.

There is enough evidence to infer that $\mu > 50$.

11.16 The value of the test statistic increases and the p-value decreases.

11.18 $z = \dfrac{\overline{x} - \mu}{\sigma / \sqrt{n}} = \dfrac{52 - 50}{20 / \sqrt{9}} = .30$ p-value = $P(Z > .30) = .5 - .1179 = .3821$.

There is not enough evidence to infer that $\mu > 50$.

11.20 $z = \dfrac{\overline{x} - \mu}{\sigma / \sqrt{n}} = \dfrac{54 - 50}{5 / \sqrt{9}} = 2.40$ p-value = $P(Z > 2.40) = .5 - .4918 = .0082$.

There is enough evidence to infer that $\mu > 50$.

11.22 The value of the test statistic increases and the p-value decreases.

11.24 $z = \dfrac{\overline{x} - \mu}{\sigma / \sqrt{n}} = \dfrac{99 - 100}{8 / \sqrt{50}} = -.88$ p-value = $P(< -.88) = .5 - .3106 = .1894$

There is not enough evidence to infer that $\mu < 100$.

11.26 The value of the test statistic increases (becomes less negative) and the p-value increases.

11.28 $z = \dfrac{\overline{x} - \mu}{\sigma / \sqrt{n}} = \dfrac{99 - 100}{15 / \sqrt{100}} = -.67$ p-value = $P(Z < -.67) = .5 - .2486 = .2514$.

There is not enough evidence to infer that $\mu < 100$.

11.30 $z = \dfrac{\overline{x} - \mu}{\sigma / \sqrt{n}} = \dfrac{98 - 100}{8 / \sqrt{100}} = -2.50$ p-value = $P(Z < -2.50) = .5 - .4938 = .0062$

There is enough evidence to infer that $\mu < 100$.

11.32 The value of the test statistic decreases (it becomes more negative) and the p-value decreases.

11.34 a $z = \dfrac{\bar{x} - \mu}{\sigma/\sqrt{n}} = \dfrac{178 - 170}{35/\sqrt{400}} = 4.57$ p-value $= P(Z > 4.57) = 0.$

b $z = \dfrac{\bar{x} - \mu}{\sigma/\sqrt{n}} = \dfrac{178 - 170}{100/\sqrt{400}} = 1.60$ p-value $= P(Z > 1.60) = .5 - .4452 = .0548.$

The value of the test statistic decreases and the p-value increases.

11.36 a $z = \dfrac{\bar{x} - \mu}{\sigma/\sqrt{n}} = \dfrac{21.63 - 22}{6/\sqrt{100}} = -.62$ p-value $= P(Z < -.62) = .5 - .2324 = .2676$

b $z = \dfrac{\bar{x} - \mu}{\sigma/\sqrt{n}} = \dfrac{21.63 - 22}{6/\sqrt{500}} = -1.38$ p-value $= P(Z < -1.38) = .5 - .4162 = .0838.$

The value of the test statistic decreases (it becomes more negative) and the p-value decreases.

11.38

$\bar{x}$	$z = \dfrac{\bar{x} - 22}{6/\sqrt{220}}$	p-value
22.0	0	.5
21.8	-.49	.3121
21.6	-.99	.1611
21.4	-1.48	.0694
21.2	-1.98	.0239
21.0	-2.47	.0062
20.8	-2.97	.0015
20.6	-3.46	0
20.4	-3.96	0

11.40 a $z = \dfrac{\bar{x} - \mu}{\sigma/\sqrt{n}} = \dfrac{17.55 - 17.09}{2/\sqrt{100}} = 2.30$ p-value $= 2P(Z > 2.30) = 2(.5 - .4893) = 2(.0107) = .0214.$

b $z = \dfrac{\bar{x} - \mu}{\sigma/\sqrt{n}} = \dfrac{17.55 - 17.09}{10/\sqrt{100}} = .46$ p-value $= 2P(Z > .46) = 2(.5 - .1772) = 2(.3228) = .6456.$

The value of the test statistic decreases and the p-value increases.

11.42 $H_0 : \mu = 50$

   $H_1 : \mu > 50$

$z = \dfrac{\bar{x} - \mu}{\sigma / \sqrt{n}} = \dfrac{59.17 - 50}{10 / \sqrt{18}} = 3.89$

p-value = P(Z > 3.89) = 0

There is enough evidence to infer that the mean is greater than 50 minutes.

11.44 $H_0 : \mu = .50$

   $H_1 : \mu \neq .50$

$z = \dfrac{\bar{x} - \mu}{\sigma / \sqrt{n}} = \dfrac{.493 - .50}{.05 / \sqrt{10}} = -.44$

p-value = 2P(Z < -.44) = 2(.5 - .1700) = 2(.3300) = .6600

There is not enough evidence to infer that the mean diameter is not .50 inch.

11.46 $H_0 : \mu = 30000$

   $H_1 : \mu < 30000$

$z = \dfrac{\bar{x} - \mu}{\sigma / \sqrt{n}} = \dfrac{29,120 - 30,000}{8000 / \sqrt{350}} = -2.06$

p-value = (P(Z < -2.06) = .5 - .4803 = .0197

There is enough evidence to infer that the president is correct

11.48a $H_0 : \mu = 17.85$

   $H_1 : \mu > 17.85$

$z = \dfrac{\bar{x} - \mu}{\sigma / \sqrt{n}} = \dfrac{19.13 - 17.85}{3.87 / \sqrt{25}} = 1.66$

p-value = P(Z > 1.66) = .5 - .4515 = .0485

There is enough evidence to infer that the campaign was successful.

b We must assume that the population standard deviation is unchanged.

11.50 $H_0 : \mu = 55$

   $H_1 : \mu > 55$

$$z = \frac{\bar{x} - \mu}{\sigma / \sqrt{n}} = \frac{55.8 - 55}{5 / \sqrt{200}} = 2.26$$

p-value = P(Z > 2.26) = .5 - .4881 = .0119

There is not enough evidence to support the officer's belief.

11.52　$H_0 : \mu = 20$

$\quad\quad H_1 : \mu < 20$

$$z = \frac{\bar{x} - \mu}{\sigma / \sqrt{n}} = \frac{19.39 - 20}{3 / \sqrt{36}} = -1.22$$

p-value = P(Z < -1.22) = .5 - .3888 = .1112

There is not enough evidence to infer that the manager is correct.

11.54　$H_0 : \mu = 4$

$\quad\quad H_1 : \mu \neq 4$

$$z = \frac{\bar{x} - \mu}{\sigma / \sqrt{n}} = \frac{4.84 - 4}{2 / \sqrt{63}} = 3.34$$

p-value = 2P(Z > 3.34) = 0

There is enough evidence to infer that the average Alpine skier does not ski 4 times per year.

11.56　$H_0 : \mu = 32$

$\quad\quad H_1 : \mu < 32$

$$z = \frac{\bar{x} - \mu}{\sigma / \sqrt{n}} = \frac{29.92 - 32}{6 / \sqrt{110}} = -3.64$$

p-value = P(Z < -3.64) = 0

There is enough evidence to infer that there has been a decrease in the mean time away from desks. A type I error occurs when we conclude that the plan decreases the mean time away from desks when it actually does not. This error is quite expensive. Consequently we demand a low p-value. The p-value is small enough to infer that there has been a decrease.

11.58 Rejection region: $\dfrac{\bar{x} - \mu}{\sigma / \sqrt{n}} > z_{\alpha/2}$ or $\dfrac{\bar{x} - \mu}{\sigma / \sqrt{n}} < -z_{\alpha/2}$

$$\frac{\bar{x} - 200}{10/\sqrt{100}} > z_{.025} = 1.96 \ \text{ or } \ \frac{\bar{x} - 200}{10/\sqrt{100}} < \text{-}1.96$$

$\bar{x} > 201.96$ or $\bar{x} < 198.04$

$\beta = P(198.04 < \bar{x} < 201.96 \ \text{given } \mu = 203)$

$$= P\left(\frac{198.04 - 203}{10/\sqrt{100}} < \frac{\bar{x} - \mu}{\sigma/\sqrt{n}} < \frac{201.96 - 203}{10/\sqrt{100}}\right) = P(\text{-}4.96 < z < \text{-}1.04) = .5 - .3508 = .1492$$

11.60 Rejection region: $\dfrac{\bar{x} - \mu}{\sigma/\sqrt{n}} < -z_\alpha$

$$\frac{\bar{x} - 50}{10/\sqrt{40}} < -z_{.05} = -1.645$$

$\bar{x} < 47.40$

$\beta = P(\bar{x} > 47.40 \ \text{given } \mu = 48) = P\left(\dfrac{\bar{x} - \mu}{\sigma/\sqrt{n}} > \dfrac{47.40 - 48}{10/\sqrt{40}}\right) = P(z > -.38) = .5 + .1480 = .6480$

11.62

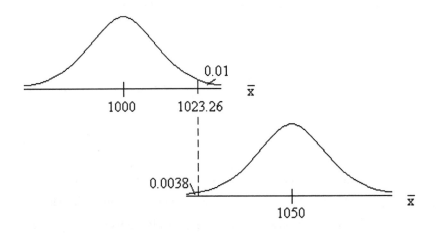

11.64 a Rejection region: $\dfrac{\bar{x}-\mu}{\sigma/\sqrt{n}} < -z_\alpha$

$\dfrac{\bar{x}-22}{6/\sqrt{220}} < -z_{.10} = -1.28$

$\bar{x} < 21.48$

$\beta = P(\bar{x} > 21.48 \text{ given } \mu = 21.5) = P\left(\dfrac{\bar{x}-\mu}{\sigma/\sqrt{n}} > \dfrac{21.48-21.5}{6/\sqrt{220}}\right) = P(z > -.05) = .5 + .0199 = .5199$

b Rejection region: $\dfrac{\bar{x}-\mu}{\sigma/\sqrt{n}} < -z_\alpha$

$\dfrac{\bar{x}-22}{6/\sqrt{220}} < -z_{.10} = -1.28$

$\bar{x} < 21.33$

$\beta = P(\bar{x} > 21.48 \text{ given } \mu = 21) = P\left(\dfrac{\bar{x}-\mu}{\sigma/\sqrt{n}} > \dfrac{21.48-21}{6/\sqrt{220}}\right) = P(z > 1.19 = .5 - .3830 = .1170$

c As μ decreases β decreases.

11.66 a Rejection region: $\dfrac{\bar{x}-\mu}{\sigma/\sqrt{n}} < -z_\alpha$

$\dfrac{\bar{x}-22}{6/\sqrt{300}} < -z_{.10} = -1.28$

$\bar{x} < 21.56$

$\beta = P(\bar{x} > 21.56 \text{ given } \mu = 21.0) = P\left(\dfrac{\bar{x}-\mu}{\sigma/\sqrt{n}} > \dfrac{21.56-21.0}{6/\sqrt{300}}\right) = P(z > 1.62) = .5 - .4474 = .0526$

b Rejection region: $\dfrac{\bar{x}-\mu}{\sigma/\sqrt{n}} < -z_\alpha$

$\dfrac{\bar{x}-22}{6/\sqrt{400}} < -z_{.10} = -1.28$

$\bar{x} < 21.62$

$\beta = P(\bar{x} > 21.62 \text{ given } \mu = 21.0) = P\left(\dfrac{\bar{x}-\mu}{\sigma/\sqrt{n}} > \dfrac{21.62-21.0}{6/\sqrt{400}}\right) = P(z > 2.07) = .5 - .4808 = .0192$

c As n increases β decreases.

11.68 a Rejection region: $\dfrac{\bar{x}-\mu}{\sigma/\sqrt{n}} > z_{\alpha/2}$ or $\dfrac{\bar{x}-\mu}{\sigma/\sqrt{n}} < -z_{\alpha/2}$

$\dfrac{\bar{x}-17.09}{3.87/\sqrt{100}} > z_{.0375} = 1.78$ or $\dfrac{\bar{x}-17.09}{3.87/\sqrt{100}} < -1.78$

$\bar{x} > 17.78$ or $\bar{x} < 16.40$

$\beta = P(16.40 < \bar{x} < 17.78 \text{ given } \mu = 18.00)$

$= P\left(\dfrac{16.40-18.00}{3.87/\sqrt{100}} < \dfrac{\bar{x}-\mu}{\sigma/\sqrt{n}} < \dfrac{17.78-18.00}{3.87/\sqrt{100}} \right) = P(-4.13 < z < -.57) = .5 - .2157 = .2843$

b Rejection region: $\dfrac{\bar{x}-\mu}{\sigma/\sqrt{n}} > z_{\alpha/2}$ or $\dfrac{\bar{x}-\mu}{\sigma/\sqrt{n}} < -z_{\alpha/2}$

$\dfrac{\bar{x}-17.09}{3.87/\sqrt{100}} > z_{.05} = 1.645$ or $\dfrac{\bar{x}-17.09}{3.87/\sqrt{100}} < -1.645$

$\bar{x} > 17.73$ or $\bar{x} < 16.45$

$\beta = P(16.45 < \bar{x} < 17.73 \text{ given } \mu = 18.00)$

$= P\left(\dfrac{16.45-18.00}{3.87/\sqrt{100}} < \dfrac{\bar{x}-\mu}{\sigma/\sqrt{n}} < \dfrac{17.73-18.00}{3.87/\sqrt{100}} \right) = P(-4.01 < z < -.70) = .5 - .2580 = .2420$

c As α increases β decreases.

11.70

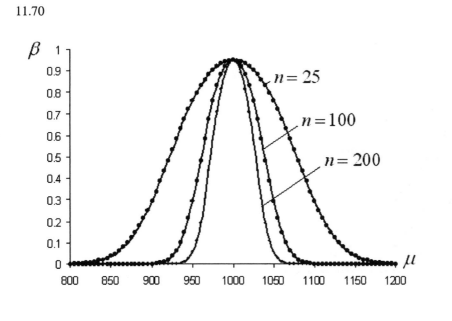

11.72 Rejection region: $\dfrac{\bar{x}-\mu}{\sigma/\sqrt{n}} > z_\alpha$

$\dfrac{\bar{x}-5000}{400/\sqrt{100}} > z_{.05} = 1.645$

$\bar{x} > 5065.8$

$\beta = P(\bar{x} < 5065.8 \text{ given } \mu = 5100) = P\left(\dfrac{\bar{x}-\mu}{\sigma/\sqrt{n}} < \dfrac{5065.8-5100}{400/\sqrt{100}}\right) = P(z < -.86) = .5 - .3051 = .1949$

11.74 Rejection region: $\dfrac{\bar{x}-\mu}{\sigma/\sqrt{n}} > z_\alpha$

$\dfrac{\bar{x}-560}{50/\sqrt{20}} > z_{.05} = 1.645$

$\bar{x} > 578.4$

$\beta = P(\bar{x} < 578.4 \text{ given } \mu = 600) = P\left(\dfrac{\bar{x}-\mu}{\sigma/\sqrt{n}} < \dfrac{578.4-600}{50/\sqrt{20}}\right) = P(z < -1.93) = .5 - .4732 = .0268$

11.76

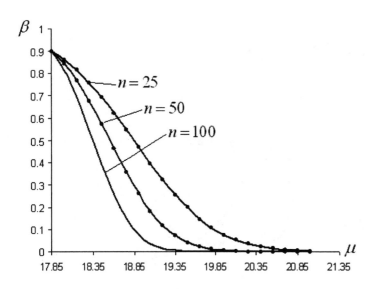

11.78 Rejection region: $\dfrac{\bar{x} - \mu}{\sigma / \sqrt{n}} > z_\alpha$

$\dfrac{\bar{x} - 55}{5 / \sqrt{200}} > z_{.01} = 2.33$

$\bar{x} > 55.8$

$\beta = P(\bar{x} < 55.8 \ \text{given} \ \mu = 57) = P\left(\dfrac{\bar{x} - \mu}{\sigma / \sqrt{n}} < \dfrac{55.8 - 57}{5 / \sqrt{200}} \right) = P(z < -3.39) = 0$

11.80 Rejection region: $\dfrac{\bar{x} - \mu}{\sigma / \sqrt{n}} < -z_\alpha$

$\dfrac{\bar{x} - 20}{3 / \sqrt{36}} < -z_{.05} = -1.645$

$\bar{x} < 19.18$

$\beta = P(\bar{x} > 19.18 \ \text{given} \ \mu = 18.5) = P\left(\dfrac{\bar{x} - \mu}{\sigma / \sqrt{n}} > \dfrac{19.18 - 18.5}{3 / \sqrt{36}} \right) = P(z > 1.36) = .5 - .4131 = .0869$

11.82

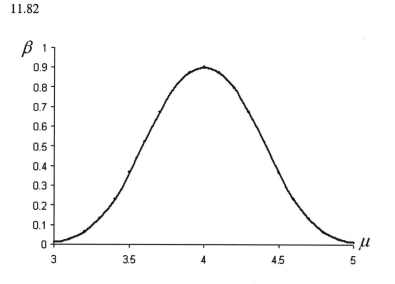

11.84 $H_0 : \mu = 170$

$H_1 : \mu < 170$

A Type I error occurs when we conclude that the new system is not cost effective when it actually is. A Type II error occurs when we conclude that the new system is cost effective when it actually is not.

The test statistic is the same. However, the p-value equals 1 minus the p-value calculated Example 10.1. That is,

p-value = 1 - .0069 = .9931

We conclude that there is no evidence to infer that the mean is less than 170. That is, there is no evidence to infer that the new system will not be cost effective.

Chapter 12

12.2 $\bar{x} \pm t_{\alpha/2} s/\sqrt{n} = 510 \pm 1.984(125/\sqrt{100}) = 510 \pm 24.80$; LCL = 485.20, UCL = 534.80

12.4 The interval narrows as the sample size increases.

12.6 $\bar{x} \pm t_{\alpha/2} s/\sqrt{n} = 510 \pm 2.009(75/\sqrt{50}) = 510 \pm 21.31$; LCL = 488.69, UCL = 531.31

12.8 $\bar{x} \pm t_{\alpha/2} s/\sqrt{n} = 510 \pm 1.676(125/\sqrt{50}) = 510 \pm 29.63$; LCL = 480.37, UCL = 539.63

12.10 As the confidence level increases the interval widens.

12.11 to 12.20 $H_0 : \mu = 20$

$H_1 : \mu > 20$

12.12 Rejection region: $t > t_{\alpha, n-1} = t_{.05,9} = 1.833$

$t = \dfrac{\bar{x} - \mu}{s/\sqrt{n}} = \dfrac{23 - 20}{9/\sqrt{10}} = 1.05$ p-value = .1597 (Excel). There is not enough evidence to infer that the

population mean is greater than 20.

12.14 As the sample size increases the test statistic increases [and the p-value decreases].

12.16 Rejection region: $t > t_{\alpha, n-1} = t_{.05,19} = 1.729$

$t = \dfrac{\bar{x} - \mu}{s/\sqrt{n}} = \dfrac{23 - 20}{29/\sqrt{20}} = .67$, p-value = .2552 (Excel). There is not enough evidence to infer that the

population mean is greater than 20.

12.18 $t = \dfrac{\bar{x} - \mu}{s/\sqrt{n}} = \dfrac{21 - 20}{9/\sqrt{20}} = .50$, p-value = .3125 (Excel). There is not enough evidence to infer that

the population mean is greater than 20.

12.20 When the sample mean increases, the test statistic increases [and the p-value decreases].

12.22 $\bar{x} \pm z_{\alpha/2}\sigma/\sqrt{n} = 50 \pm 1.96(15/\sqrt{10}) = 50 \pm 9.30$; LCL = 40.70, UCL = 59.30

12.24 $H_0 : \mu = 100$

$H_1 : \mu < 100$

Rejection region: $t < -t_{\alpha,n-1} = -t_{.10,7} = -1.415$

$t = \dfrac{\bar{x} - \mu}{s/\sqrt{n}} = \dfrac{75 - 100}{50/\sqrt{8}} = -1.41$, p-value = .1001 (Excel). There is not enough evidence to infer that the

population mean is less than 100.

12.26 The Student t distribution is more dispersed than the standard normal.

12.28 $\bar{x} \pm z_{\alpha/2}\sigma/\sqrt{n} = 15{,}500 \pm 1.645(9950/\sqrt{1000}) = 15{,}500 \pm 517.59$; LCL = 14,982.41,

UCL = 16,017.59

12.30 $H_0 : \mu = 6$

$H_1 : \mu < 6$

Rejection region: $t < -t_{\alpha,n-1} = -t_{.05,11} = -1.796$

$t = \dfrac{\bar{x} - \mu}{s/\sqrt{n}} = \dfrac{5.69 - 6}{1.58/\sqrt{12}} = -.69$, p-value = .2538 (Excel). There is not enough evidence to support the

courier's advertisement.

12.32 $H_0 : \mu = 20$

$H_1 : \mu > 20$

Rejection region: $t > t_{\alpha,n-1} = t_{.05,19} = 1.729$

$t = \dfrac{\bar{x} - \mu}{s/\sqrt{n}} = \dfrac{20.85 - 20}{6.76/\sqrt{20}} = .56$, p-value = .2903 (Excel). There is not enough evidence to infer that the

doctor's claim is true.

12.34 $\bar{x} \pm t_{\alpha/2} s / \sqrt{n} = 7.15 \pm 1.972(1.65/\sqrt{200}) = 7.15 \pm .23$; LCL = 6.92, UCL = 7.38

12.36 $H_0 : \mu = 60$

   $H_1 : \mu > 60$

Rejection region: $t > t_{\alpha,n-1} = t_{.05,161} = 1.654$

$t = \dfrac{\bar{x} - \mu}{s / \sqrt{n}} = \dfrac{63.70 - 60}{18.94 / \sqrt{162}} = 2.48$, p-value = .0070 (Excel). There is enough evidence to infer that the

mean time exceeds 60 minutes.

12.38 $\bar{x} \pm t_{\alpha/2} s / \sqrt{n} = 2.67 \pm 1.973(2.50/\sqrt{188}) = 2.67 \pm .36$; LCL = 2.31, UCL = 3.03

12.40 a $\bar{x} \pm t_{\alpha/2} s / \sqrt{n} = 62.79 \pm 2.052(5.32/\sqrt{28}) = 62.79 \pm 2.06$; LCL = 60.73, UCL = 64.85

b Prices are required to be normally distributed. The histogram (not shown) is bell shaped.

12.42 $\bar{x} \pm t_{\alpha/2} s / \sqrt{n} = 13.94 \pm 1.960(2.16/\sqrt{212}) = 13.94 \pm .29$; LCL = 13.65, UCL = 14.23

LCL = 13.65(10) = 136.5 days, UCL = 14.23(10) = 142.3 days.

12.44 $\bar{x} \pm t_{\alpha/2} s / \sqrt{n} = 3.44 \pm 1.960(3.33/\sqrt{471}) = 3.44 \pm .30$; LCL = 3.14, UCL = 3.74

12.46 $H_0 : \mu = 2$

   $H_1 : \mu > 2$

Rejection region: $t > t_{\alpha,n-1} = t_{.01,99} \approx 2.364$

$t = \dfrac{\bar{x} - \mu}{s / \sqrt{n}} = \dfrac{2.10 - 2}{.76 / \sqrt{100}} = 1.32$, p-value = .1001. There is not enough evidence to infer that the

recycling plant will be profitable.

12.48 $H_0 : \sigma^2 = 300$

   $H_1 : \sigma^2 \neq 300$

Rejection region: $\chi^2 < \chi^2_{1-\alpha/2,n-1} = \chi^2_{.975,49} \approx 32.3574$ or $\chi^2 > \chi^2_{\alpha/2,n-1} = \chi^2_{.025,49} \approx 71.4202$

$\chi^2 = \dfrac{(n-1)s^2}{\sigma^2} = \dfrac{(50-1)(220)}{300} = 35.93$, p-value = .1643 (Excel). There is not enough evidence to infer that the population variance differs from 300. Decreasing the sample size decreases the test statistic and increases the p-value of the test.

12.50 $H_0 : \sigma^2 = 100$

       $H_1 : \sigma^2 < 100$

Rejection region: $\chi^2 < \chi^2_{1-\alpha,n-1} = \chi^2_{.99,99} \approx 70.0648$

$\chi^2 = \dfrac{(n-1)s^2}{\sigma^2} = \dfrac{(100-1)(80)}{100} = 79.20$, p-value = .0714 (Excel). There is not enough evidence to infer that the population variance is less than 100. Increasing the sample size increases the test statistic and decreases the p-value.

12.52 LCL = $\dfrac{(n-1)s^2}{\chi^2_{\alpha/2,n-1}} = \dfrac{(n-1)s^2}{\chi^2_{.05,29}} = \dfrac{(30-1)(12)}{42.5569} = 8.18$,

UCL = $\dfrac{(n-1)s^2}{\chi^2_{1-\alpha/2,n-1}} = \dfrac{(n-1)s^2}{\chi^2_{.95,29}} = \dfrac{(15-1)(12)}{17.7083} = 19.65$; increasing the sample size narrows the interval.

12.54 $H_0 : \sigma^2 = .001$

       $H_1 : \sigma^2 < .001$

Rejection region: $\chi^2 < \chi^2_{1-\alpha,n-1} = \chi^2_{.95,7} = 2.16735$

$\chi^2 = \dfrac{(n-1)s^2}{\sigma^2} = \dfrac{(8-1)(.00093)}{.001} = 6.49$, p-value = .4841 (Excel). There is not enough evidence to infer that the population variance is less than .001.

12.56 LCL = $\dfrac{(n-1)s^2}{\chi^2_{\alpha/2,n-1}} = \dfrac{(n-1)s^2}{\chi^2_{.025,11}} = \dfrac{(12-1)(2.4976)}{21.9200} = 1.2533$,

$$UCL = \frac{(n-1)s^2}{\chi^2_{1-\alpha/2,n-1}} = \frac{(n-1)s^2}{\chi^2_{.975,11}} = \frac{(12-1)(2.4976)}{3.81575} = 7.2000$$

12.58 a $H_0: \sigma^2 = 250$

$H_1: \sigma^2 \neq 250$

Rejection region: $\chi^2 < \chi^2_{1-\alpha/2,n-1} = \chi^2_{.975,24} = 12.4011$ or $\chi^2 > \chi^2_{\alpha/2,n-1} = \chi^2_{.025,24} = 39.3641$

$$\chi^2 = \frac{(n-1)s^2}{\sigma^2} = \frac{(25-1)(270.58)}{250} = 25.9760, \text{ p-value} = .7088 \text{ (Excel). There is not enough evidence}$$

to infer that the population variance is not equal to 250.

b Demand is required to be normally distributed.

c The histogram is approximately bell shaped.

12.60 a $LCL = \dfrac{(n-1)s^2}{\chi^2_{\alpha/2,n-1}} = \dfrac{(n-1)s^2}{\chi^2_{.05,199}} = \dfrac{(200-1)(2.7111)}{232.912} = 2.3163,$

$UCL = \dfrac{(n-1)s^2}{\chi^2_{1-\alpha/2,n-1}} = \dfrac{(n-1)s^2}{\chi^2_{.95,199}} = \dfrac{(200-1)(2.7111)}{167.361} = 3.2236$

b The histogram is bell shaped.

12.62 $H_0: \sigma^2 = 200$

$H_1: \sigma^2 < 200$

Rejection region: $\chi^2 < \chi^2_{1-\alpha,n-1} = \chi^2_{.95,99} \approx 77.9295$

$$\chi^2 = \frac{(n-1)s^2}{\sigma^2} = \frac{(100-1)(174.47)}{200} = 86.36; \text{ p-value} = .1863 \text{ (Excel). There is not enough evidence to}$$

infer that the population variance is less than 200. Replace the bulbs as they burn out.

12.64 $\hat{p} \pm z_{\alpha/2}\sqrt{\hat{p}(1-\hat{p})/n} = .48 \pm 1.96\sqrt{.48(1-.48)/200} = .48 \pm .0692$

12.66 The interval narrows when the sample size increases.

12.68 $\hat{p} \pm z_{\alpha/2}\sqrt{\hat{p}(1-\hat{p})/n} = .10 \pm 1.96\sqrt{.10(1-.10)/500} = .10 \pm .0263$

12.70 to 12.76 $H_0 : p = .60$

$H_1 : p > .60$

12.70 $z = \dfrac{\hat{p}-p}{\sqrt{p(1-p)/n}} = \dfrac{.63-.60}{\sqrt{.60(1-.60)/100}} = .61$, p-value $= P(Z > .61) = .5 - .2291 = .2709$

12.72 $z = \dfrac{\hat{p}-p}{\sqrt{p(1-p)/n}} = \dfrac{.63-.60}{\sqrt{.60(1-.60)/400}} = 1.22$, p-value $= P(Z > 1.22) = .5 - .3888 = .1112$

12.74 $z = \dfrac{\hat{p}-p}{\sqrt{p(1-p)/n}} = \dfrac{.62-.60}{\sqrt{.62(1-.62)/100}} = .41$, p-value $= P(Z > .41) = .5 - 1591 = .3409$

12.76 Decreasing the sample proportion decreases the value of the test statistic and increases the p-value.

12.78 a.5 $\pm$ .03

b Yes, because the sample size was chosen to produce this interval.

12.80 n $= \left(\dfrac{z_{\alpha/2}\sqrt{\hat{p}(1-\hat{p})}}{B}\right)^2 = \left(\dfrac{1.645\sqrt{.75(1-.75)}}{.03}\right)^2 = 564$

12.82 a $\hat{p} \pm z_{\alpha/2}\sqrt{\hat{p}(1-\hat{p})/n} = .92 \pm 1.645\sqrt{.92(1-.92)/564} = .92 \pm .0188$

b The interval is narrower.

c Yes, because the interval estimate is better than specified.

12.84 $\hat{p} \pm z_{\alpha/2}\sqrt{\hat{p}(1-\hat{p})/n} = .84 \pm 1.645\sqrt{.84(1-.84)/600} = .84 \pm .0246$

12.86 $H_0 : p = .50$

   $H_1 : p > .50$

$z = \dfrac{\hat{p} - p}{\sqrt{p(1-p)/n}} = \dfrac{.59 - .5}{\sqrt{.5(1-.5)/100}} = 1.80$, p-value $= P(Z > 1.80) = .5 - .4641 = .0359$. There is

enough evidence to infer that p is greater than .5.

12.88 $H_0 : p = .65$

   $H_1 : p > .65$

$z = \dfrac{\hat{p} - p}{\sqrt{p(1-p)/n}} = \dfrac{.70 - .65}{\sqrt{.65(1-.65)/200}} = 1.48$, p-value $= P(Z > 1.48) = .5 - .4306 = .0694$

There is not enough evidence to conclude that the proportion of successes is greater than 65%.

12.90 $H_0 : p = .90$

   $H_1 : p < .90$

$z = \dfrac{\hat{p} - p}{\sqrt{p(1-p)/n}} = \dfrac{.8644 - .90}{\sqrt{.90(1-.90)/177}} = -1.58$, p-value $= P(Z < -1.58) = .5 - .4429 = .0571$. There is

not enough evidence to infer that the satisfaction rate is less than 90%.

12.92 $H_0 : p = .80$

   $H_1 : p > .80$

$z = \dfrac{\hat{p} - p}{\sqrt{p(1-p)/n}} = \dfrac{.8225 - .80}{\sqrt{.80(1-.80)/400}} = 1.13$, p-value $= P(Z > 1.13) = .5 - .3708 = .1292$. There is

not enough evidence to infer that the claim is true.

12.94 $H_0 : p = .50$

   $H_1 : p > .50$

$z = \dfrac{\hat{p} - p}{\sqrt{p(1-p)/n}} = \dfrac{.57 - .50}{\sqrt{.50(1-.50)/100}} = 1.40$, p-value $= P(Z > 1.40) = .5 - .4192 = .0808$. There is

enough evidence to conclude that more than 50% of all business students would rate the book as

excellent.

12.96 $\hat{p} \pm z_{\alpha/2}\sqrt{\hat{p}(1-\hat{p})/n} = .0975 \pm 1.96\sqrt{.0975(1-.0975)/2000} = .0975 \pm .0130$; LCL = .0845,

UCL = .1105

Number: LCL = 100 million (.0845) = 8.45 million, UCL = 100 million (.1105) = 11.05 million

12.98 $H_0 : p = .12$

$H_1 : p > .12$

$z = \dfrac{\hat{p}-p}{\sqrt{p(1-p)/n}} = \dfrac{.1475-.12}{\sqrt{.12(1-.12)/400}} = 1.69$, p-value = $P(Z > 1.69) = .5 - .4545 = .0455$. There is

enough evidence to infer that the proposed newspaper will be financially viable.

12.100 $\hat{p} \pm z_{\alpha/2}\sqrt{\hat{p}(1-\hat{p})/n} = .2031 \pm 1.96\sqrt{.2031(1-.2031)/650} = .2031 \pm .0309$; LCL = .1722,

UCL = .2340

Number: LCL = 5million (.1722) = .861 million, UCL = 5million (.2340) = 1.17 million

12.102 Code 2 was changed to 3.

$\hat{p} \pm z_{\alpha/2}\sqrt{\hat{p}(1-\hat{p})/n} = .5313 \pm 1.96\sqrt{.5313(1-.5313)/320} = .5313 \pm .0547$; LCL = .4766,

UCL = .5860

Number: LCL = 14,814,000 (.4766) = 7,060,352 , UCL = 14,814,000 (.5860) = 8,681,004

The answers to the chapter review exercises will be produced by Excel only.

12.104 a $H_0 : \mu = 30$

$H_1 : \mu > 30$

t-Test: Mean			
			Costs
Mean			31.95
Standard Deviation			7.19
Hypothesized Mean			30
df			124
t Stat			3.04
P(T<=t) one-tail			0.0015
t Critical one-tail			1.6572
P(T<=t) two-tail			0.003
t Critical two-tail			1.9793

t = 3.04, p-value = .0015; there is enough evidence to infer that the candidate is correct.

b

t-Estimate: Mean			
			Costs
Mean			31.95
Standard Deviation			7.19
LCL			30.68
UCL			33.23

LCL = 30.68, UCL = 33.23

c The costs are required to be normally distributed.

12.106 $H_0 : \sigma^2 = 17$

$H_1 : \sigma^2 > 17$

Chi Squared Test: Variance			
			Times
Sample Variance			27.47
Hypothesized Variance			17
df			19
chi-squared Stat			30.71
P (CHI<=chi) one-tail			0.0435
chi-squared Critical one tail	Left-tail		11.6509
	Right-tail		27.2036
P (CHI<=chi) two-tail			0.0869
chi-squared Critical two tail	Left-tail		10.1170
	Right-tail		30.1435

$\chi^2 = 30.71$, p-value = .0435. There is enough evidence to infer that problems are likely.

12.108 a

t-Estimate: Mean			
			Marks
Mean			71.88
Standard Deviation			10.03
LCL			69.03
UCL			74.73

LCL = 69.03, UCL = 74.73

b $H_0 : \mu = 68$

         $H_1 : \mu > 68$

t-Test: Mean			
			Marks
Mean			71.88
Standard Deviation			10.03
Hypothesized Mean			68
df			49
t Stat			2.74
P(T<=t) one-tail			0.0043
t Critical one-tail			1.6766
P(T<=t) two-tail			0.0086
t Critical two-tail			2.0096

$t = 2.74$, p-value = .0043; there is enough evidence to infer that students with a calculus background would perform better in statistics than students with no calculus?

12.110

z-Estimate: Proportion	
	Insurance
Sample Proportion	0.632
Observations	250
LCL	0.582
UCL	0.682

LCL = .582, UCL = .682

12.112

t-Estimate: Mean			
			Time
Mean			6.35
Standard Deviation			2.16
LCL			6.05
UCL			6.65

LCL = 6.05, UCL = 6.65

12.114

z-Estimate: Proportion	
	Tourist
Sample Proportion	0.667
Observations	72
LCL	0.558
UCL	0.776

LCL = .558, UCL = .776

12.116 $H_0 : p = .90$

$H_1 : p < .90$

z-Test: Proportion			
			Springs
Sample Proportion			0.86
Observations			100
Hypothesized Proportion			0.9
z Stat			-1.33
P(Z<=z) one-tail			0.0912
z Critical one-tail			1.6449
P(Z<=z) two-tail			0.1824
z Critical two-tail			1.96

z = -1.33, p-value = .0912; there is enough evidence to infer that less than 90% of the springs are the correct length.

12.118 a $H_0 : \mu = 9.8$

$H_1 : \mu < 9.8$

t-Test: Mean			
			Time
Mean			9.16
Standard Deviation			2.64
Hypothesized Mean			9.8
df			149
t Stat			-2.97
P(T<=t) one-tail			0.0018
t Critical one-tail			1.6551
P(T<=t) two-tail			0.0036
t Critical two-tail			1.976

$t = -2.97$, p-value = .0018; there is enough evidence to infer that enclosure of preaddressed envelopes improves the average speed of payments?

b $H_0 : \sigma^2 = 10.24\ (3.2^2)$

$H_1 : \sigma^2 < 10.24$

Chi Squared Test: Variance			
			Time
Sample Variance			6.98
Hypothesized Variance			10.24
df			149
chi-squared Stat			101.58
P (CHI<=chi) one-tail			0.0011
chi-squared Critical one tail	Left-tail		121.7870
	Right-tail		178.4853
P (CHI<=chi) two-tail			0.0021
chi-squared Critical two tail	Left-tail		117.0980
	Right-tail		184.6869

$\chi^2 = 101.58$, p-value = .0011; there is enough evidence to infer that the variability in payment speeds decreases when a preaddressed envelope is sent.

12.120

z-Estimate: Proportion	
	Concert
Sample Proportion	0.153
Observations	600
LCL	0.125
UCL	0.182

Proportion: LCL = .1245, UCL = .1821

Total: LCL = 400,000(.1245) = 49,800 UCL = 400,000(.1821) = 72,840

Chapter 13

For all exercises in Chapters 13, 14, and 24 we employed the F-test of two variances at the 5%
significance level to decide which one of the equal-variances or unequal-variances t-test and
estimator of the difference between two means to use to solve the problem. Additionally, for exercises
that compare two populations and are accompanied by data files, our answers were derived by
defining the sample from population 1 as the data stored in the first column (often column A in Excel
and column 1 in Minitab). The data stored in the second column represent the sample from population
2. Paired differences were defined as the difference between the variable in the first column minus the
variable in the second column.

13.2 $(\bar{x}_1 - \bar{x}_2) \pm t_{\alpha/2} \sqrt{s_p^2 \left(\frac{1}{n_1} + \frac{1}{n_2} \right)} = (524 - 469) \pm 2.009 \sqrt{79,637 \left(\frac{1}{25} + \frac{1}{25} \right)} = 55 \pm 160.35$

13.4 $(\bar{x}_1 - \bar{x}_2) \pm t_{\alpha/2} \sqrt{s_p^2 \left(\frac{1}{n_1} + \frac{1}{n_2} \right)} = (524 - 469) \pm 1.972 \sqrt{18,261 \left(\frac{1}{100} + \frac{1}{100} \right)} = 55 \pm 37.69$

13.6 to 13.12 $\quad H_0 : (\mu_1 - \mu_2) = 0$

$\qquad\qquad\qquad H_1 : (\mu_1 - \mu_2) \neq 0$

13.6 Rejection region: $t < -t_{\alpha/2, n-1} = -t_{.025, 22} = -2.074$ or $t > t_{\alpha/2, n-1} = t_{.025, 22} = 2.074$

$t = \dfrac{(\bar{x}_1 - \bar{x}_2) - (\mu_1 - \mu_2)}{\sqrt{s_p^2 \left(\frac{1}{n_1} + \frac{1}{n_2} \right)}} = \dfrac{(74 - 71) - 0}{\sqrt{275 \left(\frac{1}{12} + \frac{1}{12} \right)}} = .44$, p-value = .6617 (Excel). There is not enough

evidence to infer that the population means differ.

13.8 The value of the test statistic decreases and the p-value increases.

13.10 The value of the test statistic increases and the p-value decreases.

13.12 The value of the test statistic increases and the p-value decreases.

$$13.14 \ (\bar{x}_1 - \bar{x}_2) \pm t_{\alpha/2} \sqrt{\left(\frac{s_1^2}{n_1} + \frac{s_2^2}{n_2} \right)} = (63 - 60) \pm 1.671 \sqrt{\left(\frac{1681}{50} + \frac{225}{45} \right)} = 3 \pm 10.38$$

$$13.16 \ (\bar{x}_1 - \bar{x}_2) \pm t_{\alpha/2} \sqrt{\left(\frac{s_1^2}{n_1} + \frac{s_2^2}{n_2} \right)} = (63 - 60) \pm 1.671 \sqrt{\left(\frac{324}{100} + \frac{49}{90} \right)} = 3 \pm 3.22$$

13.18 to 13.24 $\quad H_0 : (\mu_1 - \mu_2) = 0$

$\quad\quad\quad\quad\quad\quad H_1 : (\mu_1 - \mu_2) > 0$

13.18 Rejection region: $t > t_{\alpha,v} = t_{.05,200} = 1.653$

$$t = \frac{(\bar{x}_1 - \bar{x}_2) - (\mu_1 - \mu_2)}{\sqrt{\left(\frac{s_1^2}{n_1} + \frac{s_2^2}{n_2} \right)}} = \frac{(412 - 405) - 0}{\sqrt{\left(\frac{16,384}{150} + \frac{2,916}{150} \right)}} = .62,$$ p-value = .2689 (Excel). There is not enough

evidence to infer that μ_1 is greater than μ_2.

13.20 The value of the test statistic increases and the p-value decreases.

13.22 The value of the test statistic decreases and the p-value increases.

13.24 The value of the test statistic decreases and the p-value increases.

13.26 a In all cases the equal-variances t-test degrees of freedom is greater than the unequal-variances t-test degrees of freedom.

13.28 $\quad H_0 : (\mu_1 - \mu_2) = 0$

$\quad\quad\quad H_1 : (\mu_1 - \mu_2) \neq 0$

Rejection region: $t < -t_{\alpha/2,v} = -t_{.025,10} = -2.228$ or $t > t_{\alpha/2,v} = t_{.025,10} = 2.228$

$$t = \frac{(\bar{x}_1 - \bar{x}_2) - (\mu_1 - \mu_2)}{\sqrt{s_p^2\left(\frac{1}{n_1} + \frac{1}{n_2}\right)}} = \frac{(7.83 - 8.50) - 0}{\sqrt{9.03\left(\frac{1}{6} + \frac{1}{6}\right)}} = -.38$$, p- value = .7089 (Excel). There is not enough

evidence to conclude that the population means differ.

13.30a $H_0 : (\mu_1 - \mu_2) = 0$

$\quad\quad H_1 : (\mu_1 - \mu_2) > 0$

Rejection region: $t > t_{\alpha,v} = t_{.10,203} \approx 1.286$

$$t = \frac{(\bar{x}_1 - \bar{x}_2) - (\mu_1 - \mu_2)}{\sqrt{s_p^2\left(\frac{1}{n_1} + \frac{1}{n_2}\right)}} = \frac{(21.51 - 19.76) - 0}{\sqrt{20.33\left(\frac{1}{121} + \frac{1}{84}\right)}} = 2.72$$, p-value = .0036 (Excel). There is enough

evidence to infer that the mean of population 1 is greater than the mean of population 2.

b $(\bar{x}_1 - \bar{x}_2) \pm t_{\alpha/2}\sqrt{s_p^2\left(\frac{1}{n_1} + \frac{1}{n_2}\right)} = (21.51 - 19.76) \pm 1.653\sqrt{20.33\left(\frac{1}{121} + \frac{1}{84}\right)} = 1.75 \pm 1.06$;

LCL = .69, UCL = 2.81

c The two populations must be normally distributed.

d The histograms (not shown here) are bell shaped.

13.32 $\quad H_0 : (\mu_1 - \mu_2) = 0$

$\quad\quad H_1 : (\mu_1 - \mu_2) < 0$

Rejection region: $t < -t_{\alpha,v} = -t_{.10,485} = -1.28$

$$t = \frac{(\bar{x}_1 - \bar{x}_2) - (\mu_1 - \mu_2)}{\sqrt{\left(\frac{s_1^2}{n_1} + \frac{s_2^2}{n_2}\right)}} = \frac{(72.93 - 73.99) - 0}{\sqrt{\left(\frac{26.32}{400} + \frac{241.66}{400}\right)}} = -1.30$$, p-value = .0974 (Excel). There is enough

evidence to infer that the mean of population 1 is less than the mean of population 2.

13.34 $\quad H_0 : (\mu_1 - \mu_2) = 0$

$\quad\quad H_1 : (\mu_1 - \mu_2) < 0$

Rejection region: $t < -t_{\alpha,v} = -t_{.05,94} \approx -1.662$

$$t = \frac{(\bar{x}_1 - \bar{x}_2) - (\mu_1 - \mu_2)}{\sqrt{s_p^2\left(\dfrac{1}{n_1} + \dfrac{1}{n_2}\right)}} = \frac{(19.02 - 21.85) - 0}{\sqrt{33.41\left(\dfrac{1}{48} + \dfrac{1}{48}\right)}} = -2.40,$$ p-value = .0092 (Excel). There is enough

evidence to infer that taking vitamin and mineral supplements daily increases the body's immune system?

13.36 $\quad H_0 : (\mu_1 - \mu_2) = 0$

$\quad\quad\quad H_1 : (\mu_1 - \mu_2) < 0$

Rejection region: $t < -t_{\alpha,v} = -t_{.05,220} = -1.645$

$$t = \frac{(\bar{x}_1 - \bar{x}_2) - (\mu_1 - \mu_2)}{\sqrt{s_p^2\left(\dfrac{1}{n_1} + \dfrac{1}{n_2}\right)}} = \frac{(3.19 - 4.35 - 0)}{\sqrt{14.18\left(\dfrac{1}{124} + \dfrac{1}{98}\right)}} = -2.27,$$ p-value = .0122 (Excel). There is enough

evidence to infer that the number of visits to health professionals grew between 1997 and 1998.

13.38 $\quad H_0 : (\mu_1 - \mu_2) = 0$

$\quad\quad\quad H_1 : (\mu_1 - \mu_2) > 0$

Rejection region: $t > t_{\alpha,v} = t_{.05,56} \approx 1.671$

$$t = \frac{(\bar{x}_1 - \bar{x}_2) - (\mu_1 - \mu_2)}{\sqrt{s_p^2\left(\dfrac{1}{n_1} + \dfrac{1}{n_2}\right)}} = \frac{(115.50 - 110.32) - 0}{\sqrt{492.28\left(\dfrac{1}{30} + \dfrac{1}{28}\right)}} = .89,$$ p-value = .1891 (Excel). There is not enough

evidence to retain supplier A—switch to supplier B.

13.40a $\quad H_0 : (\mu_1 - \mu_2) = 0$

$\quad\quad\quad\;\; H_1 : (\mu_1 - \mu_2) \neq 0$

Rejection region: $t < -t_{\alpha/2,v} = -t_{.005,29} = -2.756$ or $t > t_{\alpha/2,v} = t_{.005,29} = 2.756$

$$t = \frac{(\bar{x}_1 - \bar{x}_2) - (\mu_1 - \mu_2)}{\sqrt{\left(\frac{s_1^2}{n_1} + \frac{s_2^2}{n_2}\right)}} = \frac{(74.91 - 53.40) - 0}{\sqrt{\left(\frac{601.90}{23} + \frac{73.69}{15}\right)}} = 3.86,$$ p-value = .0006 (Excel). There is enough

evidence to conclude that the two packages differ in the amount of time needed to learn how to use them.

b $(\bar{x}_1 - \bar{x}_2) \pm t_{\alpha/2} \sqrt{\left(\frac{s_1^2}{n_1} + \frac{s_2^2}{n_2}\right)} = (74.91 - 53.40) \pm 2.045 \sqrt{\left(\frac{601.90}{23} + \frac{73.69}{15}\right)} = 21.51 \pm 11.40;$

LCL = 10.11, UCL = 32.92

c The amount of time is required to be normally distributed.

d The histograms are somewhat bell shaped.

13.42 $H_0 : (\mu_1 - \mu_2) = 0$

$H_1 : (\mu_1 - \mu_2) > 0$

Rejection region: $t > t_{\alpha,\nu} = t_{.05,268} = 1.645$

$$t = \frac{(\bar{x}_1 - \bar{x}_2) - (\mu_1 - \mu_2)}{\sqrt{s_p^2 \left(\frac{1}{n_1} + \frac{1}{n_2}\right)}} = \frac{(.646 - .601) - 0}{\sqrt{.00243 \left(\frac{1}{125} + \frac{1}{145}\right)}} = 7.44,$$ p-value = 0. There is enough evidence to

conclude that the reaction time of drivers using cell phones is slower that for non-cell phone users.

13.44 $H_0 : (\mu_1 - \mu_2) = 0$

$H_1 : (\mu_1 - \mu_2) > 0$

Rejection region: $t > t_{\alpha,\nu} = t_{.05,143} \approx 1.656$

$$t = \frac{(\bar{x}_1 - \bar{x}_2) - (\mu_1 - \mu_2)}{\sqrt{s_p^2 \left(\frac{1}{n_1} + \frac{1}{n_2}\right)}} = \frac{(6.18 - 5.94) - 0}{\sqrt{2.57 \left(\frac{1}{64} + \frac{1}{81}\right)}} = .87,$$ p-value = .1917 (Excel). There is not enough

evidence to infer that people spend more time researching for a financial planner than they do for a stock broker.

13.46 $H_0 : (\mu_1 - \mu_2) = 0$

$H_1 : (\mu_1 - \mu_2) \neq 0$

Rejection region: $t < -t_{\alpha/2,v} = -t_{.025,413} \approx -1.960$ or $t > t_{\alpha/2,v} = t_{.025,413} \approx 1.960$

$$t = \frac{(\bar{x}_1 - \bar{x}_2) - (\mu_1 - \mu_2)}{\sqrt{s_p^2\left(\frac{1}{n_1} + \frac{1}{n_2}\right)}} = \frac{(149.85 - 154.43) - 0}{\sqrt{516.40\left(\frac{1}{213} + \frac{1}{202}\right)}} = -2.05, \text{ p-value} = .0407 \text{ (Excel). There is enough}$$

evidence to conclude that there are differences in service times between the two chains.

13.48 $H_0 : (\mu_1 - \mu_2) = 0$

$H_1 : (\mu_1 - \mu_2) \neq 0$

Rejection region: $t < -t_{\alpha/2,v} = -t_{.025,190} \approx -1.973$ or $t > t_{\alpha/2,v} = t_{.025,190} \approx 1.973$

$$t = \frac{(\bar{x}_1 - \bar{x}_2) - (\mu_1 - \mu_2)}{\sqrt{\frac{s_1^2}{n_1} + \frac{s_2^2}{n_2}}} = \frac{(130.93 - 126.14) - 0}{\sqrt{\frac{1023.36}{100} + \frac{675.85}{100}}} = 1.16, \text{ p-value} = .2467 \text{ (Excel). There is not}$$

enough evidence to infer that differences exist between the two types of customers.

13.50 $H_0 : (\mu_1 - \mu_2) = 0$

$H_1 : (\mu_1 - \mu_2) < 0$

Rejection region: $t < -t_{\alpha,v} = -t_{.05,531} = -1.645$

$$t = \frac{(\bar{x}_1 - \bar{x}_2) - (\mu_1 - \mu_2)}{\sqrt{\frac{s_1^2}{n_1} + \frac{s_2^2}{n_2}}} = \frac{(237.99 - 251.99) - 0}{\sqrt{\frac{149.91}{263} + \frac{220.25}{279}}} = -12.00, \text{ p-value} = 0. \text{ There is enough evidence to}$$

infer that British golfers play golf in less time than do American golfers.

13.52 $H_0 : (\mu_1 - \mu_2) = 0$

$H_1 : (\mu_1 - \mu_2) < 0$

Rejection region: $t < -t_{\alpha,v} = -t_{.05,53} \approx -1.676$

$$t = \frac{(\bar{x}_1 - \bar{x}_2) - (\mu_1 - \mu_2)}{\sqrt{\frac{s_1^2}{n_1} + \frac{s_2^2}{n_2}}} = \frac{(7,137 - 9,304) - 0}{\sqrt{\frac{38,051}{28} + \frac{110,151}{33}}} = -31.61, \text{ p-value} = 0. \text{ There is enough evidence to}$$

conclude that the total distance of American golf courses is greater than that of British courses.

13.54 More affluent mothers use Tastee and babies with more affluent mothers gain weight faster.

13.56a The data are observational.

b Randomly assign students to use either of the software packages.

c Better students tend to choose Program B and better students learn how to use computer software more quickly.

13.58a Randomly select finance and marketing MBA graduates and determine their starting salaries.

b Randomly assign some MBA students to major in finance and others to major in marketing. Compare starting salaries after they graduate.

c Better students may be attracted to finance and better students draw higher starting salaries.

13.60 $H_0 : \mu_D = 0$

$H_1 : \mu_D > 0$

Rejection region: $t > t_{\alpha,v} = t_{.01,4} = 3.747$

$t = \dfrac{\bar{x}_D - \mu_D}{s_D / \sqrt{n_D}} = \dfrac{3.8 - 0}{3.11 / \sqrt{5}} = 2.73$, p-value = .0263 (Excel). There is not enough evidence to infer that

the mean of population 1 exceeds the mean of population 2.

13.62 a $\bar{x}_D \pm t_{\alpha/2} \dfrac{s_D}{\sqrt{n_D}} = -2.10 \pm 1.833 \dfrac{2.23}{\sqrt{10}} = -2.10 \pm 1.29$; LCL = -3.39, UCL = -.81

b The mean difference is estimated to lie between -3.39 and -.81. This type of estimate is correct 90% of the time.

13.64a $H_0 : \mu_D = 0$

$H_1 : \mu_D \neq 0$

Rejection region: $t < -t_{\alpha/2,v} = -t_{.025,5} = -2.571$ or $t > t_{\alpha/2,v} = t_{.025,5} = 2.571$

$t = \dfrac{\bar{x}_D - \mu_D}{s_D / \sqrt{n_D}} = \dfrac{-.67 - 0}{5.16 / \sqrt{6}} = -.32$, p-value = .7646 (Excel). There is not enough evidence at the 5%

significance level to infer that the population means differ.

b The variable used to match the pairs was not strongly related to the variable being tested. As a consequence the matched pairs experiment did not reduce the variation. The smaller number of degrees of freedom produced a larger p-value.

13.66 a $H_0 : \mu_D = 0$

$H_1 : \mu_D > 0$

Rejection region: $t > t_{\alpha,v} = t_{.05,11} = 1.796$

$t = \dfrac{\bar{x}_D - \mu_D}{s_D / \sqrt{n_D}} = \dfrac{3.08 - 0}{5.88 / \sqrt{12}} = 1.81$, p-value = .0484 (Excel). There is enough evidence to infer that

companies with exercise programs have lower medical expenses.

b $\bar{x}_D \pm t_{\alpha/2} \dfrac{s_D}{\sqrt{n_D}} = 3.08 \pm 2.201 \dfrac{5.88}{\sqrt{12}} = 3.08 \pm 3.74$; LCL = -.66, UCL = 6.82

c Yes because medical expenses will vary by the month of the year.

13.68 $H_0 : \mu_D = 0$

$H_1 : \mu_D \neq 0$

Rejection region: $t < -t_{\alpha/2,v} = -t_{.025,49} = -2.009$ or $t > t_{\alpha/2,v} = t_{.025,49} = 2.009$

$t = \dfrac{\bar{x}_D - \mu_D}{s_D / \sqrt{n_D}} = \dfrac{-1.16 - 0}{2.22 / \sqrt{50}} = -3.70$, p-value = .0006 (Excel). There is enough evidence to infer that

waiters and waitresses earn different amounts in tips.

13.70 $H_0 : \mu_D = 0$

$H_1 : \mu_D < 0$

Rejection region: $t < -t_{\alpha,v} = -t_{.05,99} \approx -1.660$

$t = \dfrac{\bar{x}_D - \mu_D}{s_D / \sqrt{n_D}} = \dfrac{-3.6 - 0}{5.91 / \sqrt{100}} = -6.09$, p-value = 0. There is enough evidence to infer that the new drug

is effective.

13.72 $H_0 : \mu_D = 0$

$H_1 : \mu_D < 0$

Rejection region: $t < -t_{\alpha,v} = -t_{.05,169} = -1.654$

$t = \dfrac{\bar{x}_D - \mu_D}{s_D / \sqrt{n_D}} = \dfrac{-183.35 - 0}{1568.94 / \sqrt{170}} = -1.52$, p-value = .0647 (Excel). There is not enough to infer stock

holdings have decreased.

13.74 $H_0 : \mu_D = 0$

$H_1 : \mu_D > 0$

Rejection region: $t > t_{\alpha,v} = t_{.05,54} \approx 1.676$

$t = \dfrac{\bar{x}_D - \mu_D}{s_D / \sqrt{n_D}} = \dfrac{520.85 - 0}{1854.92 / \sqrt{55}} = 2.08$, p-value = .0210 (Excel). There is enough evidence to infer that

company 1's calculated tax payable is higher than company 2's.

13.76 The matched pairs experiment reduced the variation caused by different drivers.

13.78 $H_0 : \sigma_1^2 / \sigma_2^2 = 1$

$H_1 : \sigma_1^2 / \sigma_2^2 \neq 1$

Rejection region: $F > F_{\alpha/2,v_1,v_2} = F_{.025,29,29} \approx 2.09$ or

$F < F_{1-\alpha/2,v_1,v_2} = 1/ F_{\alpha/2,v_2,v_1} = 1/ F_{.025,29,29} \approx 1/2.09 = .48$

F = s_1^2 / s_2^2 = 350/700 =.50, p-value = .0669 (Excel). There is not enough evidence to conclude that

the population variances differ.

13.80 The value of the test statistic is unchanged. The p-value increases.

13.82 LCL = $\left(\dfrac{s_1^2}{s_2^2}\right)\dfrac{1}{F_{\alpha/2,v_1,v_2}} = \left(\dfrac{28}{19}\right)\dfrac{1}{2.27} = .649$, UCL = $\left(\dfrac{s_1^2}{s_2^2}\right)F_{\alpha/2,v_2,v_1} = \left(\dfrac{28}{19}\right)2.27 = 3.35$

13.84 $H_0 : \sigma_1^2 / \sigma_2^2 = 1$

$H_1 : \sigma_1^2 / \sigma_2^2 > 1$

Rejection region: $F > F_{\alpha, v_1, v_2} = F_{.05,19,19} \approx 2.16$

F = $s_1^2 / s_2^2 = 60/25 = 2.40$, p-value = .0318 (Excel). There is enough evidence to infer that variance of population 1 is greater than the variance of population 2.

13.86 $H_0 : \sigma_1^2 / \sigma_2^2 = 1$

$H_1 : \sigma_1^2 / \sigma_2^2 \neq 1$

Rejection region: $F > F_{\alpha/2, v_1, v_2} = F_{.025,9,9} = 4.03$ or

$F < F_{1-\alpha/2, v_1, v_2} = 1/ F_{\alpha/2, v_2, v_1} = 1/ F_{.025,9,9} = 1/4.03 = .25$

F = $s_1^2 / s_2^2 = 163.88/233.38 = .70$, p-value = .6068 (Excel). There is no evidence to conclude that the population variances differ.

13.88 LCL $= \left(\dfrac{s_1^2}{s_2^2} \right) \dfrac{1}{F_{\alpha/2, v_1, v_2}} = \left(\dfrac{15{,}800}{18{,}734} \right) \dfrac{1}{1.43} = .590$, UCL $= \left(\dfrac{s_1^2}{s_2^2} \right) F_{\alpha/2, v_2, v_1} = \left(\dfrac{15{,}800}{18{,}734} \right) 1.43 = 1.21$

13.90 $H_0 : \sigma_1^2 / \sigma_2^2 = 1$

$H_1 : \sigma_1^2 / \sigma_2^2 \neq 1$

Rejection region: $F > F_{\alpha/2, v_1, v_2} = F_{.05,78,90} \approx 1.43$ or

$F < F_{1-\alpha/2, v_1, v_2} = 1/ F_{\alpha/2, v_2, v_1} = 1/ F_{.05,90,78} \approx 1/1.53 = .65$

F = $s_1^2 / s_2^2 = 9.38/13.22 = .71$, p-value = .1214 (Excel). There is not enough evidence to conclude that the population variances are not equal.

13.92 $H_0 : \sigma_1^2 / \sigma_2^2 = 1$

$H_1 : \sigma_1^2 / \sigma_2^2 < 1$

Rejection region: $F < F_{1-\alpha, v_1, v_2} = 1/ F_{\alpha, v_2, v_1} = 1/ F_{.05,51,51} \approx 1/1.53 = .65$

$F = s_1^2 / s_2^2 = .026/.087 = .30$, p-value = 0 (Excel). There is enough evidence to infer that portfolio 2 is riskier than portfolio 1.

13.94 to 13.100 $H_0 : (p_1 - p_2) = 0$

$\qquad\qquad\quad H_1 : (p_1 - p_2) \neq 0$

Rejection region: $z < -z_{\alpha/2} = -z_{.025} = -1.96$ or $z > z_{\alpha/2} = z_{.025} = 1.96$

13.94 $z = \dfrac{(\hat{p}_1 - \hat{p}_2)}{\sqrt{\hat{p}(1-\hat{p})\left(\dfrac{1}{n_1} + \dfrac{1}{n_2}\right)}} = \dfrac{(.45 - .40)}{\sqrt{.425(1-.425)\left(\dfrac{1}{100} + \dfrac{1}{100}\right)}} = .72$, p-value = 2P(Z > .72) = 2(.5 -

.2642) = .4716.

13.96 The p-value decreases.

13.98 The p-value decreases.

13.100 The p-value deceases.

13.102 $(\hat{p}_1 - \hat{p}_2) \pm z_{\alpha/2} \sqrt{\dfrac{\hat{p}_1(1-\hat{p}_1)}{n_1} + \dfrac{\hat{p}_2(1-\hat{p}_2)}{n_2}} = (.48 - .52) \pm 1.645 \sqrt{\dfrac{.48(1-.48)}{100} + \dfrac{.52(1-.52)}{100}}$

$= -.040 \pm .116$

13.104 $H_0 : (p_1 - p_2) = 0$

$\qquad\quad H_1 : (p_1 - p_2) > 0$

Rejection region: $z > z_{\alpha} = z_{.05} = 1.645$

$z = \dfrac{(\hat{p}_1 - \hat{p}_2)}{\sqrt{\hat{p}(1-\hat{p})\left(\dfrac{1}{n_1} + \dfrac{1}{n_2}\right)}} = \dfrac{(.071 - .064)}{\sqrt{.068(1-.068)\left(\dfrac{1}{1604} + \dfrac{1}{1109}\right)}} = .71$, p-value = P(Z > .71) = .5 - .2611

= .2389. There is not enough evidence to infer that the claim is false.

13.106 $H_0 : (p_1 - p_2) = -.08$

$H_1 : (p_1 - p_2) < -.08$

Rejection region: $z < -z_\alpha = -z_{.01} = -2.33$

$$z = \frac{(\hat{p}_1 - \hat{p}_2) - (p_1 - p_2)}{\sqrt{\dfrac{\hat{p}_1(1 - \hat{p}_1)}{n_1} + \dfrac{\hat{p}_2(1 - \hat{p}_2)}{n_2}}} = \frac{(.11 - .28) - (-.08)}{\sqrt{\dfrac{.11(1 - .11)}{300} + \dfrac{.28(1 - .28)}{300}}} = -2.85, \text{ p-value} = P(Z < -2.85) = .5 -$$

.4978 = .0022. There is enough evidence to conclude that management should adopt process 1.

13.108 $H_0 : (p_1 - p_2) = 0$

$H_1 : (p_1 - p_2) \neq 0$

Rejection region: $z < -z_{\alpha/2} = -z_{.05} = -1.96$ or $z > z_{\alpha/2} = z_{.05} = 1.96$

$$z = \frac{(\hat{p}_1 - \hat{p}_2)}{\sqrt{\hat{p}(1 - \hat{p})\left(\dfrac{1}{n_1} + \dfrac{1}{n_2}\right)}} = \frac{(.0995 - .1297)}{\sqrt{.1132(1 - .1132)\left(\dfrac{1}{382} + \dfrac{1}{316}\right)}} = -1.26, \text{ p-value} = 2P(Z < -1.26)$$

= 2(.5 - .3962) = .2076. There is not enough evidence to infer differences between the two sources.

13.110 $H_0 : (p_1 - p_2) = 0$

$H_1 : (p_1 - p_2) < 0$

Rejection region: $z < -z_\alpha = -z_{.05} = -1.645$

$$z = \frac{(\hat{p}_1 - \hat{p}_2)}{\sqrt{\hat{p}(1 - \hat{p})\left(\dfrac{1}{n_1} + \dfrac{1}{n_2}\right)}} = \frac{(.2462 - .2691)}{\sqrt{.2579(1 - .2579)\left(\dfrac{1}{662} + \dfrac{1}{695}\right)}} = -.96, \text{ p-value} = P(Z < -.96) = .5 - .3315$$

= .1685. There is not enough evidence to infer that the proportion of smokers has decreased in the last 10 years.

13.112a $H_0 : (p_1 - p_2) = 0$

$H_1 : (p_1 - p_2) > 0$

Rejection region: $z > z_\alpha = z_{.10} = 1.28$

$$z = \frac{(\hat{p}_1 - \hat{p}_2)}{\sqrt{\hat{p}(1-\hat{p})\left(\dfrac{1}{n_1} + \dfrac{1}{n_2}\right)}} = \frac{(.62 - .52)}{\sqrt{.56(1-.56)\left(\dfrac{1}{400} + \dfrac{1}{500}\right)}} = 3.01, \text{p-value} = P(Z > 3.01) = .5 - .4987 =$$

.0013. There is enough evidence to infer that there has been a decrease in belief in the greenhouse effect.

$$\text{b } (\hat{p}_1 - \hat{p}_2) \pm z_{\alpha/2}\sqrt{\frac{\hat{p}_1(1-\hat{p}_1)}{n_1} + \frac{\hat{p}_2(1-\hat{p}_2)}{n_2}} = (.62-.52) \pm 1.645\sqrt{\frac{.62(1-.62)}{400} + \frac{.52(1-.52)}{500}} = .10$$

$\pm .0543$; LCL = .0457 and UCL = .1543; the change in the public's opinion is estimated to lie between 4.57 and 15.43%

13.114 $H_0 : (p_1 - p_2) = -.02$

        $H_1 : (p_1 - p_2) < -.02$

Rejection region: $z < -z_\alpha = -z_{.05} = -1.645$

$$z = \frac{(\hat{p}_1 - \hat{p}_2) - (p_1 - p_2)}{\sqrt{\dfrac{\hat{p}_1(1-\hat{p}_1)}{n_1} + \dfrac{\hat{p}_2(1-\hat{p}_2)}{n_2}}} = \frac{(.055 - .11) - (-.02)}{\sqrt{\dfrac{.055(1-.055)}{200} + \dfrac{.11(1-.11)}{200}}} = -1.28, \text{p-value} = P(Z < -1.28)$$

= .5 - .3997 = .1003. There is not enough evidence to choose machine A.

13.116 $H_0 : (p_1 - p_2) = 0$

        $H_1 : (p_1 - p_2) > 0$

Rejection region: $z > z_\alpha = z_{.05} = 1.645$

$$z = \frac{(\hat{p}_1 - \hat{p}_2)}{\sqrt{\hat{p}(1-\hat{p})\left(\dfrac{1}{n_1} + \dfrac{1}{n_2}\right)}} = \frac{(.1561 - .0921)}{\sqrt{.1377(1-.1377)\left(\dfrac{1}{378} + \dfrac{1}{152}\right)}} = 1.93, \text{p-value} = P(Z > 1.93)$$

= .5 - .4732 = .0268. There is enough evidence to infer that low-income individuals are more likely to use the company's services.

The answers to the chapter review exercises will be produced by Excel only.

13.118 $H_0 : (\mu_1 - \mu_2) = 0$

$H_1 : (\mu_1 - \mu_2) \neq 0$

t-Test: Two-Sample Assuming Equal Variances		
	Oat bran	Other
Mean	10.01	9.12
Variance	19.64	19.84
Observations	120	120
Pooled Variance	19.74	
Hypothesized Mean Difference	0	
df	238	
t Stat	1.56	
P(T<=t) one-tail	0.0602	
t Critical one-tail	1.6513	
P(T<=t) two-tail	0.1204	
t Critical two-tail	1.9700	

$t = 1.56$, p-value = .1204. There is not enough evidence to infer that oat bran is different from other cereals in terms of cholesterol reduction?

13.120 $H_0 : (\mu_1 - \mu_2) = 0$

$H_1 : (\mu_1 - \mu_2) > 0$

t-Test: Two-Sample Assuming Equal Variances		
	During	Before
Mean	5746.07	5372.13
Variance	167289	194772
Observations	15	24
Pooled Variance	184373	
Hypothesized Mean Difference	0	
df	37	
t Stat	2.65	
P(T<=t) one-tail	0.0059	
t Critical one-tail	1.6871	
P(T<=t) two-tail	0.0119	
t Critical two-tail	2.0262	

$t = 2.65$, p-value = .0059. There is enough evidence to conclude that the campaign is successful.

13.122　$H_0 : (\mu_1 - \mu_2) = 0$

$H_1 : (\mu_1 - \mu_2) < 0$

t-Test: Two-Sample Assuming Unequal Variances		
	Group 1	*Group 2*
Mean	4.94	9.48
Variance	11.19	20.29
Observations	68	193
Hypothesized Mean Difference	0	
df	158	
t Stat	-8.73	
P(T<=t) one-tail	0.0000	
t Critical one-tail	1.6546	
P(T<=t) two-tail	0.0000	
t Critical two-tail	1.9751	

t = -8.73, p-value = 0. There is enough evidence to conclude that men and women who suffer heart attacks vacation less than those who do not suffer heart attacks.

13.124　$H_0 : (\mu_1 - \mu_2) = 0$

$H_1 : (\mu_1 - \mu_2) \neq 0$

t-Test: Two-Sample Assuming Equal Variances		
	Vendor	*Delivered*
Mean	19.50	20.03
Variance	14.35	14.97
Observations	205	155
Pooled Variance	14.62	
Hypothesized Mean Difference	0	
df	358	
t Stat	-1.29	
P(T<=t) one-tail	0.0996	
t Critical one-tail	1.6491	
P(T<=t) two-tail	0.1993	
t Critical two-tail	1.9666	

t = -1.29, p-value = .1993. There is no evidence of a difference in reading time between the two groups.

13.126a $H_0 : (\mu_1 - \mu_2) = 0$

$H_1 : (\mu_1 - \mu_2) < 0$

t-Test: Two-Sample Assuming Equal Variances		
	5 Years	This Year
Mean	32.42	33.72
Variance	36.92	45.52
Observations	200	200
Pooled Variance	41.22	
Hypothesized Mean Difference	0	
df	398	
t Stat	-2.02	
P(T<=t) one-tail	0.0218	
t Critical one-tail	1.2837	
P(T<=t) two-tail	0.0436	
t Critical two-tail	1.6487	

$t = -2.02$, p-value = .0218. There is enough evidence to infer that housing cost a percentage of total income has increased.

b The histograms are be bell shaped.

13.128a $H_0 : \mu_D = 0$

$H_1 : \mu_D \neq 0$

t-Test: Paired Two Sample for Means		
	Female	Male
Mean	55.68	56.40
Variance	105.64	116.75
Observations	25	25
Pearson Correlation	0.9553	
Hypothesized Mean Difference	0	
df	24	
t Stat	-1.13	
P(T<=t) one-tail	0.1355	
t Critical one-tail	1.3178	
P(T<=t) two-tail	0.2710	
t Critical two-tail	1.7109	

$t = -1.13$, p-value = .2710. There is no evidence to infer that gender is a factor.

135

b A large variation within each gender group was expected.

c The histogram of the differences is somewhat bell shaped.

13.130 $H_0 : (\mu_1 - \mu_2) = 25$

   $H_1 : (\mu_1 - \mu_2) > 25$

t-Test: Two-Sample Assuming Equal Variances		
	A Nondefectives	B Nondefectives
Mean	230.13	200.92
Variance	79.51	59.04
Observations	24	24
Pooled Variance	69.27	
Hypothesized Mean Difference	25	
df	46	
t Stat	1.75	
P(T<=t) one-tail	0.0433	
t Critical one-tail	1.6787	
P(T<=t) two-tail	0.0865	
t Critical two-tail	2.0129	

$t = 1.75$, p-value = .0433. There is enough evidence to conclude that machine A should be purchased.

13.132 $H_0 : \mu_D = 0$

   $H_1 : \mu_D > 0$

Dry Cleaner

t-Test: Paired Two Sample for Means		
	Dry C Before	Dry C After
Mean	168.00	165.50
Variance	351.38	321.96
Observations	14	14
Pearson Correlation	0.8590	
Hypothesized Mean Difference	0	
df	13	
t Stat	0.96	
P(T<=t) one-tail	0.1780	
t Critical one-tail	1.7709	
P(T<=t) two-tail	0.3559	
t Critical two-tail	2.1604	

t = .96, p-value = .1780. There is not enough evidence to conclude that the dry cleaner sales have decreased.

Doughnut shop

t-Test: Paired Two Sample for Means		
	Donut Before	Donut After
Mean	308.14	295.29
Variance	809.67	812.07
Observations	14	14
Pearson Correlation	0.8640	
Hypothesized Mean Difference	0	
df	13	
t Stat	3.24	
P(T<=t) one-tail	0.0032	
t Critical one-tail	1.7709	
P(T<=t) two-tail	0.0065	
t Critical two-tail	2.1604	

t = 3.24, p-value = .0032. There is enough evidence to conclude that the doughnut shop sales have decreased.

Convenience store

t-Test: Paired Two Sample for Means		
	Convenience Before	Convenience After
Mean	374.64	348.14
Variance	2270.40	2941.82
Observations	14	14
Pearson Correlation	0.9731	
Hypothesized Mean Difference	0	
df	13	
t Stat	7.34	
P(T<=t) one-tail	0.0000	
t Critical one-tail	1.7709	
P(T<=t) two-tail	0.0000	
t Critical two-tail	2.1604	

t = 7.34, p-value = 0. There is enough evidence to conclude that the convenience store sales have decreased.

13.134a $H_0 : (p_1 - p_2) = 0$

$H_1 : (p_1 - p_2) > 0$

z-Test: Two Proportions		
	Depressed	Not Depressed
Sample Proportions	0.2879	0.2004
Observations	132	1058
Hypothesized Difference	0	
z Stat	2.33	
P(Z<=z) one tail	0.0100	
z Critical one-tail	2.3263	
P(Z<=z) two-tail	0.0200	
z Critical two-tail	2.5758	

z = 2.33, p-value = .0100. There is enough evidence to infer that men who are clinically depressed are more likely to die from heart diseases.

b No, we cannot establish a causal relationship.

13.136 $H_0 : (\mu_1 - \mu_2) = 0$

$H_1 : (\mu_1 - \mu_2) < 0$

t-Test: Two-Sample Assuming Unequal Variances		
	Group 1	Group 2
Mean	7.46	8.46
Variance	25.06	12.98
Observations	50	50
Hypothesized Mean Difference	0	
df	89	
t Stat	-1.14	
P(T<=t) one-tail	0.1288	
t Critical one-tail	1.6622	
P(T<=t) two-tail	0.2575	
t Critical two-tail	1.9870	

t = -1.14, p-value = .1288. There is not enough evidence to conclude that people who exercise moderately more frequently lose weight faster

13.138 $H_0 : (p_1 - p_2) = 0$

$H_1 : (p_1 - p_2) > 0$

z-Test: Two Proportions			
		Special K	Other
Sample Proportions		0.635	0.530
Observations		200	200
Hypothesized Difference		0	
z Stat		2.13	
P(Z<=z) one tail		0.0166	
z Critical one-tail		1.6449	
P(Z<=z) two-tail		0.0332	
z Critical two-tail		1.96	

z = 2.13, p-value = .0166. There is enough evidence to conclude that Special K buyers like the ad more than non-buyers.

13.140　$H_0 : (\mu_1 - \mu_2) = 0$

　　　　$H_1 : (\mu_1 - \mu_2) < 0$

t-Test: Two-Sample Assuming Unequal Variances		
	Small space	*Large space*
Mean	1245.68	1915.84
Variance	23811.89	65566.31
Observations	25	25
Hypothesized Mean Difference	0	
df	39	
t Stat	-11.21	
P(T<=t) one-tail	0.0000	
t Critical one-tail	1.3036	
P(T<=t) two-tail	0.0000	
t Critical two-tail	1.6849	

t = -11.21, p-value = 0. There is enough evidence to infer that students write in such a way as to fill the allotted space.

13.142　$H_0 : (p_1 - p_2) = 0$

　　　　$H_1 : (p_1 - p_2) > 0$

z-Test: Two Proportions			
		New	*Older*
Sample Proportions		0.948	0.92
Observations		250	250
Hypothesized Difference		0	
z Stat		1.26	
P(Z<=z) one tail		0.1037	
z Critical one-tail		1.2816	
P(Z<=z) two-tail		0.2074	
z Critical two-tail		1.6449	

z = 1.26, p-value = .1037. There is not enough evidence to conclude that the new company is better.

13.144 $H_0 : (\mu_1 - \mu_2) = 0$

$H_1 : (\mu_1 - \mu_2) > 0$

t-Test: Two-Sample Assuming Unequal Variances		
	Teenagers	20-to-30
Mean	18.18	14.30
Variance	357.32	130.79
Observations	176	154
Hypothesized Mean Difference	0	
df	293	
t Stat	2.28	
P(T<=t) one-tail	0.0115	
t Critical one-tail	1.6501	
P(T<=t) two-tail	0.0230	
t Critical two-tail	1.9681	

t = 2.28, p-value = .0115. There is enough evidence to infer that teenagers see more movies than do twenty to thirty year olds.

Chapter 14

14.2 a z-test of $p_1 - p_2$ (case 1)

$$H_0 : (p_1 - p_2) = 0$$

$$H_1 : (p_1 - p_2) > 0$$

$$z = \frac{(\hat{p}_1 - \hat{p}_2)}{\sqrt{\hat{p}(1-\hat{p})\left(\dfrac{1}{n_1} + \dfrac{1}{n_2}\right)}}$$

z-Test of the Difference Between Two Proportions (Case 1)				
	Sample 1	Sample 2	z Stat	2.83
Sample proportion	0.4336	0.2414	P(Z<=z) one-tail	0.0024
Sample size	113	87	z Critical one-tail	1.6449
Alpha	0.05		P(Z<=z) two-tail	0.0047
			z Critical two-tail	1.9600

$z = 2.83$, p-value = .0024. There is enough evidence to infer that customers who see the ad are more likely to make a purchase than those who do not see the ad.

b Equal-variances t-test of $\mu_1 - \mu_2$

$$H_0 : (\mu_1 - \mu_2) = 0$$

$$H_1 : (\mu_1 - \mu_2) > 0$$

$$t = \frac{(\bar{x}_1 - \bar{x}_2) - (\mu_1 - \mu_2)}{\sqrt{s_p^2\left(\dfrac{1}{n_1} + \dfrac{1}{n_2}\right)}}$$

t-Test: Two-Sample Assuming Equal Variances		
	Ad	No Ad
Mean	97.38	92.01
Variance	621.97	283.26
Observations	49	21
Pooled Variance	522.35	
Hypothesized Mean Difference	0	
df	68	
t Stat	0.90	
P(T<=t) one-tail	0.1853	
t Critical one-tail	1.6676	
P(T<=t) two-tail	0.3705	
t Critical two-tail	1.9955	

t = .90, p-value = .1853. There is not enough evidence to infer that customers who see the ad and make a purchase spend more than those who do not see the ad and make a purchase.

c z-estimator of p

$$\hat{p} \pm z_{\alpha/2}\sqrt{\frac{\hat{p}(1-\hat{p})}{n}}$$

z-Estimate of a Proportion				
Sample proportion	0.4336	Confidence Interval Estimate		
Sample size	113	0.4336	±	0.0914
Confidence level	0.95	Lower confidence limit		0.3423
		Upper confidence limit		0.5250

We estimate that between 34.23% and 52.50% of all customers who see the ad will make a purchase.

d t-estimator of μ

$$\bar{x} \pm t_{\alpha/2}\frac{s}{\sqrt{n}}$$

t-Estimate: Mean			
			Ad
Mean			97.38
Standard Deviation			24.94
LCL			90.22
UCL			104.55

We estimate that the mean amount spent by customers who see the ad and make a purchase lies between $90.22 and $194.55.

14.4 a z-test of p

$$H_0 : p = .95$$

$$H_1 : p > .95$$

$$z = \frac{\hat{p} - p}{\sqrt{\dfrac{p(1-p)}{n}}}$$

z-Test: Proportion			
			Prority
Sample Proportion			0.9714
Observations			245
Hypothesized Proportion			0.95
z Stat			1.54
P(Z<=z) one-tail			0.0619
z Critical one-tail			1.6449
P(Z<=z) two-tail			0.1238
z Critical two-tail			1.96

$z = 1.54$, p-value $= .0619$. There is not enough evidence to infer that the spokesperson's claim is true.

b z-test of $p_1 - p_2$ (case 1)

$$H_0 : (p_1 - p_2) = 0$$

$$H_1 : (p_1 - p_2) > 0$$

144

$$z = \frac{(\hat{p}_1 - \hat{p}_2)}{\sqrt{\hat{p}(1-\hat{p})\left(\dfrac{1}{n_1} + \dfrac{1}{n_2}\right)}}$$

z-Test: Two Proportions			
		Prority	Ordinary
Sample Proportions		0.9714	0.9101
Observations		245	378
Hypothesized Difference		0	
z Stat		3.02	
P(Z<=z) one tail		0.0013	
z Critical one-tail		1.6449	
P(Z<=z) two-tail		0.0026	
z Critical two-tail		1.96	

$z = 3.02$, p-value $= .0013$. There is overwhelming evidence to infer that Priority Mail delivers letters within two days more frequently than does ordinary mail.

14.6 Speeds: Equal-variances t-test of $\mu_1 - \mu_2$

$$H_0 : (\mu_1 - \mu_2) = 0$$

$$H_1 : (\mu_1 - \mu_2) > 0$$

$$t = \frac{(\bar{x}_1 - \bar{x}_2) - (\mu_1 - \mu_2)}{\sqrt{s_p^2\left(\dfrac{1}{n_1} + \dfrac{1}{n_2}\right)}}$$

t-Test: Two-Sample Assuming Equal Variances		
	Speeds Before	*Speeds After*
Mean	31.74	31.42
Variance	4.50	4.41
Observations	100	100
Pooled Variance	4.45	
Hypothesized Mean Difference	0	
df	198	
t Stat	1.07	
P(T<=t) one-tail	0.1424	
t Critical one-tail	1.6526	
P(T<=t) two-tail	0.2849	
t Critical two-tail	1.9720	

t = 1.07, p-value = .1424. There is not enough evidence to infer that speed bumps reduce speeds.

Proper stops: Equal-variances t-test of $\mu_1 - \mu_2$

$$H_0 : (\mu_1 - \mu_2) = 0$$

$$H_1 : (\mu_1 - \mu_2) < 0$$

$$t = \frac{(\bar{x}_1 - \bar{x}_2) - (\mu_1 - \mu_2)}{\sqrt{s_p^2 \left(\frac{1}{n_1} + \frac{1}{n_2} \right)}}$$

t-Test: Two-Sample Assuming Equal Variances		
	Stops Before	*Stops After*
Mean	7.82	7.98
Variance	1.83	1.84
Observations	100	100
Pooled Variance	1.83	
Hypothesized Mean Difference	0	
df	198	
t Stat	-0.84	
P(T<=t) one-tail	0.2021	
t Critical one-tail	1.6526	
P(T<=t) two-tail	0.4042	
t Critical two-tail	1.9720	

146

t = -.84, p-value = .2021. There is not enough evidence to infer that speed bumps increase the number of proper stops.

14.8 t-test of μ_D

$$H_0 : \mu_D = 0$$

$$H_1 : \mu_D > 0$$

$$t = \frac{\bar{x}_D - \mu_D}{s_D / \sqrt{n_D}}$$

t-Test: Paired Two Sample for Means		
	Before	*After*
Mean	28.94	26.22
Variance	61.45	104.30
Observations	50	50
Pearson Correlation	0.8695	
Hypothesized Mean Difference	0	
df	49	
t Stat	3.73	
P(T<=t) one-tail	0.0002	
t Critical one-tail	1.6766	
P(T<=t) two-tail	0.0005	
t Critical two-tail	2.0096	

t = 3.73, p-value = .0002. There is enough evidence to infer that the law discourages bicycle use.

14.10 t-test of μ

$$H_0 : \mu = 200$$
$$H_1 : \mu > 200$$

$$t = \frac{\bar{x} - \mu}{s / \sqrt{n}}$$

t-Test: Mean			
			Pedestrians
Mean			209.13
Standard Deviation			60.01
Hypothesized Mean			200
df			39
t Stat			0.96
P(T<=t) one-tail			0.1711
t Critical one-tail			1.6849
P(T<=t) two-tail			0.3422
t Critical two-tail			2.0227

t = .96, p-value = .1711. There is not enough evidence to infer that the franchiser should build on this site.

14.12 z-test of p

$$H_0 : p = .5$$

$$H_1 : p > .5$$

$$z = \frac{\hat{p} - p}{\sqrt{\dfrac{p(1 - p)}{n}}}$$

z-Test: Proportion			
			Winner
Sample Proportion			0.5296
Observations			625
Hypothesized Proportion			0.5
z Stat			1.48
P(Z<=z) one-tail			0.0694
z Critical one-tail			1.6449
P(Z<=z) two-tail			0.1388
z Critical two-tail			1.96

z = 1.48, p-value = .0694. There is not enough evidence to conclude that more Floridians believe that Mr. Bush won than Floridians who believe Mr. Gore won.

14.14 Unequal-variances t-test of $\mu_1 - \mu_2$

$$H_0 : (\mu_1 - \mu_2) = 0$$

$$H_1 : (\mu_1 - \mu_2) > 0$$

$$t = \frac{(\bar{x}_1 - \bar{x}_2) - (\mu_1 - \mu_2)}{\sqrt{\dfrac{s_1^2}{n_1} + \dfrac{s_2^2}{n_2}}}$$

t-Test: Two-Sample Assuming Unequal Variances		
	Quit	*Did not quit*
Mean	2.038	0.721
Variance	2.052	1.398
Observations	259	1626
Hypothesized Mean Difference	0	
df	316	
t Stat	14.06	
P(T<=t) one-tail	0.0000	
t Critical one-tail	1.6497	
P(T<=t) two-tail	0.0000	
t Critical two-tail	1.9675	

t = 14.06, p-value = 0. There is overwhelming evidence to infer that quitting smoking results in weight gains.

14.16 Equal-variances t-tests of $\mu_1 - \mu_2$

Memory:

$$H_0 : (\mu_1 - \mu_2) = 0$$

$$H_1 : (\mu_1 - \mu_2) > 0$$

$$t = \frac{(\bar{x}_1 - \bar{x}_2) - (\mu_1 - \mu_2)}{\sqrt{s_p^2 \left(\dfrac{1}{n_1} + \dfrac{1}{n_2} \right)}}$$

t-Test: Two-Sample Assuming Equal Variances		
	Memory-Player	*Memory-Non*
Mean	73.12	67.34
Variance	69.99	86.60
Observations	50	50
Pooled Variance	78.29	
Hypothesized Mean Difference	0	
df	98	
t Stat	3.27	
P(T<=t) one-tail	0.0008	
t Critical one-tail	1.6606	
P(T<=t) two-tail	0.0015	
t Critical two-tail	1.9845	

Reasoning:

$$H_0 : (\mu_1 - \mu_2) = 0$$

$$H_1 : (\mu_1 - \mu_2) > 0$$

$$t = \frac{(\bar{x}_1 - \bar{x}_2) - (\mu_1 - \mu_2)}{\sqrt{s_p^2 \left(\frac{1}{n_1} + \frac{1}{n_2} \right)}}$$

t-Test: Two-Sample Assuming Equal Variances		
	Reasoning-Player	*Reasoning-Non*
Mean	78.22	72.16
Variance	41.15	67.40
Observations	50	50
Pooled Variance	54.28	
Hypothesized Mean Difference	0	
df	98	
t Stat	4.11	
P(T<=t) one-tail	0.0000	
t Critical one-tail	1.6606	
P(T<=t) two-tail	0.0001	
t Critical two-tail	1.9845	

Reaction time:

$$H_0 : (\mu_1 - \mu_2) = 0$$

$$H_1 : (\mu_1 - \mu_2) \neq 0$$

$$t = \frac{(\bar{x}_1 - \bar{x}_2) - (\mu_1 - \mu_2)}{\sqrt{s_p^2 \left(\dfrac{1}{n_1} + \dfrac{1}{n_2} \right)}}$$

t-Test: Two-Sample Assuming Equal Variances		
	Reaction-Player	*Reaction-Non*
Mean	70.60	71.22
Variance	31.18	26.09
Observations	50	50
Pooled Variance	28.64	
Hypothesized Mean Difference	0	
df	98	
t Stat	-0.58	
P(T<=t) one-tail	0.2819	
t Critical one-tail	1.6606	
P(T<=t) two-tail	0.5637	
t Critical two-tail	1.9845	

Vocabulary:

$$H_0 : (\mu_1 - \mu_2) = 0$$

$$H_1 : (\mu_1 - \mu_2) \neq 0$$

$$t = \frac{(\bar{x}_1 - \bar{x}_2) - (\mu_1 - \mu_2)}{\sqrt{s_p^2 \left(\dfrac{1}{n_1} + \dfrac{1}{n_2} \right)}}$$

t-Test: Two-Sample Assuming Equal Variances		
	Vocabulary-Player	*Vocabulary-Non*
Mean	82.22	80.12
Variance	60.66	81.70
Observations	50	50
Pooled Variance	71.18	
Hypothesized Mean Difference	0	
df	98	
t Stat	1.24	
P(T<=t) one-tail	0.1081	
t Critical one-tail	1.6606	
P(T<=t) two-tail	0.2163	
t Critical two-tail	1.9845	

Overall Conclusion: p-values are .0008, 0, .5637, and .2163. There is overwhelming evidence to indicate that bridge-players score higher on memory and reasoning tests. There is not enough evidence of a difference in reaction time and vocabulary between players and nonplayers.

14.18 t-estimator of μ

$$\bar{x} \pm t_{\alpha/2} \frac{s}{\sqrt{n}}$$

t-Estimate: Mean			
			Calls
Mean			0.320
Standard Deviation			0.717
LCL			0.204
UCL			0.436

LCL = .204, UCL = .436. On average, each copier is estimated to require between .204 and .436 service calls in the first year.

Total number of service calls: LCL = 1000(.204) = 204, UCL = 1000(.436) = 436. It is estimated that the company's copiers will require between 204 and 436 service calls in the first year.

14.20 Unequal-variances t-test of $\mu_1 - \mu_2$

$$H_0 : (\mu_1 - \mu_2) = 0$$

$$H_1 : (\mu_1 - \mu_2) < 0$$

$$t = \frac{(\bar{x}_1 - \bar{x}_2) - (\mu_1 - \mu_2)}{\sqrt{\frac{s_1^2}{n_1} + \frac{s_2^2}{n_2}}}$$

t-Test: Two-Sample Assuming Unequal Variances		
	Leftover	Returned
Mean	61.71	70.57
Variance	48.99	203.98
Observations	14	53
Hypothesized Mean Difference	0	
df	44	
t Stat	-3.27	
P(T<=t) one-tail	0.0011	
t Critical one-tail	1.6802	
P(T<=t) two-tail	0.0021	
t Critical two-tail	2.0154	

$t = -3.27$, p-value = .0011. There is overwhelming evidence to support the professor's theory.

14.22 a z-test of p

$$H_0 : p = 104,320/425,000 = .245$$

$$H_1 : p > .245$$

$$z = \frac{\hat{p} - p}{\sqrt{\dfrac{p(1-p)}{n}}}$$

z-Test: Proportion		
		Deliver
Sample Proportion		0.2825
Observations		400
Hypothesized Proportion		0.245
z Stat		1.74
P(Z<=z) one-tail		0.0406
z Critical one-tail		1.6449
P(Z<=z) two-tail		0.0812
z Critical two-tail		1.96

$z = 1.74$, p-value = .0406. There is evidence to indicate that the campaign will increase home delivery sales.

b z-test of p

$$H_0 : p = 110{,}000/425{,}000 = .259$$

$$H_1 : p > .259$$

$$z = \frac{\hat{p} - p}{\sqrt{\dfrac{p(1-p)}{n}}}$$

z-Test: Proportion			
			Deliver
Sample Proportion			0.2825
Observations			400
Hypothesized Proportion			0.259
z Stat			1.07
P(Z<=z) one-tail			0.1417
z Critical one-tail			1.6449
P(Z<=z) two-tail			0.2834
z Critical two-tail			1.96

z = 1.07, p-value = .1417. There is not enough evidence to conclude that the campaign will be successful.

14.24a Equal-variances t-test of $\mu_1 - \mu_2$

$$H_0 : (\mu_1 - \mu_2) = 0$$

$$H_1 : (\mu_1 - \mu_2) < 0$$

$$t = \frac{(\bar{x}_1 - \bar{x}_2) - (\mu_1 - \mu_2)}{\sqrt{s_p^2 \left(\dfrac{1}{n_1} + \dfrac{1}{n_2} \right)}}$$

154

t-Test: Two-Sample Assuming Equal Variances		
	Expenses MSA	Expenses Regular
Mean	347.24	479.25
Variance	21042.80	21127.51
Observations	63	141
Pooled Variance	21101.51	
Hypothesized Mean Difference	0	
df	202	
t Stat	-6.00	
P(T<=t) one-tail	0.0000	
t Critical one-tail	1.6524	
P(T<=t) two-tail	0.0000	
t Critical two-tail	1.9718	

$t = -6.00$, p-value = 0. There is overwhelming evidence to infer that medical expenses for those under the MSA plan are lower than those who are not.

b z-test of $p_1 - p_2$ (case 1)

$$H_0 : p_1 - p_2 = 0$$

$$H_1 : p_1 - p_2 < 0$$

$$z = \frac{(\hat{p}_1 - \hat{p}_2)}{\sqrt{\hat{p}(1-\hat{p})\left(\frac{1}{n_1} + \frac{1}{n_2}\right)}}$$

z-Test: Two Proportions			
		Health MSA	Health Regular
Sample Proportions		0.7619	0.7801
Observations		63	141
Hypothesized Difference		0	
z Stat		-0.29	
P(Z<=z) one tail		0.3867	
z Critical one-tail		1.6449	
P(Z<=z) two-tail		0.7734	
z Critical two-tail		1.96	

$z = -.29$, p-value = .3867. There is not enough evidence to support the critics of MSA.

Chapter 15

15.2 $\bar{\bar{x}} = \dfrac{10(10) + 10(15) + 10(20)}{10 + 10 + 10} = 15$

$SST = \sum n_j(\bar{x}_j - \bar{\bar{x}})^2 = 10(10 - 15)^2 + 10(15 - 15)^2 + 10(20 - 15)^2 = 500$

$SSE = \sum (n_j - 1)s_j^2 = (10 - 1)(50) + (10 - 1)(50) + (10 - 1)(50) = 1350$

ANOVA table

Source	Degrees of Freedom	Sum of Squares	Mean Squares	F
Treatments	k- 1=3- 1=2	SST = 500	$\dfrac{SST}{k-1} = \dfrac{500}{2} = 250$	$\dfrac{MST}{MSE} = \dfrac{125}{50} = 5.00$
Error	n - k=30- 3=27	SSE = 1350	$\dfrac{SSE}{n-k1} = \dfrac{1350}{27} = 50$	
Total	n - 1=30- 1=29	SS(Total) = 1850		

15.4 $\bar{\bar{x}} = \dfrac{5(10) + 5(15) + 5(20)}{5 + 5 + 5} = 15$

$SST = \sum n_j(\bar{x}_j - \bar{\bar{x}})^2 = 5(10 - 15)^2 + 5(15 - 15)^2 + 5(15 - 15)^2 = 250$

$SSE = \sum (n_j - 1)s_j^2 = (5 - 1)(25) + (5 - 1)(25) + (5 - 1)(25) = 300$

ANOVA table

Source	Degrees of Freedom	Sum of Squares	Mean Squares	F
Treatments	k - 1=3- 1=2	SST = 250	$\dfrac{SST}{k-1} = \dfrac{250}{2} = 125$	$\dfrac{MST}{MSE} = \dfrac{125}{25} = 5.00$
Error	n - k=15- 3=12	SSE = 300	$\dfrac{SSE}{n-k1} = \dfrac{300}{12} = 25$	
Total	n - 1=15 - 1=14	SS(Total) = 550		

15.6 $\bar{\bar{x}} = \dfrac{5(110) + 5(115) + 5(120)}{5 + 5 + 5} = 115$

$SST = \sum n_j (\bar{x}_j - \bar{\bar{x}})^2 = 5(110 - 115)^2 + 5(115 - 115)^2 + 5(115 - 115)^2 = 250$

$SSE = \sum (n_j - 1)s_j^2 = (5 - 1)(50) + (5 - 1)(50) + (5 - 1)(50) = 600$

ANOVA table

Source	Degrees of Freedom	Sum of Squares	Mean Squares	F
Treatments	k - 1=3- 1=2	SST = 250	$\dfrac{SST}{k-1} = \dfrac{250}{2} = 125$	$\dfrac{MST}{MSE} = \dfrac{125}{50} = 2.50$
Error	n - k=15- 3=12	SSE = 600	$\dfrac{SSE}{n-k1} = \dfrac{600}{12} = 50$	
Total	n - 1=15 - 1=14	SS(Total) = 850		

15.8 $\bar{\bar{x}} = \dfrac{5(5) + 5(15) + 5(25)}{5 + 5 + 5} = 15$

$SST = \sum n_j (\bar{x}_j - \bar{\bar{x}})^2 = 5(5 - 15)^2 + 5(15 - 15)^2 + 5(25 - 15)^2 = 1000$

$SSE = \sum (n_j - 1)s_j^2 = (5 - 1)(50) + (5 - 1)(50) + (5 - 1)(50) = 600$

ANOVA table

Source	Degrees of Freedom	Sum of Squares	Mean Squares	F
Treatments	k - 1=3- 1=2	SST = 1000	$\dfrac{SST}{k-1} = \dfrac{1000}{2} = 500$	$\dfrac{MST}{MSE} = \dfrac{500}{50} = 10.0$
Error	n - k=15- 3=12	SSE = 600	$\dfrac{SSE}{n-k1} = \dfrac{600}{12} = 50$	
Total	n - 1=15 - 1=14	SS(Total) = 1600		

15.10 $\bar{\bar{x}} = \dfrac{5(15) + 5(15) + 5(15)}{5 + 5 + 5} = 15$

$SST = \sum n_j (\bar{x}_j - \bar{\bar{x}})^2 = 5(15 - 15)^2 + 5(15 - 15)^2 + 5(15 - 15)^2 = 0$

$$SSE = \sum (n_j - 1)s_j^2 = (5-1)(50) + (5-1)(50) + (5-1)(50) = 600$$

ANOVA table

Source	Degrees of Freedom	Sum of Squares	Mean Squares	F
Treatments	k - 1=3- 1=2	SST = 0	$\dfrac{SST}{k-1} = \dfrac{0}{2} = 0$	$\dfrac{MST}{MSE} = \dfrac{0}{50} = 0$
Error	n - k=15- 3=12	SSE = 600	$\dfrac{SSE}{n-k1} = \dfrac{600}{12} = 50$	
Total	n - 1=15 - 1=14	SS(Total) = 600		

The sum of squares for treatments equals 0 and the F statistic equals 0.

15.12 Grand mean: $\bar{\bar{x}} = \dfrac{10(14.7) + 14(11.6) + 11(19.3)}{10 + 14 + 11} = 14.9$

$$SST = \sum n_j(\bar{x}_j - \bar{\bar{x}})^2 = 10(14.7 - 14.9)^2 + 14(11.6 - 14.9)^2 + 11(19.3 - 14.9)^2 = 365.8$$

$$SSE = \sum (n_j - 1)s_j^2 = (10-1)(5.3)^2 + (14-1)(7.1)^2 + (11-1)(6.8)^2 = 1370.5$$

ANOVA Table

Source	Degrees of Freedom	Sums of Squares	Mean Squares	F
Treatments	2	365.8	182.9	4.27
Error	32	1370.5	42.8	
Total	34	1736.3		

15.14 Grand mean: $\bar{\bar{x}} = \dfrac{9(35.0) + 13(47.3) + 8(40.2)}{9 + 13 + 8} = 41.72$

$$SST = \sum n_j(\bar{x}_j - \bar{\bar{x}})^2 = 9(35.0 - 41.72)^2 + 13(47.3 - 41.72)^2 + 8(40.2 - 41.72)^2 = 829.68$$

$$SSE = \sum (n_j - 1)s_j^2 = (9-1)(8.3)^2 + (13-1)(6.4)^2 + (8-1)(7.7)^2 = 1457.67$$

ANOVA Table

Source	Degrees of Freedom Sums	Sums of Squares	Mean Squares	F
Treatments	2	829.68	414.84	7.68
Error	27	1457.67	53.99	
Total	29	2287.35		

Rejection region: $F > F_{\alpha,k-1,n-k} = F_{.05,2,27} = 3.35$

$F = 7.68$. There is enough evidence to infer that the population means differ.

15.16a $H_0 : \mu_1 = \mu_2 = \mu_3 = \mu_4$

H_1 : At least two means differ.

Anova: Single Factor						
SUMMARY						
Groups	Count	Sum	Average	Variance		
Form 1	30	2705	90.17	991.52		
Form 2	30	2873	95.77	900.87		
Form 3	30	3205	106.83	928.70		
Form 4	30	3335	111.17	1023.04		
ANOVA						
Source of Variation	SS	df	MS	F	P-value	F crit
Between Groups	8464.10	3	2821.37	2.94	0.0363	2.68
Within Groups	111479.87	116	961.03			
Total	119943.97	119				

$F = 2.94$, p-value = .0363. There is enough evidence to infer that there are differences between the completion times of the four income tax forms.

b The times for each form must be normally distributed with the same variance.

c The histograms are approximately bell-shaped and the sample variances are similar.

15.18 $H_0 : \mu_1 = \mu_2 = \mu_3 = \mu_4 = \mu_5$

H_1 : At least two means differ.

Anova: Single Factor						
SUMMARY						
Groups	Count	Sum	Average	Variance		
Lacquer 1	24	3935	163.96	1205.61		
Lacquer 2	25	4641	185.64	1719.91		
Lacquer 3	24	3703	154.29	1156.30		
Lacquer 4	25	4565	182.60	1657.83		
Lacquer 5	23	4111	178.74	906.02		
ANOVA						
Source of Variation	SS	df	MS	F	P-value	F crit
Between Groups	17413.89	4	4353.47	3.25	0.0144	3.49
Within Groups	155322.11	116	1338.98			
Total	172736.00	120				

$F = 3.25$, p-value = .0144. There is not enough evidence to allow the manufacturer to conclude that differences exist between the five lacquers.

b The times until first sign of corrosion for each lacquer must be normally distributed with a common variance.

c The histograms are approximately bell-shaped with similar sample variances.

15.20 $H_0 : \mu_1 = \mu_2 = \mu_3$

H_1 : At least two means differ.

160

Anova: Single Factor						
SUMMARY						
Groups	*Count*	*Sum*	*Average*	*Variance*		
Fertilizer A	20	11030	551.50	2741.95		
Fertilizer B	20	11535	576.75	2641.14		
Fertilizer C	20	11189	559.45	3129.31		
ANOVA						
Source of Variation	*SS*	*df*	*MS*	*F*	*P-value*	*F crit*
Between Groups	6667.03	2	3333.52	1.17	0.3162	3.16
Within Groups	161735.70	57	2837.47			
Total	168402.73	59				

$F = 1.17$, p-value $= .3162$. There is not enough evidence of a difference between fertilizers in terms of crop yields.

15.22 $H_0 : \mu_1 = \mu_2 = \mu_3 = \mu_4$

H_1 : At least two means differ.

Anova: Single Factor						
SUMMARY						
Groups	*Count*	*Sum*	*Average*	*Variance*		
1st quarter	30	2223	74.10	249.96		
2nd quarter	30	2270	75.67	184.23		
3rd quarter	30	2355	78.50	233.36		
4th quarter	30	2439	81.30	242.91		
ANOVA						
Source of Variation	*SS*	*df*	*MS*	*F*	*P-value*	*F crit*
Between Groups	909.42	3	303.14	1.33	0.2675	2.68
Within Groups	26403.17	116	227.61			
Total	27312.59	119				

$F = 1.33$, p-value $= .2675$. There is not enough evidence of a difference between the four groups of companies.

15.24 $H_0 : \mu_1 = \mu_2 = \mu_3 = \mu_4$

   H_1 : At least two means differ.

a Ages

Anova: Single Factor						
SUMMARY						
Groups	*Count*	*Sum*	*Average*	*Variance*		
Age 1	63	1972	31.30	28.34		
Age 2	81	2788	34.42	23.20		
Age 3	40	1495	37.38	31.16		
Age 4	111	4432	39.93	72.03		
ANOVA						
Source of Variation	*SS*	*df*	*MS*	*F*	*P-value*	*F crit*
Between Groups	3365.99	3	1122.00	25.60	0.0000	2.64
Within Groups	12751.80	291	43.82			
Total	16117.78	294				

F = 25.60, p-value = 0. There is sufficient evidence to infer that the ages of the four groups of cereal buyers differ.

b Incomes

Anova: Single Factor						
SUMMARY						
Groups	*Count*	*Sum*	*Average*	*Variance*		
Income 1	63	2345	37.22	39.82		
Income 2	81	3152	38.91	40.85		
Income 3	40	1659	41.48	61.38		
Income 4	111	4634	41.75	46.59		
ANOVA						
Source of Variation	*SS*	*df*	*MS*	*F*	*P-value*	*F crit*
Between Groups	1007.47	3	335.82	7.37	0.0001	2.64
Within Groups	13256.20	291	45.55			
Total	14263.66	294				

F = 7.37, p-value = .0001. There is sufficient evidence to conclude that incomes differ between the four groups of cereal buyers.

c Education

Anova: Single Factor						
SUMMARY						
Groups	Count	Sum	Average	Variance		
Education 1	63	740	11.75	3.93		
Education 2	81	1005	12.41	3.39		
Education 3	40	469	11.73	4.26		
Education 4	111	1320	11.89	4.30		
ANOVA						
Source of Variation	SS	df	MS	F	P-value	F crit
Between Groups	21.71	3	7.24	1.82	0.1428	2.64
Within Groups	1154.17	291	3.97			
Total	1175.88	294				

F = 1.82, p-value = .1428. There is not enough evidence to infer that education differs between the four groups of cereal buyers.

d Using the F-tests and the descriptive statistics we see that the mean ages and mean household incomes are in ascending order. For example, Sugar Smacks buyers are younger and earn less than the buyers of the other three cereals. Cheerio purchasers are older and earn the most.

15.26 $H_0 : \mu_1 = \mu_2 = \mu_3$

H_1 : At least two means differ.

Anova: Single Factor						
SUMMARY						
Groups	Count	Sum	Average	Variance		
12 to 14	61	1131	18.54	177.95		
15 to 16	83	1605	19.34	171.42		
17 to 19	91	1846	20.29	297.50		
ANOVA						
Source of Variation	SS	df	MS	F	P-value	F crit
Between Groups	114.48	2	57.24	0.26	0.7730	3.03
Within Groups	51508.27	232	222.02			
Total	51622.75	234				

$F = .26$, p-value $= .7730$. There is not enough evidence of a difference between the three segments.

15.28   ANOVA Table

Source	Degrees of Freedom		Sums of Squares	Mean Squares	F
Treatments	$k-1$	2	100	50.00	24.04
Blocks	$B-1$	6	50	8.33	4.00
Error	$k \cdot B$	12	25	2.08	
Total		20	175		

a Rejection region: $F > F_{\alpha,k-1,n-k-b+1} = F_{.05,2,12} = 3.89$

Conclusion: $F = 24.04$. There is enough evidence to conclude that the treatment means differ.

b Rejection region: $F > F_{\alpha,b-1,n-k-b+1} = F_{.05,6,12} = 3.00$

$F = 4.00$. There is enough evidence to conclude that the block means differ.

15.30   ANOVA Table

Source	Degrees of Freedom	Sums of Squares	Mean Squares	F
Treatments	3	275	91.67	7.98
Blocks	9	625	69.44	6.05
Error	27	310	11.48	
Total	39	1210		

164

a Rejection region: $F > F_{\alpha,k-1,n-k-b+1} = F_{.01,3,27} = 4.60$

Conclusion: $F = 7.98$. There is enough evidence to conclude that the treatment means differ.

b Rejection region: $F > F_{\alpha,b-1,n-k-b+1} = F_{.01,9,27} = 3.15$

Conclusion: $F = 6.05$. There is enough evidence to conclude that the block means differ.

15.32

ANOVA						
Source of Variation	SS	df	MS	F	P-value	F crit
Rows	4.17	2	2.08	6.82	0.0285	5.14
Columns	8.92	3	2.97	9.73	0.0101	4.76
Error	1.83	6	0.31			
Total	14.92	11				

a Rejection region: $F > F_{\alpha,k-1,n-k-b+1} = F_{.05,3,6} = 4.76$

$F = 9.73$. There is enough evidence to conclude that the treatment means differ.

b Rejection region: $F > F_{\alpha,b-1,n-k-b+1} = F_{.05,2,6} = 5.14$

$F = 6.82$. There is enough evidence to conclude that the block means differ.

15.34

ANOVA						
Source of Variation	SS	df	MS	F	P-value	F crit
Rows	35300.00	24	1470.83	15.94	0.0000	1.67
Columns	2126.51	3	708.84	7.68	0.0002	2.73
Error	6642.24	72	92.25			
Total	44068.75	99				

a $H_0 : \mu_1 = \mu_2 = \mu_3 = \mu_4$

H_1 : At least two means differ.

Rejection region: $F > F_{\alpha,k-1,n-k-b+1} = F_{.05,3,72} \approx 2.76$

$F = 7.68$, p-value = .0002. There is enough evidence to conclude that the treatment means differ.

b $\qquad H_0 : \mu_1 = \mu_2 = \ldots = \mu_{25}$

$\qquad H_1 :$ At least two means differ.

Rejection region: $F > F_{\alpha, b-1, n-k-b+1} = F_{.05, 24, 72} \approx 1.70$

Conclusion: $F = 15.94$, p-value = 0. There is enough evidence to conclude that the block means differ.

c The response is required to be normally distributed with a common variance.

d The histograms are bell shaped and the sample variances are similar.

15.36

ANOVA						
Source of Variation	*SS*	*df*	*MS*	*F*	*P-value*	*F crit*
Rows	1150.22	11	104.57	4.65	0.0011	2.26
Columns	204.22	2	102.11	4.54	0.0224	3.44
Error	495.11	22	22.51			
Total	1849.56	35				

a $\qquad H_0 : \mu_1 = \mu_2 = \mu_3$

$\qquad H_1 :$ At least two means differ.

Rejection region: $F > F_{\alpha, k-1, n-k-b+1} = F_{.05, 2, 38} \approx 3.23$

$F = 123.36$, p-value = 0. There is sufficient evidence to conclude that the three fertilizers differ with respect to crop yield.

b $F = 323.16$, p-value = 0. There is sufficient evidence to indicate that there are differences between the plots.

15.38

ANOVA						
Source of Variation	*SS*	*df*	*MS*	*F*	*P-value*	*F crit*
Rows	126842.58	29	4373.88	66.02	0.0000	1.94
Columns	4206.09	3	1402.03	21.16	0.0000	4.02
Error	5763.66	87	66.25			
Total	136812.33	119				

a $H_0 : \mu_1 = \mu_2 = \mu_3 = \mu_4$

      H_1 : At least two means differ.

Rejection region: $F > F_{\alpha, k-1, n-k-b+1} = F_{.01, 3, 87} \approx 4.13$

F = 21.16, p-value = 0. There is sufficient evidence to conclude that differences in completion times exist between the four forms.

b $H_0 : \mu_1 = \mu_2 = \ldots = \mu_{30}$

      H_1 : At least two means differ.

F = 66.02, p-value = 0. There is sufficient evidence to indicate that there are differences between the taxpayers, which tells us that this experimental design is recommended.

15.40

ANOVA						
Source of Variation	SS	df	MS	F	P-value	F crit
Rows	7309.68	35	208.85	6.36	0.0000	1.51
Columns	1406.39	4	351.60	10.72	0.0000	2.44
Error	4593.89	140	32.81			
Total	13309.97	179				

a $H_0 : \mu_1 = \mu_2 = \mu_3 = \mu_4 = \mu_5$

      H_1 : At least two means differ.

F = 10.72, p-value = 0. There is enough evidence to infer differences between medical specialties.

b $H_0 : \mu_1 = \mu_2 = \ldots = \mu_{36}$

      H_1 : At least two means differ.

F = 6.36, p-value = 0. There is sufficient evidence to indicate that there are differences between the physicians' ages, which tells us that this experimental design is recommended.

15.42

Source	Degrees of Freedom	Sums of Squares	Mean Squares	F
Factor A	2	1,560	780	5.85
Factor B	3	2,880	960	7.20
Interaction	6	7,605	1268	9.50
Error	228	30,405	133	
Total	239	42,450		

a Rejection region: $F > F_{\alpha, a-1, n-ab} = F_{.01, 2, 228} \approx 4.61$

$F = 5.85$. There is enough evidence to conclude that differences exist between the levels of factor A.

b Rejection region: $F > F_{\alpha, b-1, n-ab} = F_{.01, 3, 228} \approx 3.78$

$F = 7.20$. There is enough evidence to conclude that differences exist between the levels of factor B.

c Rejection region: $F > F_{\alpha, (a-1)(b-1), n-ab} = F_{.01, 6, 228} \approx 2.80$

$F = 9.50$. There is enough evidence to conclude that factors A and B interact.

15.44

ANOVA						
Source of Variation	SS	df	MS	F	P-value	F crit
Sample	5.33	1	5.33	1.23	0.2995	5.32
Columns	56.33	1	56.33	13.00	0.0069	5.32
Interaction	1.33	1	1.33	0.31	0.5943	5.32
Within	34.67	8	4.33			
Total	97.67	11				

a $F = .31$, p-value $= .5943$. There is not enough evidence to conclude that factors A and B interact.

b $F = 1.23$, p-value $= .2995$. There is not enough evidence to conclude that differences exist between the levels of factor A.

c $F = 13.00$, p-value $= .0069$. There is enough evidence to conclude that differences exist between the levels of factor B.

15.46 a Factor A is the drug mixture and factor B is the schedule.

b The response variable is the improvement index.

c There are $a = 4$ drug mixtures and $b = 2$ schedules.

ANOVA						
Source of Variation	SS	df	MS	F	P-value	F crit
Sample	14.4	1	14.40	0.57	0.4548	4.15
Columns	581.8	3	193.93	7.71	0.0005	2.90
Interaction	548.6	3	182.87	7.27	0.0007	2.90
Within	804.8	32	25.15			
Total	1949.6	39				

d F = .57, p-value = .4548. There is not enough evidence to conclude that differences exist between the schedules.

e F = 7.71, p-value = .0005. There is sufficient evidence to conclude that differences exist between the four drug mixtures.

f F = 7.27, p-value = .0007. There is sufficient evidence to conclude that the schedules and drug mixtures interact.

15.48 a There are 12 treatments

b There are two factors, tax form and income group.

c There are a = 4 forms and b = 3 income groups.

ANOVA						
Source of Variation	SS	df	MS	F	P-value	F crit
Sample	6718.72	2	3359.36	4.11	0.0190	3.08
Columns	6279.87	3	2093.29	2.56	0.0586	2.69
Interaction	5101.88	6	850.31	1.04	0.4030	2.18
Within	88217.00	108	816.82			
Total	106317.47	119				

d F = 2.56, p-value = .0586. There is not enough evidence to conclude that differences exist between the forms.

e F = 4.11, p-value = .0190. There is enough evidence to conclude that differences exist between the three income groups.

f F = 1.04, p-value = .4030. There is not enough evidence to conclude that forms and income groups interact.

15.50

ANOVA						
Source of Variation	SS	df	MS	F	P-value	F crit
Sample	16.04	1	16.04	14.74	0.0005	4.11
Columns	6.77	1	6.77	6.22	0.0173	4.11
Interaction	0.025	1	0.025	0.02	0.8814	4.11
Within	39.17	36	1.09			
Total	62.00	39				

The p-values for machines, alloys, and interaction are .0173, .0005, and .8814, respectively. Both machines and alloys are sources of variation.

15.52

ANOVA						
Source of Variation	SS	df	MS	F	P-value	F crit
Sample	211.78	2	105.89	21.04	0.0000	3.22
Columns	0.59	1	0.59	0.12	0.7348	4.07
Interaction	0.128	2	0.064	0.01	0.9874	3.22
Within	211.42	42	5.03			
Total	423.91	47				

The p-values for methods, skills, and interaction are .7348, 0, and .9874. The only source of variation is skill level.

15.54 $C = 3(2)/2 = 3, \alpha_E = .05, \alpha = \alpha_E / C = .0167: t_{\alpha/2,n-k} = t_{.0083,27} = 2.552$ (from Excel)

	$\bar{x}_i$	$\bar{x}_j$	$|\bar{x}_i - \bar{x}_j|$	$LSD = t_{\alpha/2,n-k}\sqrt{MSE\left(\dfrac{1}{n_i}+\dfrac{1}{n_j}\right)}$
$i = 1, j = 2$	128.7	101.4	27.3	$2.552\sqrt{700\left(\dfrac{1}{10}+\dfrac{1}{10}\right)} = 30.20$
$i = 1, j = 3$	128.7	133.7	5.0	$2.552\sqrt{700\left(\dfrac{1}{10}+\dfrac{1}{10}\right)} = 30.20$
$i = 2, j = 3$	101.4	133.7	32.3	$2.552\sqrt{700\left(\dfrac{1}{10}+\dfrac{1}{10}\right)} = 30.20$

Conclusion: μ_2 and μ_3 differ.

15.56 $\quad \alpha = .05$: $t_{\alpha/2, n-k} = t_{.025, 20} = 2.086$

	$\bar{x}_i$	$\bar{x}_j$	$|\bar{x}_i - \bar{x}_j|$	$LSD = t_{\alpha/2, n-k}\sqrt{MSE\left(\dfrac{1}{n_i} + \dfrac{1}{n_j}\right)}$
$i = 1, j = 2$	227	205	22	$2.086\sqrt{125\left(\dfrac{1}{5} + \dfrac{1}{5}\right)} = 14.75$
$i = 1, j = 3$	227	219	8	$2.086\sqrt{125\left(\dfrac{1}{5} + \dfrac{1}{5}\right)} = 14.75$
$i = 1, j = 4$	227	248	21	$2.086\sqrt{125\left(\dfrac{1}{5} + \dfrac{1}{5}\right)} = 14.75$
$i = 1, j = 5$	227	202	25	$2.086\sqrt{125\left(\dfrac{1}{5} + \dfrac{1}{5}\right)} = 14.75$
$i = 2, j = 3$	205	219	14	$2.086\sqrt{125\left(\dfrac{1}{5} + \dfrac{1}{5}\right)} = 14.75$
$i = 2, j = 4$	205	248	43	$2.086\sqrt{125\left(\dfrac{1}{5} + \dfrac{1}{5}\right)} = 14.75$
$i = 2, j = 5$	205	202	3	$2.086\sqrt{125\left(\dfrac{1}{5} + \dfrac{1}{5}\right)} = 14.75$
$i = 3, j = 4$	219	248	29	$2.086\sqrt{125\left(\dfrac{1}{5} + \dfrac{1}{5}\right)} = 14.75$
$i = 3, j = 5$	219	202	17	$2.086\sqrt{125\left(\dfrac{1}{5} + \dfrac{1}{5}\right)} = 14.75$
$i = 4, j = 5$	248	202	46	$2.086\sqrt{125\left(\dfrac{1}{5} + \dfrac{1}{5}\right)} = 14.75$

Conclusion: The following pairs of means differ. μ_1 and μ_2, μ_1 and μ_4, μ_1 and μ_5, μ_2 and μ_4, μ_3 and μ_4, μ_3 and μ_5, and μ_4 and μ_5.

15.58 $q_\alpha(k,v) = q_{.05}(5, 20) = 4.23$

	$\bar{x}_i$	$\bar{x}_j$	$\|\bar{x}_i - \bar{x}_j\|$	$\omega = q_\alpha(k,v)\sqrt{\dfrac{MSE}{n_g}}$
$i = 1, j = 2$	227	205	22	$4.23\sqrt{\dfrac{125}{5}} = 21.15$
$i = 1, j = 3$	227	219	8	$4.23\sqrt{\dfrac{125}{5}} = 21.15$
$i = 1, j = 4$	227	248	21	$4.23\sqrt{\dfrac{125}{5}} = 21.15$
$i = 1, j = 5$	227	202	25	$4.23\sqrt{\dfrac{125}{5}} = 21.15$
$i = 2, j = 3$	205	219	14	$4.23\sqrt{\dfrac{125}{5}} = 21.15$
$i = 2, j = 4$	205	248	43	$4.23\sqrt{\dfrac{125}{5}} = 21.15$
$i = 2, j = 5$	205	202	3	$4.23\sqrt{\dfrac{125}{5}} = 21.15$
$i = 3, j = 4$	219	248	29	$4.23\sqrt{\dfrac{125}{5}} = 21.15$
$i = 3, j = 5$	219	202	17	$4.23\sqrt{\dfrac{125}{5}} = 21.15$
$i = 4, j = 5$	248	202	46	$4.23\sqrt{\dfrac{125}{5}} = 21.15$

Conclusion: The following pairs of means differ. μ_1 and μ_2, μ_1 and μ_5, μ_2 and μ_4, μ_3 and μ_4, and μ_4 and μ_5.

15.60

Multiple Comparisons				
			LSD	Omega
Treatment	Treatment	Difference	Alpha = 0.00833	Alpha = 0.05
School A	School B	3.75	5.74	5.91
	School C	6.81	6.47	5.91
	School D	4.18	6.18	5.91
School B	School C	3.06	6.13	5.91
	School D	0.43	5.82	5.91
School C	School D	-2.63	6.54	5.91

The mean grades from high schools A and C differ.

15.62

Multiple Comparisons				
			LSD	Omega
Treatment	Treatment	Difference	Alpha = 0.00833	Alpha = 0.05
Form 1	Form 2	-5.60	21.49	20.83
	Form 3	-16.67	21.49	20.83
	Form 4	-21.00	21.49	20.83
Form 2	Form 3	-11.07	21.49	20.83
	Form 4	-15.40	21.49	20.83
Form 3	Form 4	-4.33	21.49	20.83

No means differ.

15.64

Multiple Comparisons				
			LSD	Omega
Treatment	Treatment	Difference	Alpha = 0.01	Alpha = 0.05
Lacquer 1	Lacquer2	-21.68	27.39	29.17
	Lacquer3	9.67	27.66	29.17
	Lacquer4	-18.64	27.39	29.17
	Lacquer5	-14.78	27.96	29.17
Lacquer2	Lacquer3	31.35	27.39	29.17
	Lacquer4	3.04	27.10	29.17
	Lacquer5	6.90	27.69	29.17
Lacquer3	Lacquer4	-28.31	27.39	29.17
	Lacquer5	-24.45	27.96	29.17
Lacquer4	Lacquer5	3.86	27.69	29.17

The means of lacquers 2 and 3, and 3 and 4 differ.

15.66a $H_0 : \mu_1 = \mu_2 = \mu_3$

H_1 : At least two means differ.

ANOVA						
Source of Variation	SS	df	MS	F	P-value	F crit
Between Groups	1178.02	2	589.01	3.70	0.0286	3.10
Within Groups	13835.80	87	159.03			
Total	15013.82	89				

F = 3.70, p-value = .0286. There is enough evidence to infer that speed of promotion varies between the three sizes of engineering firms.

b

Multiple Comparisons				
			LSD	Omega
Treatment	Treatment	Difference	Alpha = 0.05	Alpha = 0.05
Small	Medium	3.80	6.47	7.74
	Large	8.83	6.47	7.74
Medium	Large	5.03	6.47	7.74

The means of small and large firms differ. Answer (v) is correct.

15.68 $H_0 : \mu_1 = \mu_2 = \mu_3 = \mu_4$

H_1 : At least two means differ.

ANOVA						
Source of Variation	SS	df	MS	F	P-value	F crit
Rows	43979.64	19	2314.72	21.58	0.0000	1.77
Columns	4437.64	3	1479.21	13.79	0.0000	2.77
Error	6113.11	57	107.25			
Total	54530.39	79				

F = 13.79, p-value = 0. There is sufficient evidence to conclude that the reading speeds differ between the four typefaces. The typeface that was read the fastest should be used.

15.70a $H_0 : \mu_1 = \mu_2 = \mu_3 = \mu_4$

H_1 : At least two means differ.

ANOVA						
Source of Variation	SS	df	MS	F	P-value	F crit
Between Groups	9.90	3	3.30	7.67	0.0001	2.70
Within Groups	41.33	96	0.430			
Total	51.23	99				

F = 7.67, p-value = .0001. There is sufficient evidence to infer that differences in productivity exist between the four groups of companies.

b

Multiple Comparisons				
			LSD	Omega
Treatment	Treatment	Difference	Alpha = 0.00833	Alpha = 0.05
Extensive	Some	0.534	0.500	0.483
	Little	0.722	0.500	0.483
	No	0.811	0.500	0.483
Some	Little	0.188	0.500	0.483
	No	0.277	0.500	0.483
Little	No	0.089	0.500	0.483

Using either the Bonferroni adjustment or Tukey's method we conclude that μ_1 differs from μ_2, μ_3 and μ_4. Companies that offered extensive training have productivity levels different from the other companies.

15.72a There are 4 levels of ranks and 4 levels of faculties for a total of 16 treatments.

b

ANOVA						
Source of Variation	*SS*	*df*	*MS*	*F*	*P-value*	*F crit*
Between Groups	1091.15	15	72.74	2.84	0.0019	1.83
Within Groups	1638.40	64	25.60			
Total	2729.55	79				

F = 2.84, p-value = .0019. There is enough evidence to infer that at least two treatment means differ. c Factor A (columns) is the faculty. The levels are business, engineering, arts, and science. Factor B (samples) is the rank. The levels are professor, associate professor, assistant professor, and lecturer.

ANOVA						
Source of Variation	*SS*	*df*	*MS*	*F*	*P-value*	*F crit*
Sample	46.85	3	15.62	0.61	0.6109	2.75
Columns	344.65	3	114.88	4.49	0.0064	2.75
Interaction	699.65	9	77.74	3.04	0.0044	2.03
Within	1638.40	64	25.60			
Total	2729.55	79				

d F =.61, p-value = .6109. There is not enough evidence to conclude that differences exist between the ranks.

e F =4.49, p-value = .0064. There is enough evidence to conclude that differences exist between the faculties.

f F = 3.04, p-value = .0044. There is evidence to conclude that ranks and faculties interact.

15.74 $H_0 : \mu_1 = \mu_2 = \mu_3$

H_1 : At least two means differ

177

ANOVA						
Source of Variation	SS	df	MS	F	P-value	F crit
Rows	156.44	5	31.29	9.71	0.0014	3.33
Columns	43.11	2	21.56	6.69	0.0143	4.10
Error	32.22	10	3.22			
Total	231.78	17				

$F = 6.69$, p-value $= .0143$. There is enough evidence to infer that differences in attention span exist between the three products.

15.76

ANOVA						
Source of Variation	SS	df	MS	F	P-value	F crit
Sample	123554	1	123554	3.66	0.0576	3.91
Columns	3965110	2	1982555	58.78	0.0000	3.06
Interaction	30006	2	15003	0.44	0.6418	3.06
Within	4856578	144	33726			
Total	8975248	149				

Age: $F = 58.78$, p-value $= 0$. There is sufficient evidence to conclude that differences in offers exist between the three age groups.

Gender: $F = 3.66$, p-value $= .0576$. There is not enough evidence to conclude that differences in offers exist between males and females

Interaction: $F = .44$, p-value $= .6418$. There is not enough evidence to conclude that age and gender interact.

15.78a $H_0 : \mu_1 = \mu_2 = \mu_3$

$H_1 :$ At least two means differ.

ANOVA						
Source of Variation	SS	df	MS	F	P-value	F crit
Between Groups	1913.4	2	956.70	9.54	0.0002	3.10
Within Groups	8726.6	87	100.31			
Total	10640.0	89				

F = 9.54, p-value = .0002. There is sufficient evidence to infer that there are differences between the three groups.

b

Multiple Comparisons				
			LSD	Omega
Treatment	Treatment	Difference	Alpha = 0.0167	Alpha = 0.05
Mozart	*White noise*	-9.30	6.31	6.14
	Glass	-10.20	6.31	6.14
White noise	*Glass*	-0.90	6.31	6.14

The mean time of the Mozart group differs from the mean times of white noise and the Glass groups.

15.80 $H_0 : \mu_1 = \mu_2 = \mu_3 = \mu_4$

H_1 : At least two means differ.

ANOVA						
Source of Variation	*SS*	*df*	*MS*	*F*	*P-value*	*F crit*
Between Groups	3263.41	3	1087.80	10.26	0.0000	2.64
Within Groups	29684.97	280	106.02			
Total	32948.39	283				

F = 10.26, p-value = 0. There is enough evidence of differences between the four groups of investors.

15.82 $H_0 : \mu_1 = \mu_2 = \mu_3 = \mu_4$

H_1 : At least two means differ.

ANOVA						
Source of Variation	*SS*	*df*	*MS*	*F*	*P-value*	*F crit*
Between Groups	2.12	3	0.705	9.17	0.0000	2.69
Within Groups	7.99	104	0.0769			
Total	10.11	107				

F = 9.17, p-value = 0. There is sufficient evidence to infer that there are differences in changes to the TSE depending on the loss the previous day.

Chapter 16

16.2 $H_0 : p_1 = .1, \; p_2 = .2, \; p_3 = .3, \; p_4 = .2, \; p_5 = .2$

H_1 : At least one p_i is not equal to its specified value.

Cell i	f_i	e_i	$(f_i - e_i)$	$(f_i - e_i)^2 / e_i$
1	12	$150(.1) = 15$	-3	.60
2	32	$150(.2) = 30$	2	.13
3	42	$150(.3) = 45$	-3	.20
4	36	$150(.2) = 30$	6	1.20
5	28	$150(.2) = 30$	-2	.13
Total	150	150		$\chi^2 = 2.26$

Rejection region: $\chi^2 > \chi^2_{\alpha, k-1} = \chi^2_{.01,4} = 13.2767$

$\chi^2 = 2.26$, p-value = .6868 (Excel). There is not enough evidence to infer that at least one p_i is not equal to its specified value.

16.4 The χ^2 statistic decreases.

16.6 $H_0 : p_1 = .3, \; p_2 = .3, \; p_3 = .2, \; p_4 = .2$

H_1 : At least one p_i is not equal to its specified value.

Cell i	f_i	e_i	$(f_i - e_i)$	$(f_i - e_i)^2 / e_i$
1	76	$300(.3) = 90$	-14	2.18
2	100	$300(.3) = 90$	10	1.11
3	76	$300(.2) = 60$	16	4.27
4	48	$300(.2) = 60$	-12	2.40
Total	300	300		$\chi^2 = 9.96$

Rejection region: $\chi^2 > \chi^2_{\alpha, k-1} = \chi^2_{.05,3} = 7.81473$

$\chi^2 = 9.96$, p-value = .0189 (Excel). There is enough evidence to infer that at least one p_i is not equal to its specified value.

16.8 $H_0 : p_1 = .15, \; p_2 = .40, \; p_3 = .35, \; p_4 = .10$

H_1 : At least one p_i is not equal to its specified value.

Cell i	f_i	e_i	$(f_i - e_i)$	$(f_i - e_i)^2 / e_i$
1	41	$233(.15) = 34.95$	6.05	1.05
2	107	$233(.40) = 93.20$	13.80	2.04
3	66	$233(.35) = 81.55$	-15.55	2.97
4	19	$233(.10) = 23.30$	-4.30	0.79
Total	233	233		$\chi^2 = 6.85$

Rejection region: $\chi^2 > \chi^2_{\alpha,k-1} = \chi^2_{.05,3} = 7.81473$

$\chi^2 = 6.85$, p-value = .0769 (Excel). There is not enough evidence to infer that at least one p_i is not equal to its specified value.

(Excel)

16.10 $H_0 : p_1 = .05, \; p_2 = .25 \; p_3 = .40, \; p_4 = .25 \; p_5 = .05$

H_1 : At least one p_i is not equal to its specified value.

Cell i	f_i	e_i	$(f_i - e_i)$	$(f_i - e_i)^2 / e_i$
1	11	$150(.05) = 7.5$	3.5	1.63
2	32	$150(.25) = 37.5$	-5.5	0.81
3	62	$150(.40) = 60.0$	2.0	0.07
4	29	$150(.25) = 37.5$	-8.5	1.93
5	16	$150(.05) = 7.5$	8.5	9.63
Total	150	150		$\chi^2 = 14.07$

Rejection region: $\chi^2 > \chi^2_{\alpha,k-1} = \chi^2_{.05,4} = 9.48773$

$\chi^2 = 14.07$, p-value = .0071 (Excel). There is enough evidence to infer that grades are distributed differently from grades in the past.

16.12 $H_0 : p_1 = .72, \; p_2 = .15, \; p_3 = .10, \; p_4 = .03$

H_1 : At least one p_i is not equal to its specified value.

181

Cell i	f_i	e_i	$(f_i - e_i)$	$(f_i - e_i)^2 / e_i$
1	159	250(.72) = 180.0	-21.0	2.45
2	28	250(.15) = 37.5	-9.5	2.41
3	47	250(.10) = 25.0	22.0	19.36
4	16	250(.03) = 7.5	8.5	9.63
Total	250	250		$\chi^2 = 33.85$

Rejection region: $\chi^2 > \chi^2_{\alpha, k-1} = \chi^2_{.05, 3} = 7.81473$

$\chi^2 = 33.85$, p-value = 0 (Excel). There is enough evidence to infer that the aging schedule has changed.

16.14 $H_0 : p_1 = .31, \; p_2 = .51, \; p_3 = .18$

H_1 : At least one p_i is not equal to its specified value.

Cell i	f_i	e_i	$(f_i - e_i)$	$(f_i - e_i)^2 / e_i$
1	408	1200(.31) = 372	36	3.48
2	571	1200(.51) = 612	-41	2.75
3	221	1200(.18) = 216	5	0.12
Total	1200	1200		$\chi^2 = 6.35$

Rejection region: $\chi^2 > \chi^2_{\alpha, k-1} = \chi^2_{.10, 2} = 4.60517$

$\chi^2 = 6.35$, p-value = .0419 (Excel). There is enough evidence to infer that voter support has changed since the election.

16.16 $H_0 : p_1 = .23, \; p_2 = .40, \; p_3 = .15, \; p_4 = .22$

H_1 : At least one p_i is not equal to its specified value.

Cell i	f_i	e_i	$(f_i - e_i)$	$(f_i - e_i)^2 / e_i$
1	63	$320(.23) = 73.6$	-10.6	1.53
2	125	$320(.40) = 128.0$	-3.0	0.07
3	45	$320(.15) = 48.0$	-3.0	0.19
4	87	$320(.22) = 70.4$	16.6	3.91
Total	320	320		$\chi^2 = 5.70$

Rejection region: $\chi^2 > \chi^2_{\alpha, k-1} = \chi^2_{.05,3} = 7.81473$

$\chi^2 = 5.70$, p-value = .1272 (Excel) There is not enough evidence to infer that there has been a change in proportions.

16.18 H_0 : The two variables are independent

H_1 : The two variables are dependent

Cell i	f_i	e_i	$(f_i - e_i)$	$(f_i - e_i)^2 / e_i$
1	14	$48(42)/188 = 21.45$	-7.45	2.59
2	34	$48(52)/188 = 26.55$	7.45	2.09
3	28	$46(42)/188 = 20.55$	7.45	2.70
4	18	$46(52)/188 = 25.45$	-7.45	2.18
Total	94	94		$\chi^2 = 9.56$

Rejection region: $\chi^2 > \chi^2_{\alpha,(r-1)(c-1)} = \chi^2_{.05,1} = 3.84146$

$\chi^2 = 9.56$, p-value = .0020 (Excel). There is enough evidence to infer that the two classifications L and M are dependent.

16.20 The χ^2 statistic decreases.

16.22 H_0 : The two variables are independent

H_1 : The two variables are dependent

Cell i	f_i	e_i	$(f_i - e_i)$	$(f_i - e_i)^2 / e_i$
1	67	$110(130)/200 = 71.50$	-4.50	0.28
2	32	$110(50)/200 = 27.50$	4.50	0.74
3	11	$110(20)/200 = 11.00$	0	0.00
4	63	$90(130)/200 = 58.50$	4.50	0.35
5	18	$90(50)/200 = 22.50$	-4.50	0.90
6	9	$90(20)/200 = 9.00$	0	0.00
Total	200	200		$\chi^2 = 2.27$

Rejection region: $\chi^2 > \chi^2_{\alpha,(r-1)(c-1)} = \chi^2_{.10,2} = 4.60517$

$\chi^2 = 2.27$, p-value = .3221 (Excel). There is not enough evidence to infer that responses differ among the three groups of employees.

16.24 H_0 : The two variables are independent

H_1 : The two variables are dependent

Cell i	f_i	e_i	$(f_i - e_i)$	$(f_i - e_i)^2 / e_i$
1	101	$444(331)/1000 = 146.96$	-45.96	14.376
2	282	$444(557)/1000 = 233.99$	48.01	9.852
3	61	$444(142)/1000 = 63.05$	-2.05	0.067
4	38	$130(331)/1000 = 43.03$	-5.03	0.588
5	67	$130(557)/1000 = 68.51$	-1.51	0.033
6	25	$130(142)/1000 = 18.46$	6.54	2.317
7	131	$250(331)/1000 = 82.75$	48.25	28.134
8	88	$250(557)/1000 = 131.75$	-43.75	14.528
9	31	$250(142)/1000 = 35.50$	-4.50	0.570
10	61	$176(331)/1000 = 58.26$	2.74	0.129
11	90	$176(557)/1000 = 92.75$	-2.75	0.082
12	25	$176(142)/1000 = 24.99$	0.01	0.000
Total	1000	1000		$\chi^2 = 70.675$

Rejection region: $\chi^2 > \chi^2_{\alpha,(r-1)(c-1)} = \chi^2_{.01,6} = 16.8119$

$\chi^2 = 70.675$, p-value = 0 (Excel). There is sufficient evidence to infer that political affiliation affects support for economic options.

16.26 H_0 : The two variables are independent

H_1 : The two variables are dependent

Contingency Table					
	Drug				
Outcome		1	2	3	TOTAL
	1	60	31	12	103
	2	65	22	13	100
	TOTAL	125	53	25	203
	chi-squared Stat			1.7243	
	df			2	
	p-value			0.4222	
	chi-squared Critical			5.9915	

Rejection region: $\chi^2 > \chi^2_{\alpha,(r-1)(c-1)} = \chi^2_{.05,2} = 5.99147$

$\chi^2 = 1.7243$, p-value = .4222. There is not enough evidence to infer that there are differences in outcomes for the children treated by the two drugs.

16.28a H_0 : The two variables are independent

H_1 : The two variables are dependent

Contingency Table				
	Predicted			
Actual		1	2	TOTAL
	1	65	64	129
	2	39	48	87
	TOTAL	104	112	216
	chi-squared Stat		0.6434	
	df		1	
	p-value		0.4225	
	chi-squared Critical		3.8415	

Rejection region: $\chi^2 > \chi^2_{\alpha,(r-1)(c-1)} = \chi^2_{.05,1} = 3.84146$

$\chi^2 = .6434$, p-value = .4225. There is not enough evidence to infer that the predicted and actual directions of change are related.

b Ignore the what the other investors are doing.

16.30 H_0 : The two variables are independent

H_1 : The two variables are dependent

Contingency Table					
	Segment				
Employment		1	2	3	TOTAL
	1	157	44	217	418
	2	219	53	264	536
	3	256	102	524	882
	TOTAL	632	199	1005	1836
	chi-squared Stat			23.0946	
	df			4	
	p-value			0.0001	
	chi-squared Critical			9.4877	

Rejection region: $\chi^2 > \chi^2_{\alpha,(r-1)(c-1)} = \chi^2_{.05,4} = 9.48773$

$\chi^2 = 23.0946$, p-value = .0001. There is sufficient evidence to infer that there are differences in employment status between the market segments.

16.32 H_0 : The two variables are independent

H_1 : The two variables are dependent

Contingency Table						
	Group					
Education		1	2	3	4	TOTAL
	1	31	62	72	104	269
	2	55	157	143	129	484
	3	39	83	74	45	241
	4	74	107	51	24	256
	TOTAL	199	409	340	302	1250
	chi-squared Stat			108.9699		
	df			9		
	p-value			0		
	chi-squared Critical			16.919		

Rejection region: $\chi^2 > \chi^2_{\alpha,(r-1)(c-1)} = \chi^2_{.05,9} = 16.9190$

$\chi^2 = 108.9699$, p-value = 0. There is sufficient evidence to infer that there are differences in educational levels between the market segments.

16.34　　H_0 : The data are normally distributed

　　　　H_1 : The data are not normally distributed

Interval	Probability	Expected Value e_i	Observed Value f_i	$f_i - e_i$	$(f_i - e_i)^2 / e_i$
$Z \leq -1.5$	.0668	6.68	10	3.32	1.65
$-1.5 < Z \leq -0.5$	.2417	24.17	18	-6.17	1.58
$-0.5 < Z \leq 0.5$	.3829	38.29	48	9.71	2.46
$0.5 < Z \leq 1.5$	.2417	24.17	16	-8.17	2.76
$Z > 1.5$	.0668	6.68	8	1.32	0.26
Total	1	100	100		$\chi^2 = 8.71$

Rejection region: $\chi^2 > \chi^2_{\alpha,k-3} = \chi^2_{.05,2} = 5.99147$

$\chi^2 = 8.71$, p-value = .0128 (Excel). There is enough evidence to infer that the data are not normally distributed.

16.36 H_0 : Times are normally distributed

H_1 : Times are not normally distributed.

Chi-Squared Test of Normality			
	Hours		
Mean	7.15		
Standard deviation	1.65		
Observations	200		
Intervals	Probability	Expected	Observed
(z <= -1.5)	0.0668	13.36	11
(-1.5 < z <= -0.5)	0.2417	48.35	55
(-0.5 < z <= 0.5)	0.3829	76.59	52
(0.5 < z <= 1.5)	0.2417	48.35	67
(z > 1.5)	0.0668	13.36	15
chi-squared Stat	16.6238		
df	2		
p-value	0.0002		
chi-squared Critical	5.9915		

$\chi^2 = 16.6238$, p-value = .0002. There is sufficient evidence to infer that the amount of time at part-time jobs is not normally distributed.

16.38   Successful firms:

H_0 : Productivity in successful firms is normally distributed

H_1 : Productivity in successful firms is not normally distributed

Chi-Squared Test of Normality			
	Successful		
Mean	5.02		
Standard deviation	1.39		
Observations	200		
Intervals	Probability	Expected	Observed
(z <= -1.5)	0.0668	13.36	12
(-1.5 < z <= -0.5)	0.2417	48.35	52
(-0.5 < z <= 0.5)	0.3829	76.59	72
(0.5 < z <= 1.5)	0.2417	48.35	55
(z > 1.5)	0.0668	13.36	9
chi-squared Stat	3.0288		
df	2		
p-value	0.2199		
chi-squared Critical	5.9915		

$\chi^2 = 3.0288$, p-value = .2199. There is not enough evidence to infer that productivity in successful firms is not normally distributed.

Unsuccessful firms:

H_0 : Productivity in unsuccessful firms is normally distributed

H_1 : Productivity in unsuccessful firms is not normally distributed

Chi-Squared Test of Normality			
	Unsuccessful		
Mean	7.80		
Standard deviation	3.09		
Observations	200		
Intervals	Probability	Expected	Observed
($z \le -1.5$)	0.0668	13.36	12
($-1.5 < z \le -0.5$)	0.2417	48.35	47
($-0.5 < z \le 0.5$)	0.3829	76.59	83
($0.5 < z \le 1.5$)	0.2417	48.35	44
($z > 1.5$)	0.0668	13.36	14
chi-squared Stat	1.1347		
df	2		
p-value	0.567		
chi-squared Critical	5.9915		

$\chi^2 = 1.1347$, p-value = .5670. There is not enough evidence to infer that productivity in unsuccessful firms is not normally distributed.

16.40 $H_0 : p_1 = 1/3, \ p_2 = 1/3, \ p_3 = 1/3$

H_1 : At least one p_i is not equal to its specified value.

Cell i	f_i	e_i	$(f_i - e_i)$	$(f_i - e_i)^2 / e_i$
1	14	$30(1/3) = 10$	4	1.6
2	10	$30(1/3) = 10$	0	0.0
3	6	$30(1/3) = 10$	-4	1.6
Total	30	30		$\chi^2 = 3.2$

Rejection region: $\chi^2 > \chi^2_{\alpha,k-1} = \chi^2_{.10,2} = 4.60517$

$\chi^2 = 3.2$, p-value = .2019 (Excel). There is not enough evidence to infer that the game is unfair.

16.42 $H_0 : p_1 = .2, \ p_2 = .2, \ p_3 = .2, \ p_4 = .2, \ p_5 = .2$

H_1 : At least one p_i is not equal to its specified value.

Cell i	f_i	e_i	$(f_i - e_i)$	$(f_i - e_i)^2 / e_i$
1	87	$362(.2) = 72.4$	14.6	2.94
2	62	$362(.2) = 72.4$	-10.4	1.49
3	71	$362(.2) = 72.4$	-1.4	0.03
4	68	$362(.2) = 72.4$	-4.4	0.27
5	74	$362(.2) = 72.4$	1.6	0.04
Total	362	362		$\chi^2 = 4.77$

Rejection region: $\chi^2 > \chi^2_{\alpha,k-1} = \chi^2_{.05,4} = 9.48773$

Conclusion: $\chi^2 = 4.77$, p-value = .3119 (Excel). There is not enough evidence to infer that absenteeism is higher on some days of the week.

16.44 H_0 : The two variables are independent

H_1 : The two variables are dependent

Cell i	f_i	e_i	$(f_i - e_i)$	$(f_i - e_i)^2 / e_i$
1	21	$171(91)/447 = 34.81$	-13.81	5.48
2	25	$171(122)/447 = 46.67$	-21.67	10.06
3	54	$171(114)/447 = 43.61$	10.39	2.48
4	71	$171(120)/447 = 45.91$	25.09	13.72
5	39	$176(91)/447 = 35.83$	3.17	0.28
6	49	$176(122)/447 = 48.04$	0.96	0.02
7	50	$176(114)/447 = 44.89$	5.11	0.58
8	38	$176(120)/447 = 47.25$	-9.25	1.81
9	31	$100(91)/447 = 20.36$	10.64	5 56
10	48	$100(122)/447 = 27.29$	20.71	15.71
11	10	$100(114)/447 = 25.50$	-15.50	9.42
12	11	$100(120)/447 = 26.85$	-15.85	9.35
Total	447	447		$\chi^2 = 74.47$

Rejection region: $\chi^2 > \chi^2_{\alpha,(r-1)(c-1)} = \chi^2_{.05,6} = 12.5916$

Conclusion: $\chi^2 = 74.47$, p-value = 0 (Excel). There is sufficient evidence to infer that the level of job satisfaction depends on boss/employee gender relationship.

16.46 H_0 : The two variables are independent

H_1 : The two variables are dependent

Contingency Table						
	Quit					
Method		1	2	3	4	TOTAL
	1	104	125	32	49	310
	2	14	17	5	9	45
	TOTAL	118	142	37	58	355
chi-squared Stat				0.5803		
df				3		
p-value				0.9009		
chi-squared Critical				7.8147		

$\chi^2 = .5803$, p-value = .9009. There is not enough evidence to infer that the four methods differ in their success rates.

16.48a The expected frequency is 1/49.

b H_0 : $p_1 = 1/49$, $p_2 = 1/49, \ldots, p_{49} = 1/49$

H_1 : At least one p_i is not equal to its specified value.

Number i	f_i	e_i	$(f_i - e_i)$	$(f_i - e_i)^2 / e_i$
1	5	312(1/49) = 6.37	-1.38	0.29
2	6	312(1/49) = 6.37	-0.38	0.02
3	7	312(1/49) = 6.37	0.63	0.06
.		.		
.		.		
.		.		
47	6	312(1/49) = 6.37	-0.37	0.02
48	10	312(1/49) = 6.37	3.63	2.07
49	6	312(1/49) = 6.37	-0.37	0.02
Total	312	312		$\chi^2 = 38.22$

Conclusion: $\chi^2 = 38.22$, p-value = .8427 (Excel). There is not enough evidence to infer that the numbers were not generated randomly.

16.50 Binomial probabilities with n = 5 and p = .5: P(X = 0) = .0313, P(X = 1) = .1563, P(X = 2) = .3125, P(X = 3) = .3125, P(X = 4) = .1563, P(X = 5) = .0313

$H_0 : p_0 = .0313, p_1 = .1563, p_2 = .3125, p_3 = .3125, p_4 = .1563, p_5 = .0313$

H_1 : At least one p_i is not equal to its specified value.

Cell i	f_i	e_i	$(f_i - e_i)$	$(f_i - e_i)^2 / e_i$
0	8	200(.0313) = 6.26	1.74	0.48
1	35	200(.1563) = 31.26	3.74	0.45
2	57	200(.3125) = 62.50	-5.50	0.48
3	69	200(.3125) = 62.50	6.50	0.68
4	28	200(.1563) = 31.26	-3.26	0.34
5	3	200(.0313) = 6.26	-3.26	1.70
Total	200	200		$\chi^2 = 4.13$

$\chi^2 = 4.13$, p-value = .5310 (Excel). There is not enough evidence to infer that at the number of boys in families with 5 children is not a binomial random variable with p =.5.

16.52 H_0 : The two variables are independent

H_1 : The two variables are dependent

Contingency Table				
	Results			
Financial		1	2	TOTAL
	1	29	1	30
	2	10	7	17
	3	9	14	23
	TOTAL	48	22	70
	chi-squared Stat			20.9881
	df			2
	p-value			0
	chi-squared Critical			5.9915

$\chi^2 = 20.9881$, p-value = 0. There is sufficient evidence to infer that the research findings are related to whether drug companies fund the research.

16.54 H_0 : The two variables are independent

H_1 : The two variables are dependent

Contingency Table				
	Group			
Improvement		1	2	TOTAL
	1	42	8	50
	2	32	18	50
	3	13	37	50
	TOTAL	87	63	150
	chi-squared Stat			35.6322
	df			2
	p-value			0
	chi-squared Critical			5.9915

$\chi^2 = 35.6322$, p-value = 0. There is sufficient evidence to infer there are differences between the three groups.

Chapter 17

17.2 H_0 : The two population locations are the same

        H_1 : The location of population 1 is different from the location of population 2

$$E(T) = \frac{n_1(n_1 + n_2 + 1)}{2} = \frac{15(15 + 15 + 1)}{2} = 232.5$$

$$\sigma_T = \sqrt{\frac{n_1 n_2(n_1 + n_2 + 1)}{12}} = \sqrt{\frac{(15)(15)(15 + 15 + 1)}{12}} = 24.11$$

$$z = \frac{T - E(T)}{\sigma_T} = \frac{275 - 232.5}{24.11} = 1.76,\ \text{p-value} = 2P(Z > 1.76) = 2(.5 - .4608) = .0784.$$

17.4 H_0 : The two population locations are the same

        H_1 : The location of population 1 is to the right of the location of population 2

Rejection region: $z > z_\alpha = z_{.01} = 2.33$

$$E(T) = \frac{n_1(n_1 + n_2 + 1)}{2} = \frac{30(30 + 40 + 1)}{2} = 1065$$

$$\sigma_T = \sqrt{\frac{n_1 n_2(n_1 + n_2 + 1)}{12}} = \sqrt{\frac{(30)(40)(30 + 40 + 1)}{12}} = 84.26$$

$$z = \frac{T - E(T)}{\sigma_T} = \frac{1205 - 1065}{84.26} = 1.66,\ \text{p-value} = P(Z > 1.66) = .5 - .4515 = .0485.\ \text{There is not enough}$$

evidence to infer that the location of population 1 is to the right of the location of population 2.

17.6 The value of the test statistic decreases and the p-value increases.

17.8 H_0 : The two population locations are the same

        H_1 : The location of population 1 is different from the location of population 2

Rejection region: $T \geq T_U = 127$ or $T \leq T_L = 83$

Sample 1	Rank	Sample 2	Rank
15	4.0	8	2.0
7	1.0	27	18.0
22	14.0	17	7.0
20	.5	25	16.0
32	20.0	20	11.5
18	9.5	16	5.0
26	17.0	21	13.0
17	7.0	17	7.0
23	15.0	10	3.0
30	19.0	18	9.5
	$T_1 = 118$		$T_2 = 92$

There is not enough evidence to infer that the location of population 1 is different from the location of population 2.

17.10 The printout is identical to that of Exercise 17.9.

17.12 H_0 : The two population locations are the same

H_1 : The location of population 1 is different from the location of population 2

Wilcoxon Rank Sum Test			
		Rank Sum	Observations
Business		4004	40
Economy		8086	115
z Stat		3.61	
P(Z<=z) one-tail		0.0002	
z Critical one-tail		1.6449	
P(Z<=z) two-tail		0.0004	
z Critical two-tail		1.96	

$z = 3.61$, p-value = .0004. There is enough evidence to infer that the business and economy class differ in their degree of satisfaction.

17.14 All codes that preserve the order produce the same results.

17.16 The results are identical because the codes in this exercise and in Example 17.2 are ranked identically.

17.18　　H_0 : The two population locations are the same

　　　　H_1 : The location of population 1 is to the left of the location of population 2

Rejection region: $z < -z_\alpha = -z_{.05} = -1.645$

$$E(T) = \frac{n_1(n_1 + n_2 + 1)}{2} = \frac{30(30 + 30 + 1)}{2} = 915$$

$$\sigma_T = \sqrt{\frac{n_1 n_2(n_1 + n_2 + 1)}{12}} = \sqrt{\frac{(30)(30)(30 + 30 + 1)}{12}} = 67.6$$

$$z = \frac{T - E(T)}{\sigma_T} = \frac{797 - 915}{67.6} = -1.75 \text{, p-value} = P(Z < -1.75) = .5 - .4599 = .0401. \text{ There is enough}$$

evidence to infer that companies that provide exercise programs should be given discounts.

17.20　　H_0 : The two population locations are the same

　　　　H_1 : The location of population 1 is to the right of the location of population 2

Rejection region: $z > z_\alpha = z_{.10} = 1.28$

$$E(T) = \frac{n_1(n_1 + n_2 + 1)}{2} = \frac{100(100 + 100 + 1)}{2} = 10,050$$

$$\sigma_T = \sqrt{\frac{n_1 n_2(n_1 + n_2 + 1)}{12}} = \sqrt{\frac{(100)(100)(100 + 100 + 1)}{12}} = 409.3$$

$$z = \frac{T - E(T)}{\sigma_T} = \frac{10,691 - 10,050}{409.3} = 1.57, \text{ p-value} = P(Z > 1.57) = .5 - .4418 = .0582. \text{ There is enough}$$

evidence to conclude that public support has decreased between this year and last year.

17.22　　H_0 : The two population locations are the same

　　　　H_1 : The location of population 1 is to the right of the location of population 2

Rejection region: $z > z_\alpha = z_{.05} = 1.645$

$$E(T) = \frac{n_1(n_1 + n_2 + 1)}{2} = \frac{15(15 + 25 + 1)}{2} = 307.5$$

$$\sigma_T = \sqrt{\frac{n_1 n_2(n_1 + n_2 + 1)}{12}} = \sqrt{\frac{(15)(25)(15 + 25 + 1)}{12}} = 35.8$$

$$z = \frac{T - E(T)}{\sigma_T} = \frac{383.5 - 307.55}{35.8} = 2.12,\ \text{p-value} = P(Z > 2.12) = .5 - .4830 = .0170.\ \text{There is enough}$$

evidence to infer that Tastee is superior.

17.24 H_0 : The two population locations are the same

H_1 : The location of population 1 is to the left of the location of population 2

Rejection region: $z < -z_\alpha = -z_{.05} = -1.645$

$$E(T) = \frac{n_1(n_1 + n_2 + 1)}{2} = \frac{125(125 + 125 + 1)}{2} = 15{,}687.5$$

$$\sigma_T = \sqrt{\frac{n_1 n_2 (n_1 + n_2 + 1)}{12}} = \sqrt{\frac{(125)(125)(125 + 125 + 1)}{12}} = 571.7$$

$$z = \frac{T - E(T)}{\sigma_T} = \frac{13{,}078 - 15{,}687.5}{571.7} = -4.56,\ \text{p-value} = P(Z < -4.56) = 0.\ \text{There is enough evidence to}$$

infer that changing the name of prunes to dried plums will increase the likelihood that shoppers will buy.

17.26 H_0 : The two population locations are the same

H_1 : The location of population 1 is different from the location of population 2

Rejection region: $z < -z_{\alpha/2} = -z_{.025} = -1.96$ or $z > z_{\alpha/2} = z_{.025} = 1.96$

$$z = \frac{x - .5n}{.5\sqrt{n}} = \frac{15 - .5(45)}{.5\sqrt{45}} = -2.24,\ \text{p-value} = 2P(Z < -2.24) = 2(.5 - .4875) = .0250.\ \text{There is enough}$$

evidence to infer that the population locations differ.

17.28 H_0 : The two population locations are the same

H_1 : The location of population 1 is to the right of right of the location of population 2

Rejection region: $z > z_\alpha = z_{.05} = 1.645$

$$z = \frac{x - .5n}{.5\sqrt{n}} = \frac{18 - .5(30)}{.5\sqrt{30}} = 1.10,\ \text{p-value} = P(Z > 1.10) = .5 - .3643 = .1357.\ \text{There is not enough}$$

evidence to infer that the location of population 1 is to the right of the location of population 2.

17.30 H_0 : The two population locations are the same

H_1 : The location of population 1 is different from the location of population 2

Rejection region: $z < -z_{\alpha/2} = -z_{.025} = -1.96$ or $z > z_{\alpha/2} = z_{.025} = 1.96$

$$E(T) = \frac{n(n+1)}{4} = \frac{55(56)}{4} = 770$$

$$\sigma_T = \sqrt{\frac{n(n+1)(2n+1)}{24}} = \sqrt{\frac{55(56)(111)}{24}} = 119.35$$

$z = \dfrac{T - E(T)}{\sigma_T} = \dfrac{660 - 770}{119.35} = -.92$, p-value = $2P(z < -.92) = 2(.5 - .3212) = .3576$. There is not enough

evidence to infer that the population locations differ.

17.32 H_0 : The two population locations are the same

H_1 : The location of population 1 is different from the location of population 2

Rejection region: $T \geq T_U = 19$ or $T \leq T_L = 2$

Pair	Sample 1	Sample 2	Difference	|Difference|	Ranks	
1	9	5	4	4	5.5	
2	12	10	2	2	3.5	
3	13	11	2	2	3.5	
4	8	9	-1	1		1.5
5	7	3	4	4	5.5	
6	10	9	1	1	1.5	

$$T^+ = 19.5 \quad T^- = 1.5$$

T = 19.5. There is enough evidence to infer that the population locations differ.

17.34 H_0 : The two population locations are the same

H_1 : The location of population 1 is to the right of the location of population 2

Sign Test			
Difference			New - Leading
Positive Differences			46
Negative Differences			30
Zero Differences			24
z Stat			1.84
P(Z<=z) one-tail			0.0332
z Critical one-tail			1.6449
P(Z<=z) two-tail			0.0664
z Critical two-tail			1.96

$z = 1.84$, p-value = .0332. There is enough evidence to indicate that the new beer is more highly rated than the leading brand.

17.36 All codes that preserve the order produce the same results.

17.38 The printout is identical to that of Exercise 17.37.

17.40 H_0 : The two population locations are the same

H_1 : The location of population 1 is to the right of the location of population 2

Sign Test			
Difference			European - American
Positive Differences			18
Negative Differences			5
Zero Differences			2
z Stat			2.71
P(Z<=z) one-tail			0.0034
z Critical one-tail			1.6449
P(Z<=z) two-tail			0.0068
z Critical two-tail			1.96

$z = 2.71$, p-value = .0034. There is enough evidence to infer that the European car is perceived to be more comfortable.

17.42 H_0 : The two population locations are the same

H_1 : The location of population 1 is different from the location of population 2

Sign Test		
Difference		Sample 1 - Sample 2
Positive Differences		51
Negative Differences		74
Zero Differences		0
z Stat		-2.06
P(Z<=z) one-tail		0.0198
z Critical one-tail		1.6449
P(Z<=z) two-tail		0.0396
z Critical two-tail		1.96

z = -2.06, p-value = .0396. There is enough evidence to infer that the population locations differ.

17.44 The sign test ignores the magnitudes of the paired differences whereas the Wilcoxon signed rank sum test does not.

17.46 H_0 : The two population locations are the same

H_1 : The location of population 1 is different from the location of population 2

Wilcoxon Signed Rank Sum Test		
Difference		Sample 1 - Sample 2
T+		304
T-		872
Observations (for test)		48
z Stat		-2.91
P(Z<=z) one-tail		0.0018
z Critical one-tail		1.6449
P(Z<=z) two-tail		0.0036
z Critical two-tail		1.96

z = -2.91, p-value = .0036. There is enough evidence to conclude that the population locations differ.

17.48 H_0 : The two population locations are the same

       H_1 : The location of population 1 is to the left of the location of population 2

Rejection region: $z < -z_\alpha = -z_{.05} = -1.645$

$$E(T) = \frac{n(n+1)}{4} = \frac{72(72+1)}{4} = 1314$$

$$\sigma_T = \sqrt{\frac{n(n+1)(2n+1)}{24}} = \sqrt{\frac{72(72+1)(2[72]+1)}{24}} = 178.2$$

$$z = \frac{T - E(T)}{\sigma_T} = \frac{378.5 - 1314}{178.2} = -5.25,$$ p-value = P(Z < -5.25) = 0. There is enough evidence to infer

that the drug is effective.

17.50 H_0 : The two population locations are the same

       H_1 : The location of population 1 is to the right of the location of population 2

Rejection region: $z > z_\alpha = z_{.05} = 1.645$

$$z = \frac{x - .5n}{.5\sqrt{n}} = \frac{60 - .5(98)}{.5\sqrt{98}} = 2.22,$$ p-value = P(Z > 2.22) = .5 - .4868 = .0132. There is enough evidence

to conclude that concern about a gasoline shortage exceeded concern about an electricity shortage.

17.52 H_0 : The two population locations are the same

       H_1 : The location of population 1 is to the left of the location of population 2

Rejection region: $z < -z_\alpha = -z_{.05} = -1.645$

$$E(T) = \frac{n(n+1)}{4} = \frac{26(26+1)}{4} = 175.5$$

$$\sigma_T = \sqrt{\frac{n(n+1)(2n+1)}{24}} = \sqrt{\frac{26(26+1)(2[26]+1)}{24}} = 39.4$$

$$z = \frac{T - E(T)}{\sigma_T} = \frac{111 - 175.5}{39.4} = -1.64,$$ p-value = P(z < -1.64) = .5 - .4495 = .0505. There is not enough

evidence to infer that the swimming department has higher gross sales.

17.54 H_0 : The two population locations are the same

H_1 : The location of population 1 is to the left of the location of population 2

Rejection region: $z < -z_\alpha = -z_{.01} = -2.33$

$z = \dfrac{x - .5n}{.5\sqrt{n}} = \dfrac{5 - .5(20)}{.5\sqrt{20}} = -2.24$, p-value = P(Z < -2.24) = .5 - .4875 = .0125. There is not enough
evidence to conclude that children feel less pain.

17.56 H_0 : The two population locations are the same

H_1 : The location of population 1 is to the right of the location of population 2

Sign Test			
Difference			High School 1 - High School 2
Positive Differences			32
Negative Differences			21
Zero Differences			47
z Stat			1.51
P(Z<=z) one-tail			0.0654
z Critical one-tail			1.6449
P(Z<=z) two-tail			0.1308
z Critical two-tail			1.96

Rejection region: $z > z_\alpha = z_{.05} = 1.645$

$z = \dfrac{x - .5n}{.5\sqrt{n}} = \dfrac{32 - .5(53)}{.5\sqrt{53}} = 1.51$, p-value = P(Z > 1.51) = .5 - .4345 = .0655. There is not enough
evidence to infer that preference should be given to students for high school 1.

17.58 H_0 : The locations of all 3 populations are the same.

H_1 : At least two population locations differ.

Rejection region: $H > \chi^2_{\alpha, k-1} = \chi^2_{.05, 2} = 5.99147$

$H = \left[\dfrac{12}{n(n+1)} \sum \dfrac{T_j^2}{n_j} \right] - 3(n+1) = \left[\dfrac{12}{88(88+1)} \left(\dfrac{984^2}{23} + \dfrac{1502^2}{36} + \dfrac{1430^2}{29} \right) \right] - 3(88+1) = 1.56.$ There is

not enough evidence to conclude that the population locations differ.

17.60 H_0 : The locations of all 3 populations are the same.

H_1 : At least two population locations differ.

Rejection region: $H > \chi^2_{\alpha,k-1} = \chi^2_{.10,2} = 4.60517$

$$H = \left[\frac{12}{n(n+1)} \sum \frac{T_j^2}{n_j} \right] - 3(n+1) = \left[\frac{12}{143(143+1)} \left(\frac{3741^2}{47} + \frac{1610^2}{29} + \frac{4945^2}{67} \right) \right] - 3(143+1) = 6.30.$$

There is enough evidence to conclude that the population locations differ.

17.62 H_0 : The locations of all 3 populations are the same.

H_1 : At least two population locations differ.

Rejection region: $H > \chi^2_{\alpha,k-1} = \chi^2_{.05,2} = 5.99147$

1	Rank	2	Rank	3	Rank
25	10.5	19	2	27	12
15	1	21	4	25	10.5
20	3	23	8.5	22	6
22	6	22	6	29	15
23	8.5	28	13.5	28	13.5
$T_1 = 29$		$T_2 = 34$		$T_3 = 57$	

$$H = \left[\frac{12}{n(n+1)} \sum \frac{T_j^2}{n_j} \right] - 3(n+1) = \left[\frac{12}{15(15+1)} \left(\frac{29^2}{5} + \frac{34^2}{5} + \frac{57^2}{5} \right) \right] - 3(15+1) = 4.46, \text{ p-value} = .1075$$

(Excel). There is not enough evidence to conclude that at least two population locations differ.

17.64 H_0 : The locations of all 4 populations are the same.

H_1 : At least two population locations differ.

Kruskal-Wallis Test		
Group	Rank Sum	Observations
Printer 1	4889.5	50
Printer 2	5350	50
Printer 3	4864.5	50
Printer 4	4996	50
H Stat		0.899
df		3
p-value		0.8257
chi-squared Critical		7.8147

H = .899, p-value = .8257. There is not enough evidence to conclude that differences exist between the ratings of the four printings.

17.66 All codes that preserve the order produce the same results.

17.68 All codes that preserve the order produce the same results.

17.70 H_0 : The locations of all 4 populations are the same.

H_1 : At least two population locations differ.

Rejection region: $H > \chi^2_{\alpha,k-1} = \chi^2_{.05,3} = 7.81473$

$$H = \left[\frac{12}{n(n+1)} \sum_{j=1}^{k} \frac{T_j^2}{n_j} \right] - 3(n+1)$$

$$= \frac{12}{401(401+1)} \left(\frac{17,116.5^2}{80} + \frac{16,816.5^2}{90} + \frac{17,277^2}{77} + \frac{29,391^2}{154} \right) - 3(401+1) \ = 6.65, \text{p-value} = .0838$$

(Excel). There is not enough evidence to infer that there are differences between the four groups of GMAT scores.

17.72a The one-way analysis of variance and the Kruskal-Wallis test should be considered.

b H_0 : The locations of all 4 populations are the same.

H_1 : At least two population locations differ.

Rejection region: $H > \chi^2_{\alpha,k-1} = \chi^2_{.05,3} = 7.81473$

$$H = \left[\frac{12}{n(n+1)} \sum_{j=1}^{k} \frac{T_j^2}{n_j} \right] - 3(n+1) \ = \frac{12}{200(200+1)} \left(\frac{4180^2}{50} + \frac{5262^2}{50} + \frac{5653^2}{50} + \frac{5005^2}{50} \right) - 3(200+1) =$$

6.96, p-value = .0733 (Excel). There is not enough evidence to infer that differences exist between the speeds at which the four brands perform.

17.74 H_0 : The locations of all 4 populations are the same.

H_1 : At least two population locations differ.

Rejection region: $H > \chi^2_{\alpha,k-1} = \chi^2_{.05,3} = 7.81473$

$$H = \left[\frac{12}{n(n+1)} \sum_{j=1}^{k} \frac{T_j^2}{n_j} \right] - 3(n+1)$$

$$= \frac{12}{400(400+1)} \left(\frac{21{,}246^2}{100} + \frac{19{,}784^2}{100} + \frac{20{,}976}{100} + \frac{18{,}194^2}{100} \right) - 3(400+1) = 4.34, \text{ p-value} = .2269 \text{ (Excel)}.$$

There is not enough evidence to infer that differences in believability exist between the four ads.

17.76 H_0 : The locations of all 5 populations are the same.

H_1 : At least two population locations differ.

Rejection region: $H > \chi^2_{\alpha,k-1} = \chi^2_{.05,4} = 9.48773$

$$H = \left[\frac{12}{n(n+1)} \sum_{j=1}^{k} \frac{T_j^2}{n_j} \right] - 3(n+1)$$

$$= \frac{12}{133(133+1)} \left(\frac{638.5^2}{18} + \frac{1233.5^2}{14} + \frac{1814.5^2}{26} + \frac{3159.5^2}{42} + \frac{2065^2}{33} \right) - 3(133+1) = 18.73, \text{ p-value} =$$

.0009 (Excel). There is enough evidence to infer that differences in perceived ease of use between the five brands of scanners.

17.78 H_0 : The locations of all 3 populations are the same.

H_1 : At least two population locations differ.

Rejection region: $F_r > \chi^2_{\alpha,k-1} = \chi^2_{.05,2} = 5.99147$

| | | Treatment | | | | |
Block	1	Rank	2	Rank	3	Rank
1	7.3	2	6.9	1	8.4	3
2	8.2	3	7.0	1	7.3	2
3	5.7	1	6.0	2	8.1	3
4	6.1	1	6.5	2	9.1	3
5	5.9	1	6.1	2	8.0	3
	$T_1 = 8$		$T_2 = 8$		$T_3 = 14$	

$$F_r = \left[\frac{12}{b(k)(k+1)} \sum_{j=1}^{k} T_j^2 \right] - 3b(k+1) = \left[\frac{12}{(5)(3)(4)} (8^2 + 8^2 + 14^2) \right] - 3(5)(4) = 4.8, \text{ p-value} = .0907$$

(Excel). There is not enough evidence to infer that at least two population locations differ.

17.80a The randomized block experimental design of the analysis of variance and the Friedman test.

b $\quad H_0$: The locations of all 3 populations are the same.

$\quad H_1$: At least two population locations differ.

Rejection region: $F_r > \chi_{\alpha,k-1}^2 = \chi_{.05,2}^2 = 5.99147$

| | | Newspaper | | | | |
Job Advertised	1	Rank	2	Rank	3	Rank
Receptionist	14	2	17	3	12	1
Systems analyst	8	2	9	3	6	1
Junior secretary	25	3	20	1	23	2
Computer programmer	12	2	15	3	10	1
Legal secretary	7	2	10	3	5	1
Office manager	5	2	9	3	4	1
	$T_1 = 13$		$T_2 = 16$		$T_3 = 7$	

$$F_r = \left[\frac{12}{b(k)(k+1)} \sum_{j=1}^{k} T_j^2 \right] - 3b(k+1) = \left[\frac{12}{(6)(3)(4)} (13^2 + 16^2 + 7^2) \right] - 3(6)(4) = 7.00, \text{ p-value} = .0302$$

(Excel). There is enough evidence to infer that differences exist between the newspapers.

17.82 Printout is identical to that of Exercise 17.81.

17.84 $\quad H_0$: The locations of all 4 populations are the same.

$\quad H_1$: At least two population locations differ.

Friedman Test		
Group		Rank Sum
Manager 1		21
Manager 2		10
Manager 3		24.5
Manager 4		24.5
Fr Stat		10.613
df		3
p-value		0.014
chi-squared Critical		7.8147

F_r = 10.613, p-value = .0140. There is enough evidence to infer that differences exist between the ratings of the four managers.

17.86 H_0 : The locations of all 3 populations are the same.

H_1 : At least two population locations differ.

Rejection region: $F_r > \chi^2_{\alpha, k-1} = \chi^2_{.05, 2} = 5.99147$

$$F_r = \left[\frac{12}{b(k)(k+1)} \sum_{j=1}^{k} T_j^2 \right] - 3b(k+1) = \left[\frac{12}{(20)(3)(4)} (33^2 + 39.5^2 + 47.5^2) \right] - 3(20)(4) = 5.28, \text{p-value} =$$

.0715 (Excel). There is not enough evidence to infer that there are differences in the ratings of the three recipes.

17.88 H_0 : The locations of all 3 populations are the same.

H_1 : At least two population locations differ.

Rejection region: $F_r > \chi^2_{\alpha, k-1} = \chi^2_{.05, 2} = 5.99147$

$$F_r = \left[\frac{12}{b(k)(k+1)} \sum_{j=1}^{k} T_j^2 \right] - 3b(k+1) = \left[\frac{12}{(12)(3)(4)} (28.5^2 + 22.5^2 + 21^2) \right] - 3(12)(4) = 2.63, \text{p-value} =$$

.2691 (Excel). There is not enough evidence to infer that there are differences in delivery times between the three couriers.

17.90 H_0 : The two population locations are the same

H_1 : The location of population 1 is different from the location of population 2

Wilcoxon Rank Sum Test			
		Rank Sum	Observations
Section 1		15297.5	113
Section 2		14592.5	131
z Stat		2.65	
P(Z<=z) one-tail		0.0041	
z Critical one-tail		2.3263	
P(Z<=z) two-tail		0.0082	
z Critical two-tail		2.5758	

z = 2.65, p-value = .0082. There is enough evidence to infer that the two teaching methods differ

17.92 H_0 : The locations of all 4 populations are the same.

H_1 : At least two population locations differ.

Friedman Test		
Group		Rank Sum
Typeface 1		50.5
Typeface 2		38
Typeface 3		66
Typeface 4		45.5
Fr Stat		12.615
df		3
p-value		0.0055
chi-squared Critical		7.8147

F_r = 12.615, p-value = .0055. There is enough evidence to conclude that there are differences between typefaces.

17.94 H_0 : The two population locations are the same

H_1 : The location of population 1 is to the left of the location of population 2

Wilcoxon Signed Rank Sum Test		
Difference		Drug A - Drug B
T+		36
T-		342
Observations (for test)		27
z Stat		-3.68
P(Z<=z) one-tail		0.0001
z Critical one-tail		1.6449
P(Z<=z) two-tail		0.0002
z Critical two-tail		1.96

z = -3.68, p-value = .0001. There is enough evidence to conclude that drug B is more effective.

17.96 H_0 : The two population locations are the same

H_1 : The location of population 1 is to the right of the location of population 2

Wilcoxon Rank Sum Test			
		Rank Sum	Observations
New Material		2747	50
Old Material		2303	50
z Stat		1.5304	
P(Z<=z) one-tail		0.063	
z Critical one-tail		1.6449	
P(Z<=z) two-tail		0.126	
z Critical two-tail		1.96	

z = 1.53, p-value = .0630. There is not enough evidence to conclude that the new material takes longer to burst into flames.

17.98 H_0 : The two population locations are the same

H_1 : The location of population 1 is different from the location of population 2

210

Sign Test			
Difference			*Commercial 1 - Commercial 2*
Positive Differences			15
Negative Differences			21
Zero Differences			24
z Stat			-1.00
P(Z<=z) one-tail			0.1587
z Critical one-tail			1.6449
P(Z<=z) two-tail			0.3174
z Critical two-tail			1.96

$z = -1.00$, p-value = .3174. There is not enough evidence to infer differences in believability between the two commercials.

17.100 H_0 : The two population locations are the same

H_1 : The location of population 1 is to the left of the location of population 2

Wilcoxon Rank Sum Test		Rank Sum	Observations
This Year		37525.5	200
10 Years Ago		42674.5	200
z Stat		-2.23	
P(Z<=z) one-tail		0.013	
z Critical one-tail		1.6449	
P(Z<=z) two-tail		0.026	
z Critical two-tail		1.96	

$z = -2.23$, p-value = .0130. There is enough evidence to infer that people perceive newspapers as doing a better job 10 years ago than today.

17.102 H_0 : The two population locations are the same

H_1 : The location of population 1 is to the right of the location of population 2

Sign Test			
Difference			*Before - After*
Positive Differences			19
Negative Differences			5
Zero Differences			16
z Stat			2.86
P(Z<=z) one-tail			0.0021
z Critical one-tail			1.6449
P(Z<=z) two-tail			0.0042
z Critical two-tail			1.96

$z = 2.86$, p-value = .0021. There is enough evidence to infer that the midterm test negatively influences student opinion.

17.104　H_0 : The two population locations are the same

H_1 : The location of population 1 is to the left of the location of population 2

Wilcoxon Rank Sum Test			
		Rank Sum	Observations
Low		9055	100
High		11045	100
z Stat		-2.43	
P(Z<=z) one-tail		0.0075	
z Critical one-tail		1.6449	
P(Z<=z) two-tail		0.015	
z Critical two-tail		1.96	

$z = -2.43$, p-value = .0075. There is enough evidence to conclude that boys with high levels of lead are more aggressive than boys with low levels.

17.106　H_0 : The locations of all 3 populations are the same.

H_1 : At least two population locations differ.

Kruskal-Wallis Test		
Group	Rank Sum	Observations
Unattractive	16844.5	134
Neutral	13313	68
Attractive	26122.5	133
H Stat		42.5935
df		2
p-value		0
chi-squared Critical		5.9915

H = 42.59, p-value = 0. There is enough evidence to conclude that incomes of lawyers are affected by physical attractiveness.

17.108 H_0 : The two population locations are the same

H_1 : The location of population 1 is to the right of the location of population 2

Day 1 versus Before

Sign Test			
Difference			*Before - Day 1*
Positive Differences			67
Negative Differences			0
Zero Differences			5
z Stat			8.19
P(Z<=z) one-tail			0
z Critical one-tail			1.6449
P(Z<=z) two-tail			0
z Critical two-tail			1.96

z = 8.19, p-value = 0

Day 2 versus Before

Sign Test			
Difference			*Before - Day 2*
			-
Positive Differences			59
Negative Differences			0
Zero Differences			13
z Stat			7.68
P(Z<=z) one-tail			0
z Critical one-tail			1.6449
P(Z<=z) two-tail			0
z Critical two-tail			1.96

$z = 7.68$, p-value $= 0$

Day 3 versus Before

Sign Test			
Difference			*Before - Day 3*
Positive Differences			35
Negative Differences			0
Zero Differences			37
z Stat			5.92
P(Z<=z) one-tail			0
z Critical one-tail			1.6449
P(Z<=z) two-tail			0
z Critical two-tail			1.96

$z = 5.92$, p-value $= 0$

There is enough evidence to infer that exercisers who abstain from physical activity are less happy than when they are exercising.

b H_0 : The two population locations are the same

H_1 : The location of population 1 (Day 2) is to the left of the location of population 2 (Day 3)

214

Sign Test			
Difference			Day 2 - Day 3
Positive Differences			3
Negative Differences			37
Zero Differences			32
z Stat			-5.38
P(Z<=z) one-tail			0
z Critical one-tail			1.6449
P(Z<=z) two-tail			0
z Critical two-tail			1.96

z = -5.38, p-value = 0. There is enough evidence to conclude that by the third day their moods were improving.

c 1. Exercisers who abstained were adjusting to their inactivity by the third day. 2. By the third day exercisers realized that they were closer to the end of their inactivity.

Chapter 18

18.2 a $b_1 = \dfrac{\text{cov}(x, y)}{s_x^2} = \dfrac{7.87}{16.43} = .479$, $b_0 = \bar{y} - b_1\bar{x} = 68.70 - .479(67.14) = 36.54$. (Excel: $\hat{y} = 36.54 +$

.479x).

b Nothing

c For each additional inch of father's height, the son's height increases on average by .479 inch.

18.4 a $b_1 = \dfrac{\text{cov}(x, y)}{s_x^2} = \dfrac{.121}{2.56} = .047$, $b_0 = \bar{y} - b_1\bar{x} = 10.05 - .047(3.47) = 9.89$. (Excel: $\hat{y} = 9.88 +$

.048x).

b Nothing

c The slope coefficient tells us that on average for each one-point increase in the inflation rate the return on common stocks increases by .048.

18.6 a

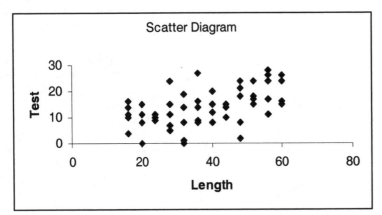

b $b_1 = \dfrac{\text{cov}(x, y)}{s_x^2} = \dfrac{51.86}{193.90} = .267$, $b_0 = \bar{y} - b_1\bar{x} = 13.80 - .267(38.00) = 3.65$. (Excel: $\hat{y} = 3.64 +$

.267x).

c $b_1 = .267$; for each additional second of commercial, the memory test score increases on average by

.267. $b_0 = 3.64$ is the y-intercept.

18.8 a $b_1 = \dfrac{\text{cov}(x, y)}{s_x^2} = \dfrac{3.08}{3.90} = .790$, $b_0 = \bar{y} - b_1\bar{x} = 6.67 - .790(11.04) = -2.05$. (Excel: $\hat{y} = -2.03 +$

.788x).

b $b_1 = .788$; for each additional year of education, Internet use increases on average by .788 hour. $b_0 =$ -2.03 is the y-intercept.

18.10 $b_1 = \dfrac{\text{cov}(x, y)}{s_x^2} = \dfrac{2.03}{21.39} = .0949$, $b_0 = \bar{y} - b_1\bar{x} = 12.73 - .0949(34.61) = 9.45$. (Excel: $\hat{y} = 9.44 +$

.0949x). The appropriate compensation is 9.49 cents per degree API.

18.12 a $b_1 = \dfrac{\text{cov}(x, y)}{s_x^2} = \dfrac{12.00}{.00323} = 3715$, $b_0 = \bar{y} - b_1\bar{x} = 500.08 - 3715(.204) = -257.8$. (Excel:

$\hat{y} = -259.6 + 3721x$).

b $b_1 = 3721$; for each additional carat of weight, the price increases on average by \$3721. $b_0 = -259.6$ cannot be interpreted.

18.14 It is normally distributed with constant variance and a mean that is a linear function of the quality of oil.

18.16 a $SSE = (n-1)\left(s_y^2 - \dfrac{[\text{cov}(x, y)]^2}{s_x^2} \right) = (400-1)\left(14.14 - \dfrac{7.87^2}{16.43} \right) = 4137.7$

$s_\varepsilon = \sqrt{\dfrac{SSE}{n-2}} = \sqrt{\dfrac{4137.7}{400-2}} = 3.22$ (Excel: $s_\varepsilon = 3.22$). This statistic is an estimate of the standard

deviation of the error variable.

b $R^2 = \dfrac{[\text{cov}(x, y)]^2}{s_x^2 s_y^2} = \dfrac{7.87^2}{(16.43)(14.14)} = .2666$ (Excel: $R^2 = .2665$)

c $H_0 : \beta_1 = 0$

        $H_1 : \beta_1 \neq 0$

Rejection region: $t < -t_{\alpha/2,\nu} = -t_{.025,398} = -1.96$ or $t > t_{\alpha/2,\nu} = t_{.025,398} = 1.96$

$$s_{b_1} = \frac{s_\varepsilon}{\sqrt{(n-1)s_x^2}} = \frac{3.22}{\sqrt{(400-1)16.43}} = .040$$

$$t = \frac{b_1 - \beta_1}{s_{b_1}} = \frac{.479 - 0}{.040} = .11.98 \text{ (Excel: t = 12.03, p-value = 0). There is enough evidence to infer that}$$

the height of sons and fathers are linearly related.

$$18.18 \quad SSE = (n-1)\left(s_y^2 - \frac{[\text{cov}(x, y)]^2}{s_x^2}\right) = (10-1)\left(193.06 - \frac{.121^2}{2.56}\right) = 1737.49$$

$$s_\varepsilon = \sqrt{\frac{SSE}{n-2}} = \sqrt{\frac{1737.48}{10-2}} = 14.74 \text{ (Excel: } s_\varepsilon = 14.74\text{).}$$

$$H_0 : \beta_1 = 0$$

$$H_1 : \beta_1 \neq 0$$

Rejection region: $t < -t_{\alpha/2,v} = -t_{.05,8} = -1.860$ or $t > t_{\alpha/2,v} = t_{.05,8} = 1.860$

$$s_{b_1} = \frac{s_\varepsilon}{\sqrt{(n-1)s_x^2}} = \frac{14.74}{\sqrt{(10-1)2.56}} = 3.07$$

$$t = \frac{b_1 - \beta_1}{s_{b_1}} = \frac{.047 - 0}{3.07} = .02 \text{ (Excel: t = .02, p-value = .9880). There is no evidence to infer that the}$$

two variables are linearly related.

$$18.20 \text{ a } SSE = (n-1)\left(s_y^2 - \frac{[\text{cov}(x, y)]^2}{s_x^2}\right) = (60-1)\left(47.96 - \frac{51.86^2}{193.90}\right) = 2011.3$$

$$s_\varepsilon = \sqrt{\frac{SSE}{n-2}} = \sqrt{\frac{2011.3}{60-2}} = 5.89 \text{ (Excel: } s_\varepsilon = 5.89\text{). This statistic is an estimate of the standard}$$

deviation of the error variable.

b $R^2 = \dfrac{[\text{cov}(x, y)]^2}{s_x^2 s_y^2} = \dfrac{51.86^2}{(193.90)(47.96)} = .2892$ (Excel: $R^2 = .2893$). 28.93% of the variation in

memory test scores is explained by the variation in commercial lengths.

c $\qquad H_0 : \beta_1 = 0$

$\qquad H_1 : \beta_1 \neq 0$

Rejection region: $t < -t_{\alpha/2,v} = -t_{.025,58} \approx -2.000$ or $t > t_{\alpha/2,v} = t_{.025,58} \approx 2.000$

$s_{b_1} = \dfrac{s_\varepsilon}{\sqrt{(n-1)s_x^2}} = \dfrac{5.89}{\sqrt{(60-1)193.90}} = .055$

$t = \dfrac{b_1 - \beta_1}{s_{b_1}} = \dfrac{.267 - 0}{.055} = 4.85$ (Excel: t = 4.86, p-value = 0). There is enough evidence to infer that the

length of commercial and memory test score are linearly related.

18.22 a $SSE = (n-1)\left(s_y^2 - \dfrac{[\text{cov}(x, y)]^2}{s_x^2} \right) = (200-1)\left(22.16 - \dfrac{3.08^2}{3.90} \right) = 3925.8$

$s_\varepsilon = \sqrt{\dfrac{SSE}{n-2}} = \sqrt{\dfrac{3925.8}{200-2}} = 4.45$ (Excel: $s_\varepsilon = 4.45$). This statistic is an estimate of the standard

deviation of the error variable

b $\qquad H_0 : \beta_1 = 0$

$\qquad H_1 : \beta_1 \neq 0$

Rejection region: $t < -t_{\alpha/2,v} = -t_{.005,198} \approx -2.601$ or $t > t_{\alpha/2,v} = t_{.005,198} \approx 2.601$

$s_{b_1} = \dfrac{s_\varepsilon}{\sqrt{(n-1)s_x^2}} = \dfrac{4.45}{\sqrt{(200-1)3.90}} = .160$

$t = \dfrac{b_1 - \beta_1}{s_{b_1}} = \dfrac{.790 - 0}{.160} = 4.94$ (Excel: t = 4.93, p-value = 0). There is enough evidence to infer that

educational level and Internet use are linearly related.

c $R^2 = \dfrac{[\text{cov}(x, y)]^2}{s_x^2 s_y^2} = \dfrac{3.08^2}{(3.90)(22.16)} = .1098$ (Excel: $R^2 = .1094$). 10.94% of the variation in Internet

use is explained by the variation in education.

18.24 $H_0 : \beta_1 = 0$

     $H_1 : \beta_1 \neq 0$

Rejection region: $t < -t_{\alpha/2,v} = -t_{.025,11} = -2.201$ or $t > t_{\alpha/2,v} = t_{.025,11} = 2.201$

$$SSE = (n-1)\left(s_y^2 - \dfrac{[\text{cov}(x, y)]^2}{s_x^2}\right) = (13-1)\left(.21 - \dfrac{2.03^2}{21.39}\right) = .208$$

$$s_\varepsilon = \sqrt{\dfrac{SSE}{n-2}} = \sqrt{\dfrac{.208}{13-2}} = .138 \text{ (Excel: } s_\varepsilon = .1325), \quad s_{b_1} = \dfrac{s_\varepsilon}{\sqrt{(n-1)s_x^2}} = \dfrac{.138}{\sqrt{(13-1)21.39}} = .0086$$

$$t = \dfrac{b_1 - \beta_1}{s_{b_1}} = \dfrac{.0949 - 0}{.0086} = 11.02 \text{ (Excel: } t = 11.48, \text{ p-value} = 0).$$ There is enough evidence to infer

that oil quality and price are linearly related.

$$R^2 = \dfrac{[\text{cov}(x, y)]^2}{s_x^2 s_y^2} = \dfrac{2.03^2}{(21.39)(.21)} = .9174 \text{ (Excel: } R^2 = .9229).$$

18.26 a $SSE = (n-1)\left(s_y^2 - \dfrac{[\text{cov}(x, y)]^2}{s_x^2}\right) = (48-1)\left(45,643 - \dfrac{12.00^2}{.00323}\right) = 49,865$

$$s_\varepsilon = \sqrt{\dfrac{SSE}{n-2}} = \sqrt{\dfrac{49,865}{48-2}} = 32.92 \text{ (Excel: } s_\varepsilon = 31.84).$$ This statistic is an estimate of the standard

deviation of the error variable.

b $R^2 = \dfrac{[\text{cov}(x, y)]^2}{s_x^2 s_y^2} = \dfrac{12.00^2}{(.00323)(45,643)} = .9768 \text{ (Excel: } R^2 = .9783).$ 97.83% of the variation in price

is explained by the variation in weight.

c $H_0 : \beta_1 = 0$

       $H_1 : \beta_1 \neq 0$

Rejection region: $t < -t_{\alpha/2,\nu} = -t_{.025,46} \approx -2.014$ or $t > t_{\alpha/2,\nu} = t_{.025,46} \approx 2.014$

$$s_{b_1} = \frac{s_\varepsilon}{\sqrt{(n-1)s_x^2}} = \frac{32.92}{\sqrt{(48-1).00323}} = 84.49$$

$$t = \frac{b_1 - \beta_1}{s_{b_1}} = \frac{3715 - 0}{84.49} = 43.97 \text{ (Excel: } t = 45.50, \text{ p-value = 0). There is enough evidence to infer that}$$

the price and weight of diamonds are linearly related.

18.28a $b_1 = \dfrac{\text{cov}(x, y)}{s_x^2} = \dfrac{1240.60}{13,641} = .0909$, $b_0 = \bar{y} - b_1\bar{x} = 27.80 - .0909(283.14) = 2.06$. (Excel: $\hat{y} =$

2.05 + .0909x).

b $b_1 = .0909$; for each additional minute of exercise, cholesterol is reduced on average by .0909. $b_0 =$

2.05 is the y-intercept.

c $\qquad H_0 : \beta_1 = 0$

$\qquad H_1 : \beta_1 < 0$

Rejection region: $t < -t_{\alpha/2,\nu} = -t_{.025,48} \approx -2.009$ or $t > t_{\alpha/2,\nu} = t_{.025,48} \approx 2.009$

$$SSE = (n-1)\left(s_y^2 - \frac{[\text{cov}(x, y)]^2}{s_x^2} \right) = (50-1)\left(221.43 - \frac{1240.69^2}{13,641} \right) = 5321.5$$

$$s_\varepsilon = \sqrt{\frac{SSE}{n-2}} = \sqrt{\frac{5321.5}{50-2}} = 10.53 \text{ (Excel: } s_\varepsilon = 10.53\text{)}, \quad s_{b_1} = \frac{s_\varepsilon}{\sqrt{(n-1)s_x^2}} = \frac{10.53}{\sqrt{(50-1)13,641}} = .0129$$

$$t = \frac{b_1 - \beta_1}{s_{b_1}} = \frac{.0909 - 0}{.0129} = 7.05 \text{ (Excel: } t = 7.06, \text{ p-value = 0). There is enough evidence to infer that}$$

exercise and cholesterol reduction are linearly related.

d $R^2 = \dfrac{[\text{cov}(x, y)]^2}{s_x^2 s_y^2} = \dfrac{1240.60^2}{(13,641)(221.43)} = .5095$ (Excel: $R^2 = .5095$). The model fits moderately well.

18.30 Intel's beta is 1.47, which means its stock is more volatile than the market. The coefficient of determination is .1480, which means that only 14.80% of the total risk is market related. The remaining 85.20% of the total risk is associated specifically with Intel.

18.32 General Motor's beta is .8429, which means its stock is less volatile than the market. The coefficient of determination is .1280, which means that only 12.80% of the total risk is market related. The remaining 87.20% of the total risk is associated specifically with General Motors.

18.34 General Electric's beta is 1.09, which means its stock is more volatile than the market. The coefficient of determination is .4049, which means that 40.49% of the total risk is market related. The remaining 59.51% of the total risk is associated specifically with General Electric.

18.36 Coca Cola's beta is .506, which means its stock is less volatile than the market. The coefficient of determination is .0962, which means that only 9.62% of the total risk is market related. The remaining 90.38 of the total risk is associated specifically with Coca Cola.

18.38 The stock that is least sensitive is Coca Cola whose beta is .506. The most sensitive is Intel with a beta of 1.47. Coca Cola's R^2 is 9.62%, which means that its firm-specific risk is 90.38%. The stock with the smallest firm-specific risk is General Electric (59.51%).

18.40 Lorus's beta is 1.69, which means its stock is more volatile than the market. The coefficient of determination is .1145, which means that only 11.45% of the total risk is market related. The remaining 88.55% of the total risk is associated specifically with Lorus Therapeutics.

18.42 Suncor's beta is .326, which means its stock is very much less volatile than the market. The coefficient of determination is .0575, which means that only 5.75% of the total risk is market related. The remaining 94.25% of the total risk is associated specifically with Suncor.

18.44 Laurentian Bank's beta is .485, which means its stock is less volatile than the market. The coefficient of determination is .1293, which means that only 12.93% of the total risk is market related. The remaining 87.07% of the total risk is associated specifically with Laurentian Bank.

18.46 ATI's beta is 1.19, which means its stock is more volatile than the market. The coefficient of determination is .1541, which means that only 15.41% of the total risk is market related. The remaining 84.59% of the total risk is associated specifically with ATI.

18.48 The prediction interval provides a prediction for a value of y. The confidence interval estimator of the expected value of y is an estimator of the population mean for a given x.

18.50 $\hat{y} = 475.19 - 39.17x = 475.19 - 39.17(8) = 161.83$

$$\hat{y} \pm t_{\alpha/2,n-2} s_\varepsilon \sqrt{1 + \frac{1}{n} + \frac{(x_g - \bar{x})^2}{(n-1)s_x^2}} = 161.83 \pm 2.306(31.48) \sqrt{1 + \frac{1}{10} + \frac{(8-8.2)^2}{(10-1)(.24)}} = 161.83 \pm 76.77$$

Excel: Lower prediction limit = 85.07, upper prediction limit = 238.60

18.52 $\hat{y} = 21.59 + 1.88x = 21.59 + 1.88(25) = 68.59$

$$a\ \hat{y} \pm t_{\alpha/2,n-2} s_\varepsilon \sqrt{1 + \frac{1}{n} + \frac{(x_g - \bar{x})^2}{(n-1)s_x^2}} = 68.59 \pm 1.660(8.70) \sqrt{1 + \frac{1}{100} + \frac{(25-27.95)^2}{(100-1)(82.01)}} = 68.59 \pm 14.52$$

Excel: Lower prediction limit = 54.00, upper prediction limit = 83.05

$$b\ \hat{y} \pm t_{\alpha/2,n-2} s_\varepsilon \sqrt{\frac{1}{n} + \frac{(x_g - \bar{x})^2}{(n-1)s_x^2}} = 68.59 \pm 1.660(8.70) \sqrt{\frac{1}{100} + \frac{(25-27.95)^2}{(100-1)(82.01)}} = 68.59 \pm 1.52$$

Excel: Lower confidence limit = 67.00, upper confidence limit = 70.04

18.54 $\hat{y} = 30.64 - .117x = 30.64 - .117(25) = 27.72$

$$a\ \hat{y} \pm t_{\alpha/2,n-2} s_\varepsilon \sqrt{1 + \frac{1}{n} + \frac{(x_g - \bar{x})^2}{(n-1)s_x^2}} = 27.72 \pm 1.990(1.81) \sqrt{1 + \frac{1}{80} + \frac{(25-37.29)^2}{(80-1)(55.11)}} = 27.72 \pm 3.69$$

Excel: Lower prediction limit = 24.02, upper prediction limit = 31.40

18.56 $\hat{y} = -5.99 + .226x = -5.99 + .226(65) = 8.70$

$$a\ \hat{y} \pm t_{\alpha/2,n-2} s_\varepsilon \sqrt{1 + \frac{1}{n} + \frac{(x_g - \bar{x})^2}{(n-1)s_x^2}} = 8.70 \pm 1.96(12.98) \sqrt{1 + \frac{1}{1348} + \frac{(65-56.00)^2}{(1348-1)(228.26)}} = 8.70 \pm 25.45$$

Excel: Lower prediction limit = -16.76 (increased to 0), upper prediction limit = 34.17

$$b \ \hat{y} \pm t_{\alpha/2,n-2} s_\varepsilon \sqrt{\frac{1}{n} + \frac{(x_g - \bar{x})^2}{(n-1)s_x^2}} = 8.70 \pm 1.96(12.98) \sqrt{\frac{1}{1348} + \frac{(65-56.00)^2}{(1348-1)(228.26)}} = 8.70 \pm .81$$

Excel: Lower confidence limit = 7.90, upper confidence limit = 9.51

18.58 $\hat{y} = 20.64 - .304x = 20.64 - .304(10) = 17.60$

$$\hat{y} \pm t_{\alpha/2,n-2} s_\varepsilon \sqrt{1 + \frac{1}{n} + \frac{(x_g - \bar{x})^2}{(n-1)s_x^2}} = 17.60 \pm 2.048(2.87) \sqrt{1 + \frac{1}{30} + \frac{(10-11.33)^2}{(30-1)(35.47)}} = 17.60 \pm 5.98$$

Excel: Lower prediction limit = 11.61, upper prediction limit = 23.59

18.60 a $H_0 : \rho = 0$

$H_1 : \rho \neq 0$

Correlation		
X and Y		
Pearson Coefficient of Correlation		0.9375
t Stat		5.39
df		4
P(T<=t) one tail		0.0029
t Critical one tail		2.1318
P(T<=t) two tail		0.0058
t Critical two tail		2.7765

r = .9375, t = 5.39, p-value = .0058. There is enough evidence of a linear relationship.

b $\qquad H_0 : \rho_S = 0$

$H_1 : \rho_S \neq 0$

Spearman Rank Correlation			
X and Y			
Spearman Rank Correlation			0.9429
z Stat			2.11
P(Z<=z) one tail			0.0175
z Critical one tail			1.6449
P(Z<=z) two tail			0.035
z Critical two tail			1.96

$r_S = .9429$, $z = 2.11$, p-value = .0350. There is enough evidence of a linear relationship.

18.62　　$H_0 : \rho_S = 0$

　　　　$H_1 : \rho_S \neq 0$

Spearman Rank Correlation			
Experience and Rating			
Spearman Rank Correlation			0.2336
z Stat			1.12
P(Z<=z) one tail			0.1313
z Critical one tail			1.2816
P(Z<=z) two tail			0.2626
z Critical two tail			1.6449

$z = 1.12$, p-value = .2626. There is not enough evidence to infer that the two variables are related.

18.64a The required condition is that odometer reading and price are bivariate normally distributed.

b　　　$H_0 : \rho_S = 0$

　　　　$H_1 : \rho_S \neq 0$

Spearman Rank Correlation			
Odometer and Price			
Spearman Rank Correlation			-0.8038
z Stat			-8.00
P(Z<=z) one tail			0
z Critical one tail			1.6449
P(Z<=z) two tail			0
z Critical two tail			1.96

z = -8.00, p-value = 0. There is enough evidence to infer that odometer reading and price are related.

18.66 $H_0 : \rho_S = 0$

$H_1 : \rho_S > 0$

Spearman Rank Correlation			
Time and Mark			
Spearman Rank Correlation			0.7894
z Stat			7.85
P(Z<=z) one tail			0
z Critical one tail			1.6449
P(Z<=z) two tail			0
z Critical two tail			1.96

z = 7.85, p-value = 0. There is enough evidence to infer that mark and study time are positively related.

18.68 $H_0 : \rho_S = 0$

$H_1 : \rho_S \neq 0$

Spearman Rank Correlation		
Age and Employment		
Spearman Rank Correlation		-0.4654
z Stat		-4.14
P(Z<=z) one tail		0
z Critical one tail		1.6449
P(Z<=z) two tail		0
z Critical two tail		1.96

$z = -4.14$, p-value = 0. There is enough to infer that age and length of employment are related.

18.70

Correlation		
Age and Expense		
Pearson Coefficient of Correlation		0.2543
t Stat		9.65
df		1346
P(T<=t) one tail		0
t Critical one tail		1.646
P(T<=t) two tail		0
t Critical two tail		1.9617

a r = .2543

b $\qquad H_0 : \rho = 0$

$\qquad H_1 : \rho \neq 0$

$t = 9.65$, p-value = 0. There is enough evidence to infer that there is a linear relationship between age and medical expense.

c $\qquad H_0 : \rho_S = 0$

$\qquad H_1 : \rho_S > 0$

Spearman Rank Correlation			
Age and Expense			
Spearman Rank Correlation			0.1848
z Stat			6.78
P(Z<=z) one tail			0
z Critical one tail			1.6449
P(Z<=z) two tail			0
z Critical two tail			1.96

$z = 6.78$, p-value = 0. There is enough evidence to infer that older Canadians incur higher medical expenses.

18.72 $H_0 : \rho_S = 0$

$H_1 : \rho_S \neq 0$

Spearman Rank Correlation			
US Index and Japanese Index			
Spearman Rank Correlation			0.42
z Stat			3.20
P(Z<=z) one tail			0.0007
z Critical one tail			1.6449
P(Z<=z) two tail			0.0014
z Critical two tail			1.96

$z = 3.20$, p-value = .0014. There is enough evidence to conclude that the returns are related.

18.74 $H_0 : \rho_S = 0$

$H_1 : \rho_S \neq 0$

Spearman Rank Correlation	
Italian Index and Hong Kong Index	
Spearman Rank Correlation	0.2485
z Stat	1.89
P(Z<=z) one tail	0.0292
z Critical one tail	1.6449
P(Z<=z) two tail	0.0584
z Critical two tail	1.96

z = 1.89, p-value = .0584. There is not enough evidence to infer that the returns on the indexes are linearly related.

18.76

SUMMARY OUTPUT					
Regression Statistics					
Multiple R	0.9714				
R Square	0.9436				
Adjusted R Square	0.9295				
Standard Error	1.27				
Observations	6				
ANOVA					
	df	*SS*	*MS*	*F*	*Significance F*
Regression	1	107.57	107.57	66.8918	0.0012
Residual	4	6.43	1.61		
Total	5	114.00			
	Coefficients	*Standard Error*	*t Stat*	*P-value*	
Intercept	8.24	0.54	15.28	0.0001	
X	-1.07	0.13	-8.18	0.0012	
RESIDUAL OUTPUT					
Observation	*Predicted Y*	*Residuals*	*Standard Residuals*		
1	13.57	1.43	1.26		
2	10.37	-1.37	-1.21		
3	8.24	-1.24	-1.10		
4	5.05	0.95	0.84		
5	3.98	0.02	0.02		
6	0.79	0.21	0.19		

a $\hat{y} = 8.24 - 1.07x$

e There are no outliers.

18.78a

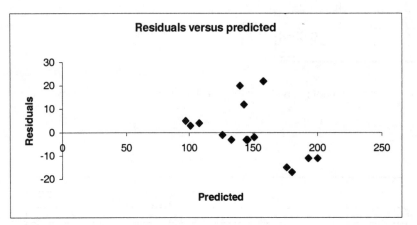

The variance increases as the predicted value of y increases.

b

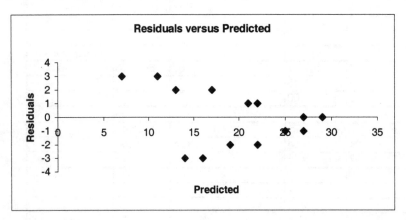

The variance decreases as the predicted value of y increases.

c

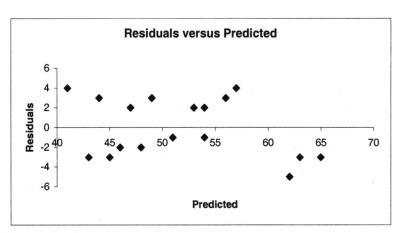

The variance is constant.

18.80a

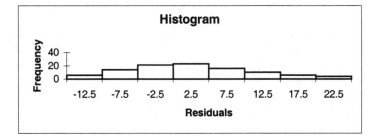

b

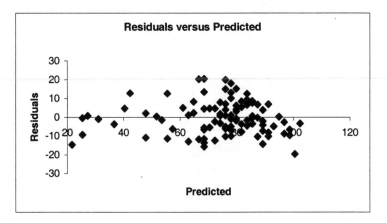

The errors appear to be normally distributed and the variance is constant.

18.82b

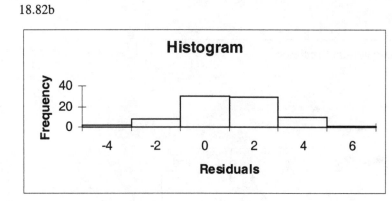

c Observations 1, 15, 21, 31, and 64 have standardized residuals whose absolute values exceed 2.0.

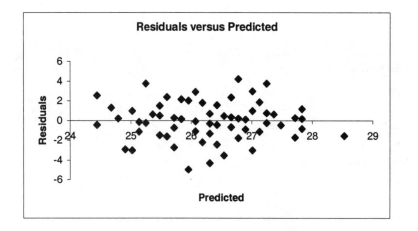

d Heteroscedasticity is not a problem.

18.84

SUMMARY OUTPUT					
Regression Statistics					
Multiple R	0.2919				
R Square	0.0852				
Adjusted R Square	0.0471				
Standard Error	132.96				
Observations	26				
ANOVA					
	df	*SS*	*MS*	*F*	*Significance F*
Regression	1	39521	39521	2.24	0.1479
Residual	24	424281	17678		
Total	25	463802			
	Coefficients	*Standard Error*	*t Stat*	*P-value*	
Intercept	296.92	64.31	4.62	0.0001	
Ads	21.36	14.28	1.50	0.1479	

a $\hat{y} = 296.92 + 21.36x$

b On average each ad generates 21.36 customers.

c t = 1.50, p-value = .1479/2 = .0740; there is not enough evidence to infer that the larger the number of ads the larger the number of customers.

d R^2 = .0852; 8.52% of the variation in the number of customers is explained by the variation in the number of ads.

e The poor fit of the model precludes its use for prediction.

18.86

Spearman Rank Correlation		
Rating and Sugar		
Spearman Rank Correlation		0.7993
z Stat		11.28
P(Z<=z) one tail		0
z Critical one tail		1.6449
P(Z<=z) two tail		0
z Critical two tail		1.96

z = 11.28, p-value = 0. There is enough evidence to infer that sugar content and drinkers' ratings of the cola are related.

18.88

Correlation			
CO and NO3			
Pearson Coefficient of Correlation			0.8913
t Stat			13.62
df			48
P(T<=t) one tail			0
t Critical one tail			1.6772
P(T<=t) two tail			0
t Critical two tail			2.0106

Assuming normality: t = 13.62, p-value = 0; there is enough evidence to infer that the belief is correct.

18.90

SUMMARY OUTPUT					
Regression Statistics					
Multiple R	0.4930				
R Square	0.2431				
Adjusted R Square	0.1800				
Standard Error	0.0549				
Observations	14				
ANOVA					
	df	SS	MS	F	Significance F
Regression	1	0.0116	0.0116	3.85	0.0733
Residual	12	0.0362	0.0030		
Total	13	0.0478			
	Coefficients	Standard Error	t Stat	P-value	
Intercept	0.83	0.17	4.94	0.0003	
Team ERA	-0.080	0.041	-1.96	0.0733	

$\hat{y} = .83 - .080x$. The slope is -.080; for each additional point increase in ERA, the team's winning percentage decreases on average by .080 points.

b $s_\varepsilon = .0549$. This statistic is large relative to the average winning percentage, .500. The model is poor.

c $t = -1.96$, p-value $= .0733/2 = .0367$; there is enough evidence to infer a negative linear relationship between ERA and winning percentage.

d $R^2 = .2431$; 24.31% of the variation in winning percentage is explained by the variation in ERA.

e

Prediction Interval		
	Winning%	
Predicted value	0.508	
Prediction Interval		
Lower limit	0.406	
Upper limit	0.609	
Interval Estimate of Expected Value		
Lower limit	0.481	
Upper limit	0.535	

Lower prediction limit $= .406$, upper prediction limit $= .609$

18.92

Correlation		
Winning times and Temperature		
Pearson Coefficient of Correlation		0.5984
t Stat		3.26
df		19
P(T<=t) one tail		0.0021
t Critical one tail		1.7291
P(T<=t) two tail		0.0042
t Critical two tail		2.093

$t = 3.26$, p-value $= .0042$. There is enough evidence of a linearly relation between temperature and winning times.

18.94

SUMMARY OUTPUT					
Regression Statistics					
Multiple R	0.2248				
R Square	0.0505				
Adjusted R Square	0.0467				
Standard Error	8.28				
Observations	250				
ANOVA					
	df	*SS*	*MS*	*F*	*Significance F*
Regression	1	905.60	905.60	13.20	0.0003
Residual	248	17010.97	68.59		
Total	249	17916.56			
	Coefficients	*Standard Error*	*t Stat*	*P-value*	
Intercept	17.93	11.48	1.56	0.1194	
Height	0.604	0.166	3.63	0.0003	

$\hat{y} = 17.93 + .60x$. The slope is .60; for each additional inch of height, annual income increases on average by .60 thousand dollars ($600).

b $t = 3.63$, p-value $= .0003/2 = .0002$. There is enough evidence to infer a positive linear relationship between height and income.

c $R^2 = .0505$; 5.05% of the variation in incomes is explained by the variation in heights.

d The model is too poor to be used to predict or estimate.

18.96

Correlation			
Debt and Television			
Pearson Coefficient of Correlation			0.554
t Stat			13.77
df			428
P(T<=t) one tail			0
t Critical one tail			1.6484
P(T<=t) two tail			0
t Critical two tail			1.9655

$t = 13.77$, p-value $= 0$. There is enough evidence of a positive linear relationship. The theory appears to be valid.

Chapter 19

19.2

SUMMARY OUTPUT					
Regression Statistics					
Multiple R	0.8734				
R Square	0.7629				
Adjusted R Square	0.7453				
Standard Error	3.75				
Observations	30				
ANOVA					
	df	*SS*	*MS*	*F*	*Significance F*
Regression	2	1223.18	611.59	43.43	0.0000
Residual	27	380.18	14.08		
Total	29	1603.37			
	Coefficients	*Standard Error*	*t Stat*	*P-value*	
Intercept	13.01	3.528	3.69	0.0010	
Assignment	0.194	0.200	0.97	0.3417	
Midterm	1.112	0.122	9.12	0.0000	

a $\hat{y} = 13.01 + .194x_1 + 1.112x_2$

b The standard error of estimate is $s_\varepsilon = 3.75$. It is an estimate of the standard deviation of the error variable.

c The coefficient of determination is $R^2 = .7629$; 76.29% of the variation in final exam marks is explained by the model.

d The coefficient of determination adjusted for degrees of freedom is .7453. It differs from R^2 because it includes an adjustment for the number of independent variables.

e $\qquad H_0 : \beta_1 = \beta_2 = 0$

$\qquad H_1$: At least one β_i is not equal to zero

F = 43.43, p-value = 0. There is enough evidence to conclude that the model is valid.

f $b_1 = .194$; for each addition mark on assignments the final exam mark on average increases by .194 provided that the other variable remains constant.

$b_2 = 1.112$; for each addition midterm mark the final exam mark on average increases by 1.112 provided that the other variable remains constant.

g $\quad H_0 : \beta_1 = 0$

$\quad\quad H_1 : \beta_1 \neq 0$

$t = .97$, p-value $= .3417$. There is not enough evidence to infer that assignment marks and final exam marks are linearly related.

h $\quad H_0 : \beta_2 = 0$

$\quad\quad H_1 : \beta_2 \neq 0$

$t = 9.12$, p-value $= 0$. There is sufficient evidence to infer that midterm marks and final exam marks are linearly related.

19.4a

SUMMARY OUTPUT					
Regression Statistics					
Multiple R	0.5169				
R Square	0.2672				
Adjusted R Square	0.2635				
Standard Error	3.23				
Observations	400				
ANOVA					
	df	*SS*	*MS*	*F*	*Significance F*
Regression	2	1507.5	753.7	72.37	0.0000
Residual	397	4134.9	10.4		
Total	399	5642.4			
	Coefficients	*Standard Error*	*t Stat*	*P-value*	
Intercept	37.56	3.20	11.73	0.0000	
Mother	-0.023	0.039	-0.58	0.5615	
Father	0.485	0.041	11.78	0.0000	

b The standard error of estimate is $s_\varepsilon = 3.23$. It is t an estimate of the standard deviation of the error variable.

c The coefficient of determination is $R^2 = .2672$; 26.72% of the variation in heights is explained by the model.

d The coefficient of determination adjusted for degrees of freedom is .2635. It differs from R^2 because it includes an adjustment for the number of independent variables.

e $\qquad H_0 : \beta_1 = \beta_2 = 0$

$\qquad H_1$: At least one β_i is not equal to zero

F = 72.37, p-value = 0. There is enough evidence to conclude that the model is valid.

f $b_1 = -.023$; for each addition inch of height of mothers the son's height decreases on average by .023 inches provided that the other variable remains constant.

$b_2 = .485$; for each addition inch of height of fathers the son's height increases on average by .485 inches provided that the other variable remains constant.

g $\qquad H_0 : \beta_1 = 0$

$\qquad H_1 : \beta_1 \neq 0$

t = 11.78, p-value = 0. There is enough evidence to infer that fathers' and sons' height are linearly related.

h $\qquad H_0 : \beta_2 = 0$

$\qquad H_1 : \beta_2 \neq 0$

t = -.58, p-value = .5615. There is no evidence to infer that mothers' and sons' heights are linearly related.

19.6

SUMMARY OUTPUT					
Regression Statistics					
Multiple R	0.5369				
R Square	0.2882				
Adjusted R Square	0.2660				
Standard Error	2.03				
Observations	100				
ANOVA					
	df	*SS*	*MS*	*F*	*Significance F*
Regression	3	160.24	53.41	12.96	0.0000
Residual	96	395.70	4.12		
Total	99	555.93			
	Coefficients	*Standard Error*	*t Stat*	*P-value*	
Intercept	0.721	1.870	0.39	0.7006	
HS GPA	0.611	0.101	6.06	0.0000	
SAT	0.0027	0.0029	0.94	0.3482	
Activities	0.046	0.064	0.72	0.4720	

b The standard error of estimate is $s_\varepsilon = 2.03$. It is an estimate of the standard deviation of the error variable.

c The coefficient of determination is $R^2 = .2882$; 28.82% of the variation in university GPAs is explained by the model.

d The coefficient of determination adjusted for degrees of freedom is .2660.

e $\qquad H_0 : \beta_1 = \beta_2 = \beta_3 = 0$

$\qquad H_1 :$ At least one β_i is not equal to zero

F = 12.96, p-value = 0. There is enough evidence to conclude that the model is valid.

f $b_1 = .611$; for each additional point of high school GPA university GPA increases on average by .611 provided that the other variables remain constant.

$b_2 = .0027$; for each additional point of SAT university GPA increases on average by .0027 provided that the other variables remain constant.

$b_3 = .046$; for each additional hour of activities university GPA increases on average by .046 provided that the other variables remain constant.

g $H_0 : \beta_i = 0$

$H_1 : \beta_i \neq 0$

High school GPA: $t = 6.06$, p-value $= 0$

SAT: $t = .94$, p-value $= .3482$

Activities: $t = .72$, p-value $= .4720$

Only high school GPA is linearly related to university GPA.

h

Prediction Interval			
		Univ GPA	
Predicted value		8.55	
Prediction Interval			
Lower limit		4.45	
Upper limit		12.65	
Interval Estimate of Expected Value			
Lower limit		7.79	
Upper limit		9.31	

We predict that the student's GPA will fall between 4.45 and 12.00 (12 is the maximum).

i

Prediction Interval		
	Univ GPA	
Predicted value	7.56	
Prediction Interval		
Lower limit	4.13	
Upper limit	11.00	
Interval Estimate of Expected Value		
Lower limit	6.90	
Upper limit	8.22	

The mean GPA is estimated to lie between 6.90 and 8.22.

19.8

SUMMARY OUTPUT					
Regression Statistics					
Multiple R	0.8415				
R Square	0.7081				
Adjusted R Square	0.7021				
Standard Error	213.7				
Observations	100				
ANOVA					
	df	SS	MS	F	Significance F
Regression	2	10744454	5372227	117.64	0.0000
Residual	97	4429664	45667		
Total	99	15174118			
	Coefficients	Standard Error	t Stat	P-value	
Intercept	576.8	514.0	1.12	0.2646	
Space	90.61	6.48	13.99	0.0000	
Water	9.66	2.41	4.00	0.0001	

a The regression equation is $\hat{y} = 576.8 + 90.61x_1 + 9.66x_2$

b The standard error of estimate is $s_\varepsilon = 213.7$. It is an estimate of the standard deviation of the error variable.

242

c The coefficient of determination is $R^2 = .7081$; 70.81% of the variation in sales is explained by the model. The coefficient of determination adjusted for degrees of freedom is .7021. The model fits reasonably well.

d $\quad H_0 : \beta_1 = \beta_2 = 0$

$\quad H_1$: At least one β_i is not equal to zero

$F = 117.64$, p-value = 0. There is enough evidence to conclude that the model is valid.

e & f

Prediction Interval		
		Consumption
Predicted value		8175
Prediction Interval		
Lower limit		7748
Upper limit		8601
Interval Estimate of Expected Value		
Lower limit		8127
Upper limit		8222

e We predict that the house will consume between 7748 and 8601 units of electricity.

f We estimate that the average house will consume between 8127 and 8222 units of electricity.

19.10

SUMMARY OUTPUT					
Regression Statistics					
Multiple R	0.4455				
R Square	0.1985				
Adjusted R Square	0.1903				
Standard Error	4.19				
Observations	200				
ANOVA					
	df	*SS*	*MS*	*F*	*Significance F*
Regression	2	856.42	428.21	24.39	0.0000
Residual	197	3458.98	17.56		
Total	199	4315.40			
	Coefficients	*Standard Error*	*t Stat*	*P-value*	
Intercept	13.03	2.54	5.12	0.0000	
Age	-0.279	0.045	-6.22	0.0000	
Income	0.094	0.031	3.00	0.0030	

a The regression equation is $\hat{y} = 13.03 - .279x_1 + .094x_2$

b The coefficient of determination is $R^2 = .1985$; 19.85% of the variation in internet use is explained by the model. The model fits poorly.

c $H_0 : \beta_1 = \beta_2 = 0$

H_1 : At least one β_i is not equal to zero

$F = 24.39$, p-value = 0. There is enough evidence to conclude that the model is valid.

d

Prediction Interval			
		Internet	
Predicted value		6.55	
Prediction Interval			
Lower limit		-0.40	
Upper limit		13.50	
Interval Estimate of Expected Value			
Lower limit		5.98	
Upper limit		7.13	

Internet use is predicted to fall between 0 and 13.50 hours per week.

e

Prediction Interval			
		Internet	
Predicted value		7.94	
Prediction Interval			
Lower limit		-0.49	
Upper limit		16.37	
Interval Estimate of Expected Value			
Lower limit		6.27	
Upper limit		9.61	

Mean Internet use is estimated to lie between 6.27 and 9.61 hours per week.

19.12a & b

Prediction Interval		
		Final
Predicted value	.	30.9
Prediction Interval		
Lower limit		23.0
Upper limit		38.8
Interval Estimate of Expected Value		
Lower limit		29.0
Upper limit		32.9

a Pat's final exam mark is predicted to be between 23 and 38.8 (out of 50).

b Lower limit = 12/20 + 14/30 + 23/50 = 49%,

Upper limit = 12/20 + 14/30 + 38.8/50 = 64.8%,

19.14 a The histogram is roughly bell-shaped indicating that the error variable is approximately normal.

b There is no sign of heteroscedasticity. The error variable's variance is constant.

19.16

	Final	Assignment	Midterm
Final	1		
Assignment	0.1803	1	
Midterm	0.8687	0.1037	1

The two variables are very weakly correlated. The two t-tests are valid.

19.18

	Father	Son	Mother
Father	1		
Son	0.5163	1	
Mother	0.2511	0.1055	1

a The heights of mothers and fathers are weakly correlated. The amount of correlation however, is not likely a problem.

b The two test results are valid.

19.20 a The regression equation is $\hat{y} = -103.1 + 5.82x_1 + 8.56x_2$

b Observations 63, 81, 82, and 97 should be checked

c The histogram is bell-shaped. The error variable is normally distributed.

d The variance of the error variable grows as $\hat{y}$ increases. It appears that the error variable's variance is not constant.

19.22 The histogram of the residuals is bell shaped and the variance of the error variable appears to be constant.

19.24 The histogram of the residuals is bell shaped and the variance of the error variable appears to be constant.

19.26a The histogram is slightly skewed but it does appear that the errors are normally distributed. The error variable's variance appears to be constant.

b

	HS GPA	SAT	Activities
HS GPA	1		
SAT	-0.1019	1	
Activities	0.1310	-0.1653	1

The correlations among the independent variables are small. Multicollinearity is not a problem.

c Observation 91's standardized residual is greater than 2. It should be checked.

19.28a The histogram is bell-shaped; the errors appear to be normally distributed. The error variable's variance appears to be constant.

b

	Consumption	Space	Water
Consumption	1		
Space	0.8123	1	
Water	0.3451	0.1578	1

There is a weak correlation between the two independent variables.

19.30 The histogram is negatively skewed. It appears that the errors are not normally distributed. The variance of the error variable is not constant.

19.32 d_L = 1.46, d_U = 1.63. There is evidence of positive first-order autocorrelation.

19.34 4 - d_U = 4 - 1.73 = 2.27, 4 - d_L = 4 - 1.19 = 2.81. There is no evidence of negative first-order autocorrelation.

19.36 a The regression equation is $\hat{y} = 2260 + .423x$

c Check observation 4.

d The histogram is bell-shaped.

e The error variable variance appears to be constant.

f d = .7859; $d_L \approx 1.50$, $d_U \approx 1.59$, 4 - $d_U \approx 2.41$, 4 - $d_L \approx 2.50$. There is evidence of first-order autocorrelation.

g The model is $y = \beta_0 + \beta_1 x + \beta_2 t + \varepsilon$

The regression equation is $\hat{y} = 446.2 + 1.10x + 38.92t$

h First model: $s_\varepsilon = 709.7$ and $R^2 = .0146$. Second model: $s_\varepsilon = 413.7$ and $R^2 = .6718$. The second model fits better.

19.38 a The errors appear to be normally distributed.

b There does not appear to be a change in spread; there is no sign of heteroscedasticity.

19.40 d = 1.755; $d_L = 1.01$, $d_U = 1.78$, 4 - $d_U = 2.22$, 4 - $d_L = 2.99$. The test is inconclusive.

19.42 The histogram is bell-shaped; apparently the errors are normally distributed.

c Check observations 1, 11, 25, 28, and 46.

d The error variable variance appears to be constant.

e The errors appear to be independent.

f $d = 1.9547; d_L = 1.55, d_U = 1.62, 4 - d_U = 2.38, 4 - d_L = 2.45$. There is no evidence of first-order autocorrelation.

19.44 Lower prediction limit = 6.87, upper prediction limit = 10.20

Prediction Interval		
	MBA GPA	
Predicted value	8.54	
Prediction Interval		
Lower limit	6.87	
Upper limit	10.20	
Interval Estimate of Expected Value		
Lower limit	7.98	
Upper limit	9.10	

19.46a

SUMMARY OUTPUT					
Regression Statistics					
Multiple R	0.7023				
R Square	0.4933				
Adjusted R Square	0.4726				
Standard Error	558.7				
Observations	52				
ANOVA					
	df	*SS*	*MS*	*F*	*Significance F*
Regression	2	14887583	7443791	23.85	0.0000
Residual	49	15294148	312125		
Total	51	30181731			
	Coefficients	*Standard Error*	*t Stat*	*P-value*	
Intercept	3719	857.6	4.34	0.0001	
Price A	-46.77	10.83	-4.32	0.0001	
Price B	58.52	10.46	5.59	0.0000	

b $s_\varepsilon = 558.7$ and $R^2 = .4933$; the model's fit is only moderately good.

c $b_1 = -46.77$; for each one cent increase in the price of milk sales decrease on average by 46.77 provided that the competitor's price remains unchanged.

$b_2 = 58.52$; for each one cent increase in the competitor's price of milk sales increase on average by 58.52 provided that the company's price remains unchanged.

d $\qquad H_0 : \beta_i = 0$

$\qquad H_1 : \beta_i \neq 0$

Company's price: t = -4.32, p-value = .0001

Competitor's price: t = 5.59, p-value = 0

Both prices are linearly related to sales.

e $\qquad H_0 : \beta_1 = \beta_2 = 0$

$\qquad H_1$: At least one β_i is not equal to zero

$\qquad F = MSR/MSE$

F = 23.85, p-value = 0. There is enough evidence to conclude that the model is valid.

f

Prediction Interval		
	Sales	
Predicted value	3312	
Prediction Interval		
Lower limit	2341	
Upper limit	4284	
Interval Estimate of Expected Value		
Lower limit	3055	
Upper limit	3570	

We predict that sales will fall between 2341 and 4284.

19.48a

SUMMARY OUTPUT					
Regression Statistics					
Multiple R	0.5926				
R Square	0.3511				
Adjusted R Square	0.3352				
Standard Error	6.99				
Observations	126				
ANOVA					
	df	*SS*	*MS*	*F*	*Significance F*
Regression	3	3227.61	1075.87	22.01	0.0000
Residual	122	5964.52	48.89		
Total	125	9192.13			
	Coefficients	*Standard Error*	*t Stat*	*P-value*	
Intercept	-1.97	9.55	-0.21	0.8369	
Minor HR	0.67	0.09	7.64	0.0000	
Age	0.14	0.52	0.26	0.7961	
Years Pro	1.18	0.67	1.75	0.0819	

b $b_1 = .67$; for each additional minor league home run the number of major league home runs increases on average by .67 provided that the other variables remain constant.

$b_2 = .14$; for each additional year of age the number of major league home runs increases on average by .14 provided that the other variables remain constant.

$b_3 = 1.18$; for each additional year as a professional the number of major league home runs increases on average by 1.18 provided that the other variables remain constant.

c $s_\varepsilon = 6.99$ and $R^2 = .3511$; the model's fit is not very good.

d $H_0 : \beta_1 = \beta_2 = \beta_3 = 0$

H_1 : At least one β_i is not equal to zero

F = 22.01, p-value = 0. There is enough evidence to conclude that the model is valid.

e $H_0 : \beta_i = 0$

$H_1 : \beta_i \neq 0$

Minor league home runs: t = 7.64, p-value = 0

Age: t = .26, p-value = .7961

Years professional: t = 1.75, p-value = .0819

At the 5% significance level only the number of minor league home runs is linearly related to the number of major league home runs.

f

Prediction Interval		
	Major HR	
Predicted value	24.31	
Prediction Interval		
Lower limit	9.86	
Upper limit	38.76	
Interval Estimate of Expected Value		
Lower limit	20.16	
Upper limit	28.45	

We predict that the player will hit between 9.86 (rounded to 10) and 38.76 (rounded to 39) home runs.

g

Prediction Interval		
	Major HR	
Predicted value	19.56	
Prediction Interval		
Lower limit	4.88	
Upper limit	34.25	
Interval Estimate of Expected Value		
Lower limit	14.66	
Upper limit	24.47	

It is estimated that the average player will hit between 14.66 and 24.47 home runs

19.50

SUMMARY OUTPUT					
Regression Statistics					
Multiple R	0.6447				
R Square	0.4157				
Adjusted R Square	0.3724				
Standard Error	57.29				
Observations	30				
ANOVA					
	df	*SS*	*MS*	*F*	*Significance F*
Regression	2	63043	31521	9.60	0.0007
Residual	27	88626	3282		
Total	29	151669			
	Coefficients	*Standard Error*	*t Stat*	*P-value*	
Intercept	194.84	32.58	5.98	0.0000	
Fetilizer	0.12	0.07	1.66	0.1088	
Water	0.025	0.006	4.06	0.0004	

a $\hat{y} = 194.84 + .12x_1 + .025x_2$

b $\quad H_0 : \beta_1 = 0$

$\quad H_1 : \beta_1 \neq 0$

t = 1.66, p-value = .1088. There is not enough evidence to infer that the amount of fertilizer and yield are linearly related.

c $\quad H_0 : \beta_2 = 0$

$\quad H_1 : \beta_2 \neq 0$

t = 4.06, p-value = .0004. There is enough evidence to infer that the amount of water and yield are linearly related.

d $s_\varepsilon = 57.29$ and $R^2 = .4157$; the model's fit is not very good.

e

Prediction Interval			
		Yield	
Predicted value		232.0	
Prediction Interval			
Lower limit		104.7	
Upper limit		359.2	
Interval Estimate of Expected Value			
Lower limit		183.3	
Upper limit		280.6	

The yield is predicted to fall between 104.7 and 359.2.

19.52a

SUMMARY OUTPUT					
Regression Statistics					
Multiple R	0.5975				
R Square	0.3570				
Adjusted R Square	0.3034				
Standard Error	7.72				
Observations	40				
ANOVA					
	df	*SS*	*MS*	*F*	*Significance F*
Regression	3	1192.73	397.58	6.66	0.0011
Residual	36	2148.06	59.67		
Total	39	3340.79			
	Coefficients	*Standard Error*	*t Stat*	*P-value*	
Intercept	35.68	7.28	4.90	0.0000	
Math Degree	0.25	0.07	3.54	0.0011	
Age	0.24	0.19	1.32	0.1945	
Income	0.13	0.15	0.87	0.3889	

a $\hat{y} = 35.68 + .25x_1 + .24x_2 + .13x_3$

b $H_0 : \beta_1 = \beta_2 = \beta_3 = 0$

        H_1 : At least one β_i is not equal to zero

$F = 6.66$, p-value = .0011. There is enough evidence to conclude that the model is valid.

c The error variable appears to be normal. The variance of the errors appears to be constant.

d

	Test Score	Math Degree	Age	Income
Test Score	1			
Math Degree	0.5066	1		
Age	0.3325	0.0766	1	
Income	0.3120	0.0994	0.5698	1

The correlation between income and age is high enough to distort the t-tests.

e $b_1 = .25$; for each one percentage point increase in the proportion of teachers with mathematics degrees the test score increases on average by .25 provided the other variables are constant.

$b_2 = .24$; for each one year increase in mean age test score increases on average by .24 provided the other variables are constant (which may not be possible because of the multicollinearity).

$b_3 = .13$; for each one thousand dollar increase in salary test score increases on average by .13 provided the other variables are constant (which may not be possible because of the multicollinearity).

        $H_0 : \beta_i = 0$

        $H_1 : \beta_i \neq 0$

Proportion of teachers with at least one mathematics degree: $t = 3.54$, p-value = .0011

Age: $t = 1.32$, p-value = .1945

Income: $t = .87$, p-value = .3889.

The proportion of teachers with at least one mathematics degree is linearly related to test scores. The other two variables may be related to test scores but the multicollinarity makes it difficult to discern.

f

Prediction Interval		
	Test Score	
Predicted value	65.02	
Prediction Interval		
Lower limit	49.02	
Upper limit	81.02	
Interval Estimate of Expected Value		
Lower limit	61.75	
Upper limit	68.28	

The school's test score is predicted to fall between 49.02 and 81.02.

19.54

SUMMARY OUTPUT					
Regression Statistics					
Multiple R	0.8491				
R Square	0.7209				
Adjusted R Square	0.7090				
Standard Error	7.01				
Observations	50				
ANOVA					
	df	SS	MS	F	Significance F
Regression	2	5963.2	2981.6	60.70	0.0000
Residual	47	2308.8	49.12		
Total	49	8272.0			
	Coefficients	Standard Error	t Stat	P-value	
Intercept	47.77	7.63	6.26	0.0000	
Evaluation	0.78	1.30	0.60	0.5529	
Articles	1.06	0.13	8.08	0.0000	

Diagnosing violations: The error variable appears to be normal. The error variable's variance appears to be constant. The required conditions are satisfied.

Assessing the Model:

$s_\varepsilon = 7.01$ and $R^2 = .7209$; the model fits well.

Testing the validity of the model:

$$H_0 : \beta_1 = \beta_2 = 0$$

$$H_1 : \text{At least one } \beta_i \text{ is not equal to zero}$$

F = 60.70, p-value = 0. There is enough evidence to conclude that the model is valid.

Drawing inferences about the independent variables:

$$H_0 : \beta_i = 0$$

$$H_1 : \beta_i \neq 0$$

Evaluations: t = .60, p-value = .5529

Articles: t = 8.08, p-value = 0.

The number of articles a professor publishes is linearly related to salary. Teaching evaluations are not.

19.56

SUMMARY OUTPUT					
Regression Statistics					
Multiple R	0.6584				
R Square	0.4335				
Adjusted R Square	0.4096				
Standard Error	2.91				
Observations	100				
ANOVA					
	df	*SS*	*MS*	*F*	*Significance F*
Regression	4	615.44	153.86	18.17	0.0000
Residual	95	804.35	8.47		
Total	99	1419.79			
	Coefficients	*Standard Error*	*t Stat*	*P-value*	
Intercept	11.91	1.79	6.67	0.0000	
Education	-0.43	0.13	-3.26	0.0016	
Age	0.029	0.025	1.16	0.2501	
Children	0.093	0.224	0.42	0.6780	
Income	-0.074	0.028	-2.69	0.0085	

b $H_0 : \beta_1 = \beta_2 = \beta_3 = \beta_4 = 0$

$H_1 : \text{At least one } \beta_i \text{ is not equal to zero}$

F = 18.17, p-value = 0. There is enough evidence to conclude that the model is valid.

c The errors appear to be normally distributed. The variance of the errors is not constant.

d

	Lottery	Education	Age	Children	Income
Lottery	1				
Education	-0.6202	1			
Age	0.1767	-0.1782	1		
Children	-0.0230	0.1073	0.1072	1	
Income	-0.5891	0.7339	-0.0418	0.0801	1

There is a strong correlation between income and education. The t-tests of these two coefficients may be distorted.

e $H_0 : \beta_i = 0$

$H_1 : \beta_i < 0$ (for beliefs 1 and 4)

$H_1 : \beta_i > 0$ for beliefs 2 and 3)

Belief 1: t = -3.26, p-value = .0016/2 = .0008

Belief 2: t = 1.16, p-value = .2501/2 = .1251

Belief 3: t = .42, p-value = .6780/2 = .3390

Belief 4: t = -2.69, p-value = .0085/2 = .0043

Despite multicollinearity, there is enough evidence to support beliefs 1 and 4. There is no evidence to support beliefs 2 and 3.

Chapter 20

20.2 a

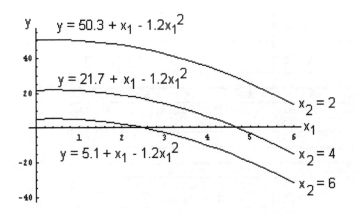

$y = 50.3 + x_1 - 1.2x_1^2$

$y = 21.7 + x_1 - 1.2x_1^2$

$x_2 = 2$

x_1

$y = 5.1 + x_1 - 1.2x_1^2$

$x_2 = 4$

$x_2 = 6$

20.4a   First-order model: a Demand $= \beta_0 + \beta_1 \text{Price} + \varepsilon$

Second-order model: a Demand $= \beta_0 + \beta_1 \text{Price} + \beta_2 \text{Price}^2 + \varepsilon$

First-order model:

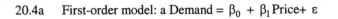

SUMMARY OUTPUT					
Regression Statistics					
Multiple R	0.9249				
R Square	0.8553				
Adjusted R Square	0.8473				
Standard Error	13.29				
Observations	20				
ANOVA					
	df	*SS*	*MS*	*F*	*Significance F*
Regression	1	18798	18798.0	106.44	0.0000
Residual	18	3179	176.6		
Total	19	21977			
	Coefficients	*Standard Error*	*t Stat*	*P-value*	
Intercept	453.6	15.18	29.87	0.0000	
Price	-68.91	6.68	-10.32	0.0000	

259

Second-order model:

SUMMARY OUTPUT					
Regression Statistics					
Multiple R	0.9862				
R Square	0.9726				
Adjusted R Square	0.9693				
Standard Error	5.96				
Observations	20				
ANOVA					
	df	*SS*	*MS*	*F*	*Significance F*
Regression	2	21374	10687	301.15	0.0000
Residual	17	603	35.49		
Total	19	21977			
	Coefficients	*Standard Error*	*t Stat*	*P-value*	
Intercept	766.9	37.40	20.50	0.0000	
Price	-359.1	34.19	-10.50	0.0000	
Price-sq	64.55	7.58	8.52	0.0000	

c The second order model fits better because its standard error of estimate is 5.96, whereas that of the first-order models is 13.29

d $\hat{y} = 766.9 - 359.1(2.95) + 64.55(2.95)^2 = 269.3$

20.6a MBA GPA = $\beta_0 + \beta_1 \text{UnderGPA} + \beta_2 \text{GMAT} + \beta_3 \text{Work} + \beta_4 \text{UnderGPA} \times \text{GMAT} + \varepsilon$

b

SUMMARY OUTPUT					
Regression Statistics					
Multiple R	0.6836				
R Square	0.4674				
Adjusted R Square	0.4420				
Standard Error	0.790				
Observations	89				
ANOVA					
	df	*SS*	*MS*	*F*	*Significance F*
Regression	4	45.97	11.49	18.43	0.0000
Residual	84	52.40	0.62		
Total	88	98.37			
	Coefficients	*Standard Error*	*t Stat*	*P-value*	
Intercept	-11.11	14.97	-0.74	0.4601	
UnderGPA	1.19	1.46	0.82	0.4159	
GMAT	0.0311	0.0255	1.2182	0.2265	
Work	0.0956	0.0312	3.0618	0.0030	
UGPA-GMAT	-0.0019	0.0025	-0.7773	0.4392	

$s_\varepsilon = .790$ and $R^2 = .4674$. The model's fit is relatively poor.

c MBA example $s_\varepsilon = .788$ and $R^2 = .4635$. There is little difference between the fits of the two models.

20.8a

SUMMARY OUTPUT					
Regression Statistics					
Multiple R	0.9255				
R Square	0.8566				
Adjusted R Square	0.8362				
Standard Error	5.20				
Observations	25				
ANOVA					
	df	*SS*	*MS*	*F*	*Significance F*
Regression	3	3398.7	1132.9	41.83	0.0000
Residual	21	568.78	27.08		
Total	24	3967.4			
	Coefficients	*Standard Error*	*t Stat*	*P-value*	
Intercept	260.7	162.27	1.61	0.1230	
Temperature	-3.32	2.09	-1.59	0.1270	
Currency	-164.3	667.12	-0.25	0.8078	
Temp Curr	3.64	8.54	0.43	0.6741	

b

SUMMARY OUTPUT					
Regression Statistics					
Multiple R	0.9312				
R Square	0.8671				
Adjusted R Square	0.8322				
Standard Error	5.27				
Observations	25				
ANOVA					
	df	*SS*	*MS*	*F*	*Significance F*
Regression	5	3440.3	688.07	24.80	0.0000
Residual	19	527.09	27.74		
Total	24	3967.4			
	Coefficients	*Standard Error*	*t Stat*	*P-value*	
Intercept	274.8	283.8	0.97	0.3449	
Temperature	-1.72	6.88	-0.25	0.8053	
Currency	-828.6	888.5	-0.93	0.3627	
Temp-sq	0.00	0.05	-0.05	0.9608	
Curr-sq	2054.0	1718.5	1.20	0.2467	
Temp Curr	-0.87	10.57	-0.08	0.9353	

c Both models fit equally well. The standard errors of estimate and coefficients of determination are quite similar.

20.10a Yield $= \beta_0 + \beta_1\,$Pressure $+ \beta_2\,$Temperature $+ \beta_3\,$Pressure^2

$+ \beta_4\,$Temperature$^2 + \beta_5\,$Pressure Temperature $+ \varepsilon$

b

SUMMARY OUTPUT					
Regression Statistics					
Multiple R	0.8290				
R Square	0.6872				
Adjusted R Square	0.6661				
Standard Error	512				
Observations	80				
ANOVA					
	df	*SS*	*MS*	*F*	*Significance F*
Regression	5	42657846	8531569	32.52	0.0000
Residual	74	19413277	262342		
Total	79	62071123			
	Coefficients	*Standard Error*	*t Stat*	*P-value*	
Intercept	74462	7526	9.89	0.0000	
Pressure	14.40	5.92	2.43	0.0174	
Temperature	-613.3	59.95	-10.23	0.0000	
Press-sq	-0.0159	0.0032	-5.04	0.0000	
Temp-sq	1.23	0.12	9.86	0.0000	
Press Temp	0.038	0.017	2.19	0.0316	

c $s_\varepsilon = 512$ and $R^2 = .6872$. The model's fit is good.

20.12 a $I_1 = 1$ if Catholic; $I_1 = 0$ otherwise

$I_2 = 1$ if Protestant, $I_2 = 0$ otherwise

b $I_1 = 1$ if 8:00 A.M. to 4:00 P.M., $I_1 = 0$ otherwise

$I_2 = 1$ if 4:00 P.M. to midnight, $I_2 = 0$ otherwise

c $I_1 = 1$ if Jack Jones, $I_1 = 0$ otherwise

$I_2 = 1$ if Mary Brown, $I_2 = 0$ otherwise

$I_3 = 1$ if George Fosse, $I_3 = 0$ otherwise

20.14a

Prediction Interval			
		MBA GPA	
Predicted value		10.11	
Prediction Interval			
Lower limit		8.55	
Upper limit		11.67	
Interval Estimate of Expected Value			
Lower limit		9.53	
Upper limit		10.68	

Prediction: MBA GPA will lie between 8.55 and 11.67

b

Prediction Interval			
		MBA GPA	
Predicted value		9.73	
Prediction Interval			
Lower limit		8.15	
Upper limit		11.31	
Interval Estimate of Expected Value			
Lower limit		9.10	
Upper limit		10.36	

Prediction: MBA GPA will lie between 8.15 and 11.31

20.16a

SUMMARY OUTPUT					
Regression Statistics					
Multiple R	0.8368				
R Square	0.7002				
Adjusted R Square	0.6659				
Standard Error	811				
Observations	40				
ANOVA					
	df	*SS*	*MS*	*F*	*Significance F*
Regression	4	53729535	13432384	20.43	0.0000
Residual	35	23007438	657355		
Total	39	76736973			
	Coefficients	*Standard Error*	*t Stat*	*P-value*	
Intercept	3490	469.16	7.44	0.0000	
Yest Att	0.37	0.078	4.73	0.0000	
I1	1623	492.55	3.30	0.0023	
I2	733.5	394.37	1.86	0.0713	
I3	-765.5	484.66	-1.58	0.1232	

b $H_0 : \beta_1 = \beta_2 = \beta_3 = \beta_4 = 0$

H_1 : At least on β_i is not equal to 0

$F = 20.43$, p-value = 0. There is enough evidence to infer that the model is valid.

c $H_0 : \beta_i = 0$

$H_1 : \beta_i \neq 0$

I_2 : t = 1.86, p-value = .0713

I_3 : t = -1.58, p-value = .1232

Weather is not a factor in attendance.

d $H_0 : \beta_4 = 0$

$H_1 : \beta_4 > 0$

t = 3.30, p-value = .0023/2 = .0012. There is sufficient evidence to infer that weekend attendance is larger than weekday attendance.

20.18a

SUMMARY OUTPUT					
Regression Statistics					
Multiple R	0.7753				
R Square	0.6011				
Adjusted R Square	0.5754				
Standard Error	24206				
Observations	100				
ANOVA					
	df	SS	MS	F	Significance F
Regression	6	82119688412	13686614735	23.36	0.0000
Residual	93	54491075988	585925548		
Total	99	136610764400			
	Coefficients	Standard Error	t Stat	P-value	
Intercept	29217	14589	2.00	0.0481	
Bedrooms	-938	6893	-0.14	0.8921	
H Size	79.9	51.5	1.55	0.1245	
Lot Size	-5.07	16.55	-0.31	0.7601	
I1	20487	6993	2.93	0.0043	
I2	12795	7259	1.76	0.0812	
I3	19512	7965	2.45	0.0162	

b $I_1 = 20,487$; in this sample on average two-story houses sell for \$20,487 more than other houses with the same number of bedrooms, square footage, and lot size.

$I_2 = 12,795$; in this sample on average side-split houses sell for \$12,795 more than other houses with the same number of bedrooms, square footage, and lot size.

$I_3 = 19,512$; in this sample on average back-split sell for \$19,512 more than other houses with the same number of bedrooms, square footage, and lot size.

Note that "other" refers to houses that are not two-story, side-split, or back-split.

$$H_0 : \beta_i = 0$$

$$H_1 : \beta_i \neq 0$$

I_1 : t = 2.93, p-value = .0043

I_2 : t = 1.76, p-value = .0812

I_3 : t = 2.45, p-value = .0162

We can infer that two-story and back-split houses sell for more than other.

20.20a

SUMMARY OUTPUT					
Regression Statistics					
Multiple R	0.5602				
R Square	0.3138				
Adjusted R Square	0.2897		.		
Standard Error	5.84				
Observations	60				
ANOVA					
	df	*SS*	*MS*	*F*	*Significance F*
Regression	2	887.90	443.95	13.03	0.0000
Residual	57	1941.70	34.06		
Total	59	2829.60			
	Coefficients	*Standard Error*	*t Stat*	*P-value*	
Intercept	7.02	3.24	2.17	0.0344	
Length	0.250	0.056	4.46	0.0000	
Type	-1.35	0.95	-1.43	0.1589	

b $\quad H_0 : \beta_2 = 0$

$\quad\quad H_1 : \beta_2 \neq 0$

t = -1.43, p-value = .1589. There is not enough evidence to infer that the type of commercial affects memory test scores.

c Let

$\quad\quad I_1 = 1$ if humorous, $I_1 = 0$ otherwise

$\quad\quad I_2 = 1$ if musical, $I_2 = 0$ otherwise

SUMMARY OUTPUT					
Regression Statistics					
Multiple R	0.6231				
R Square	0.3882				
Adjusted R Square	0.3554				
Standard Error	5.56				
Observations	60				
ANOVA					
	df	*SS*	*MS*	*F*	*Significance F*
Regression	3	1098.51	366.17	11.85	0.0000
Residual	56	1731.09	30.91		
Total	59	2829.60			
	Coefficients	*Standard Error*	*t Stat*	*P-value*	
Intercept	2.53	2.15	1.18	0.2445	
Length	0.223	0.054	4.10	0.0001	
I-1	2.91	1.81	1.61	0.1130	
I-2	5.50	1.83	3.01	0.0039	

d $\quad H_0 : \beta_i = 0$

$\quad H_1 : \beta_i \neq 0$

I_1 : t = 1.61, p-value = .1130

I_2 : t = 3.01, p-value = .0039

There is enough evidence to infer that there is a difference in memory test scores between watchers of humorous and serious commercials.

e The variable type of commercial in parts (a) and (b) is nominal. It is usually meaningless to conduct a regression analysis with such variables without converting them to indicator variables.

20.22a Let

$I_1 = 1$ if no scorecard, $I_1 = 0$ otherwise

$I_2 = 1$ if scorecard overturned more than 10% of the time, $I_2 = 0$ otherwise

b

SUMMARY OUTPUT					
Regression Statistics					
Multiple R	0.7299				
R Square	0.5327				
Adjusted R Square	0.5181				
Standard Error	4.20				
Observations	100				
ANOVA					
	df	*SS*	*MS*	*F*	*Significance F*
Regression	3	1933	644.5	36.48	0.0000
Residual	96	1696	17.67		
Total	99	3629			
	Coefficients	*Standard Error*	*t Stat*	*P-value*	
Intercept	4.65	2.06	2.26	0.0260	
Loan Size	0.00012	0.00015	0.83	0.4084	
I-1	4.08	1.14	3.57	0.0006	
I-2	10.18	1.01	10.08	0.0000	

c $s_\varepsilon = 4.20$ and $R^2 = .5327$. The model's fit is mediocre.

d

	Pct Bad	Loan Size	I-1	I-2
Pct Bad	1			
Loan Size	0.1099	1		
I-1	-0.1653	-0.0346	1	
I-2	0.6835	0.0737	-0.5471	1

There is a high correlation between I_1 and I_2 that may distort the t-tests.

e $b_1 = .00012$; in this sample for each additional dollar lent the default rate increases by .00012 provided the other variables remain the same.

$b_2 = 4.08$; In this sample banks that don't use scorecards on average have default rates 4.08 percentage points higher than banks that overturn their scorecards less than 10% of the time.

$b_3 = 10.18$; In this sample banks that overturn their scorecards more than 10% of the time on average have default rates 10.18 percentage points higher than banks that overturn their scorecards less than 10% of the time.

e

Prediction Interval		
	Pct Bad	
Predicted value	9.94	
Prediction Interval		
Lower limit	1.39	
Upper limit	18.49	
Interval Estimate of Expected Value		
Lower limit	8.08	
Upper limit	11.81	

We predict that the bank's default rate will fall between 1.39 and 18.49%.

20.24a

SUMMARY OUTPUT					
Regression Statistics					
Multiple R	0.7296				
R Square	0.5323				
Adjusted R Square	0.5075				
Standard Error	2.36				
Observations	100				
ANOVA					
	df	*SS*	*MS*	*F*	*Significance F*
Regression	5	593.90	118.78	21.40	0.0000
Residual	94	521.72	5.55		
Total	99	1115.62			
	Coefficients	*Standard Error*	*t Stat*	*P-value*	
Intercept	10.26	1.17	8.76	0.0000	
Wage	-0.00020	0.00004	-5.69	0.0000	
Pct PT	-0.11	0.03	-3.62	0.0005	
Pct U	0.060	0.012	4.83	0.0000	
Av Shift	1.56	0.50	3.11	0.0025	
U/M Rel	-2.64	0.49	-5.36	0.0000	

b $H_0 : \beta_4 = 0$

$H_1 : \beta_4 \neq 0$

t = 3.11, p-value = .0025. There is enough evidence to infer that the availability of shiftwork affects absenteeism.

c $H_0 : \beta_5 = 0$

$H_1 : \beta_5 < 0$

t = -5.36, p-value = 0. There is enough evidence to infer that in organizations where the union-management relationship is good absenteeism is lower.

20.26

SUMMARY OUTPUT					
Regression Statistics					
Multiple R	0.8311				
R Square	0.6907				
Adjusted R Square	0.5670				
Standard Error	1.856229516				
Observations	8				
ANOVA					
	df	*SS*	*MS*	*F*	*Significance F*
Regression	2	38.47	19.24	5.58	0.0532
Residual	5	17.23	3.45		
Total	7	55.70			
	Coefficients	*Standard Error*	*t Stat*	*P-value*	
Intercept	2.01	4.02	0.50	0.6385	
Score	3.25	1.00	3.25	0.0227	
Gender	-0.039	1.353	-0.03	0.9782	

In this case male-dominated jobs are paid on average $.039 (3.9 cents) *less* than female-dominated jobs after adjusting for the value of each job.

20.28 The strength of this approach lies in regression analysis. This statistical technique allows us to determine whether gender is a factor in determining salaries. However, the conclusion is very much dependent upon the subjective assignment of weights. Change the value of the weights and a totally different conclusion is achieved.

20.30 a

Results of stepwise regression					
Step 1 - Entering variable: HS_GPA					
Summary measures					
	Multiple R	0.5283			
	R-Square	0.2791			
	Adj R-Square	0.2718			
	StErr of Est	2.0222			
ANOVA Table					
	Source	df	SS	MS	F	p-value
	Explained	1	155.1690	155.1690	37.9438	0.0000
	Unexplained	98	400.7654	4.0894		
Regression coefficients					
		Coefficient	Std Err	t-value	p-value
	Constant	2.4095	0.8168	2.9501	0.0040
	HS_GPA	0.6108	0.0992	6.1599	0.0000

b In this printout only the significant variable high school GPA was included in the equation.

20.32

Results of stepwise regression					
Step 1 - Entering variable: Age					
Summary measures					
	Multiple R	0.4022			
	R-Square	0.1617			
	Adj R-Square	0.1575			
	StErr of Est	4.2743			
ANOVA Table					
	Source	df	SS	MS	F	p-value
	Explained	1	697.9702	697.9702	38.2034	0.0000
	Unexplained	198	3617.4248	18.2698		
Regression coefficients					
		Coefficient	Std Err	t-value	p-value
	Constant	18.4099	1.8394	10.0084	0.0000
	Age	-0.2826	0.0457	-6.1809	0.0000
Step 2 - Entering variable: Income					
Summary measures		Change	% Change		
	Multiple R	0.4455	0.0433	%10.8	
	R-Square	0.1985	0.0367	%22.7	
	Adj R-Square	0.1903	0.0328	%20.8	
	StErr of Est	4.1903	-0.0841	-%2.0	
ANOVA Table					
	Source	df	SS	MS	F	p-value
	Explained	2	856.4167	428.2084	24.3879	0.0000
	Unexplained	197	3458.9783	17.5583		
Regression coefficients					
		Coefficient	Std Err	t-value	p-value
	Constant	13.0272	2.5422	5.1245	0.0000
	Age	-0.2791	0.0448	-6.2248	0.0000
	Income	0.0938	0.0312	3.0040	0.0030

Both independent variables were included because both are linearly related to Internet use.

20.34

Results of stepwise regression					
Step 1 - Entering variable: Erns_Alw					
Summary measures					
	Multiple R	0.9817			
	R-Square	0.9638			
	Adj R-Square	0.9608			
	StErr of Est	12.3977			
ANOVA Table					
	Source	df	SS	MS	F	p-value
	Explained	1	49094.9973	49094.9973	319.4155	0.0000
	Unexplained	12	1844.4313	153.7026		
Regression coefficients					
		Coefficient	Std Err	t-value	p-value	
	Constant	45.7408	38.2382	1.1962	0.2547	
	Erns_Alw	1.0280	0.0575	17.8722	0.0000	

Step 2 - Entering variable: SO					
Summary measures		Change	% Change		
Multiple R	0.9897	0.0079	%0.8		
R-Square	0.9794	0.0157	%1.6		
Adj R-Square	0.9757	0.0149	%1.6		
StErr of Est	9.7554	-2.6423	-%21.3		
ANOVA Table					
Source	df	SS	MS	F	p-value
Explained	2	49892.5864	24946.2932	262.1305	0.0000
Unexplained	11	1046.8422	95.1675		
Regression coefficients					
	Coefficient	Std Err	t-value	p-value	
Constant	-5.8828	34.9758	-0.1682	0.8695	
Erns_Alw	1.0212	0.0453	22.5331	0.0000	
SO	0.4828	0.1668	2.8950	0.0146	

Step 3 - Entering variable: Hits_Alw					
Summary measures		Change	% Change		
Multiple R	0.9942	0.0045	%0.5		
R-Square	0.9884	0.0089	%0.9		
Adj R-Square	0.9849	0.0092	%0.9		
StErr of Est	7.6893	-2.0661	-%21.2		
ANOVA Table					
Source	df	SS	MS	F	p-value
Explained	3	50348.1753	16782.7251	283.8500	0.0000
Unexplained	10	591.2533	59.1253		
Regression coefficients					
	Coefficient	Std Err	t-value	p-value	
Constant	-72.0567	36.4459	-1.9771	0.0762	
Erns_Alw	0.8958	0.0576	15.5495	0.0000	
SO	0.4062	0.1343	3.0237	0.0128	
Hits_Alw	0.1096	0.0395	2.7759	0.0196	

The number of earned runs (no surprise), the number of strikeouts, and the number of hits allowed are all factors in determining the number of runs allowed.

20.36a Apply a first-order model with interaction.

b

SUMMARY OUTPUT					
Regression Statistics					
Multiple R	0.8623				
R Square	0.7436				
Adjusted R Square	0.7299				
Standard Error	1.27				
Observations	60				
ANOVA					
	df	*SS*	*MS*	*F*	*Significance F*
Regression	3	260.22	86.74	54.14	0.0000
Residual	56	89.72	1.60		
Total	59	349.93			
	Coefficients	*Standard Error*	*t Stat*	*P-value*	
Intercept	640.8	53.80	11.91	0.0000	
Cars	-64.17	5.27	-12.19	0.0000	
Speed	-10.63	0.90	-11.85	0.0000	
Cars Speed	1.08	0.09	12.26	0.0000	

c: $H_0 : \beta_1 = \beta_2 = \beta_3 = 0$

H_1 : At least on β_i is not equal to 0

F = 54.14, p-value = 0. There is enough evidence to infer that the model is valid.

20.38 a Let

$I_1 = 1$ if ad was in newspaper, $I_1 = 0$ otherwise

$I_2 = 1$ if ad was on radio, $I_2 = 0$ otherwise

b

SUMMARY OUTPUT					
Regression Statistics					
Multiple R	0.6946				
R Square	0.4824				
Adjusted R Square	0.4501				
Standard Error	44.87				
Observations	52				
ANOVA					
	df	*SS*	*MS*	*F*	*Significance F*
Regression	3	90057	30019	14.91	0.0000
Residual	48	96627	2013		
Total	51	186684			
	Coefficients	*Standard Error*	*t Stat*	*P-value*	
Intercept	282.6	17.46	16.19	0.0000	
Ads	25.23	3.98	6.34	0.0000	
I-1	-23.36	15.83	-1.48	0.1467	
I-2	-46.59	16.44	-2.83	0.0067	

$$H_0 : \beta_1 = \beta_2 = \beta_3 = 0$$

$$H_1 : \text{At least on } \beta_i \text{ is not equal to } 0$$

F = 14.91, p-value = 0. There is enough evidence to infer that the model is valid.

c $$H_0 : \beta_i = 0$$

$$H_1 : \beta_i \neq 0$$

I_1 : t = -1.48, p-value = .1467

I_2 : t = -2.83, p-value = .0067

There is enough evidence to infer that the advertising medium makes a difference.

20.40a Units $= \beta_0 + \beta_1 \text{ Years} + \beta_2 \text{ Years}^2 + \varepsilon$

b

SUMMARY OUTPUT					
Regression Statistics					
Multiple R	0.4351				
R Square	0.1893				
Adjusted R Square	0.1726				
Standard Error	87.98				
Observations	100				
ANOVA					
	df	*SS*	*MS*	*F*	*Significance F*
Regression	2	175291	87646	11.32	0.0000
Residual	97	750764	7740		
Total	99	926056			
	Coefficients	*Standard Error*	*t Stat*	*P-value*	
Intercept	331.2	17.55	18.87	0.0000	
Years	21.45	5.50	3.90	0.0002	
Years-sq	-0.85	0.32	-2.61	0.0105	

c $s_\varepsilon = 87.98$ and $R^2 = .1893$. The model fits poorly.

Chapter 21

21.2 Time series	Moving average
48	
41	
37	$(48 +41+37+32+36)/5 = 38.8$
32	$(41+37+32+36+31)/5 = 35.4$
36	$(37+32+36+31+43)/5 = 35.8$
31	$(32+36+31+43+52)/5 = 38.8$
43	$(36+31+43+52+60)/5 = 44.4$
52	$(31+43+52+60+48)/5 = 46.8$
60	$(43+52+60+48+41)/5 = 48.8$
48	$(52+60+48+41+30)/5 = 46.2$
41	
30	

21.4 Time series	Moving average
16	
22	$(16+22+19)/3 = 19.00$
19	$(22+19+24)/3 = 21.67$
24	$(19+24+30)/3 = 24.33$
30	$(24+30+26)/3 = 26.67$
26	$(30+26+24)/3 = 26.67$
24	$(26+24+29)/3 = 26.33$
29	$(24+29+21)/3 = 24.67$
21	$(29+21+23)/3 = 24.33$
23	$(21+23+19)/3 = 21.00$
19	$(23+19+15)/3 = 19.00$
15	

21.6

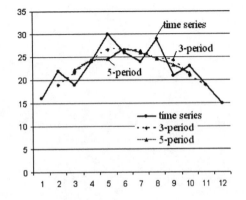

21.8 Time series	Exponentially smoothed time series
12	12
18	.8(18) +. 2(12) = 16.80
16	.8(16) +. 2(16.80) = 16.16
24	.8(24) +. 2(16.16) = 22.43
17	.8(17) +. 2(22.43) = 18.09
16	.8(16) +. 2(18.09) = 16.42
25	.8(25) +. 2(16.42) = 23.28
21	.8(21) +. 2(23.28) = 21.46
23	.8(23) + .2(21.46) = 22.69
14	.8(14) + .2(22.69) = 15.74

21.10 Time series	Exponentially smoothed time series
38	38
43	.1(43) +. 9(38) = 38.50
42	.1(42) +. 9(38.50) = 38.85
45	.1(45) +. 9(38.85) = 39.47
46	.1(46) +. 9(39.47) = 40.12
48	.1(48) +. 9(40.12) = 40.91
50	.1(50) +. 9(40.91) = 41.82
49	.1(49) +. 9(41.82) = 42.53
46	.1(46) + .9(42.53) = 42.88
45	.1(45) + .9(42.88) = 43.09

21.12

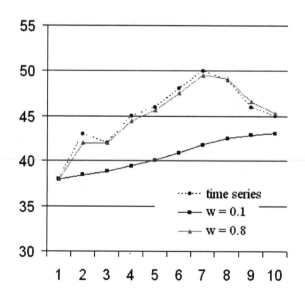

There is a trend component.

21.14

Sales	5-Day moving average
43	
45	
22	(43+45+22+25+31)/5 = 33.2
25	(45+22+25+31+51)/5 = 34.8
31	(22+25+31+51+41)/5 = 34.0
51	(25+31+51+41+37)/5 = 37.0
41	(31+51+41+37+22)/5 = 36.4
37	(51+41+37+22+25)/5 = 35.2
22	(41+37+22+25+40)/5 = 33.0
25	(37+22+25+40+57)/5 = 36.2
40	(22+25+40+57+30)/5 = 34.8
57	(25+40+57+30+33)/5 = 37.0
30	(40+57+30+33+37)/5 = 39.4
33	(57+30+33+37+64)/5 = 44.2
37	(30+33+37+64+58)/5 = 44.4
64	(33+37+64+58+33)/5 = 45.0
58	(37+64+58+33+38)/5 = 46.0
33	(64+58+33+38+25)/5 = 43.6
38	
25	

c There appears to be a seasonal (weekly) pattern.

21.16

Sales	Exponentially smoothed w = .4
18	18
22	.4(22)+.6(18) = 19.60
27	.4(27)+.6(19.6) = 22.56
31	.4(31)+.6(22.56) = 25.94
33	.4(33)+.6(25.94) = 28.76
20	.4(20)+.6(28.76) = 25.26
38	.4(38)+.6(25.26) = 30.35
26	.4(26)+.6(30.35) = 28.61
25	.4(25)+.6(28.61) = 27.17
36	.4(36)+.6(27.17) = 30.70
44	.4(44)+.6(30.70) = 36.02
29	.4(29)+.6(36.02) = 33.21
41	.4(41)+.6(33.21) = 36.33
33	.4(33)+.6(36.33) = 35.00
52	.4(52)+.6(35.00) = 41.80
45	.4(45)+.6(41.80) = 43.08

b

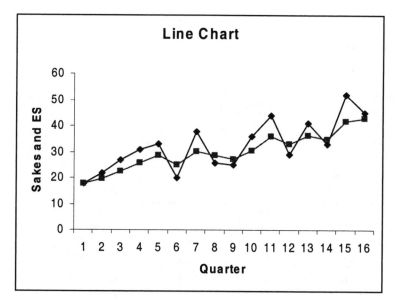

21.18

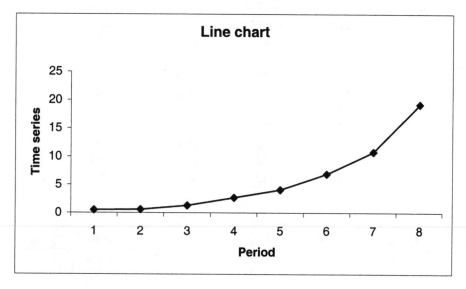

The quadratic model would appear to be the best model.

21.20

$$\hat{y} = -4.96 + 2.38t \qquad (R^2 = .81)$$
$$\hat{y} = 3.14 - 2.48t + .54t^2 \qquad (R^2 = .98)$$

The quadratic trend line fits better.

21.22

Week	Day	Period t	y	$\hat{y}$	$y/\hat{y}$
1	1	1	12	17.2	0.699
	2	2	18	17.5	1.027
	3	3	16	17.9	0.894
	4	4	25	18.3	1.369
	5	5	31	18.6	1.664
2	1	6	11	19.0	0.579
	2	7	17	19.4	0.878
	3	8	19	19.7	0.963
	4	9	24	20.1	1.194
	5	10	27	20.5	1.320
3	1	11	14	20.8	0.672
	2	12	16	21.2	0.755
	3	13	16	21.6	0.742
	4	14	28	21.9	1.277
	5	15	25	22.3	1.122
4	1	16	17	22.7	0.750
	2	17	21	23.0	0.912
	3	18	20	23.4	0.855
	4	19	24	23.8	1.010
	5	20	32	24.1	1.327

| | Day | | | | | |
Week	Monday	Tuesday	Wednesday	Thursday	Friday	Total
1	.699	1.027	.894	1.369	1.664	
2	.579	.878	.963	1.194	1.320	
3	.672	.755	.742	1.277	1.122	
4	.750	.912	.855	1.010	1.327	
Average	.675	.893	.864	1.213	1.358	5.003
Seasonal Index	.675	.892	.864	1.212	1.357	5.000

21.24

Year	Quarter	Period t	y	$\hat{y}$	$y/\hat{y}$
1997	1	1	52	62.9	0.827
	2	2	67	64.1	1.046
	3	3	85	65.2	1.303
	4	4	54	66.4	0.813
1998	1	5	57	67.6	0.843
	2	6	75	68.8	1.090
	3	7	90	70.0	1.286
	4	8	61	71.1	0.857
1999	1	9	60	72.3	0.830
	2	10	77	73.5	1.048
	3	11	94	74.7	1.259
	4	12	63	75.9	0.830
2000	1	13	66	77.0	0.857
	2	14	82	78.2	1.048
	3	15	98	79.4	1.234
	4	16	67	80.6	0.831

		Quarter			
Year	1	2	3	4	Total
1997	.827	1.046	1.303	.813	
1998	.843	1.090	1.286	.857	
1999	.830	1.048	1.259	.830	
2000	.857	1.048	1.234	.831	
Average	.839	1.058	1.271	.833	4.001
Seasonal Index	.839	1.058	1.270	.833	4.000

21.26a

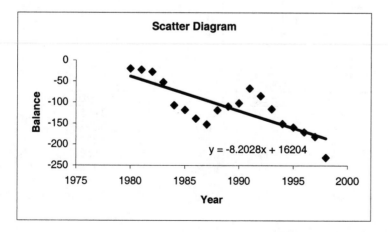

b $\hat{y} = 16{,}204 - 8.21\text{Year}$

21.28 Regression line: $\hat{y} = 145 + 1.66\,t$

Week	Day	Period t	y	$\hat{y} = 145 + 1.66t$	$y / \hat{y}$
1	1	1	240	146.66	1.636
	2	2	85	148.32	0.573
	3	3	93	149.98	0.620
	4	4	106	151.64	0.699
	5	5	125	153.3	0.815
	6	6	188	154.96	1.213
	7	7	314	156.62	2.005
2	1	8	221	158.28	1.396
	2	9	80	159.94	0.500
	3	10	75	161.6	0.464
	4	11	121	163.26	0.741
	5	12	110	164.92	0.667
	6	13	202	166.58	1.213
	7	14	386	168.24	2.294
3	1	15	235	169.9	1.383
	2	16	86	171.56	0.501
	3	17	74	173.22	0.427
	4	18	100	174.88	0.572
	5	19	117	176.54	0.663
	6	20	205	178.2	1.150
	7	21	402	179.86	2.235
4	1	22	219	181.52	1.206
	2	23	91	183.18	0.497
	3	24	102	184.84	0.552
	4	25	89	186.5	0.477
	5	26	105	188.16	0.558
	6	27	192	189.82	1.011
	7	28	377	191.48	1.969

Week	Sunday	Monday	Tuesday	Wednesday	Thursday	Friday	Saturday	Total
				Day				
1	1.636	.573	.620	.699	.815	1.213	2.005	
2	1.396	.500	.464	.741	.667	1.213	2.294	
3	1.383	.501	.427	.572	.663	1.150	2.235	
4	1.206	.497	.552	.477	.558	1.011	1.969	
Average	1.405	.518	.516	.657	.676	1.187	2.126	7.085
Seasonal Index	1.404	.517	.515	.621	.675	1.145	2.123	7.000

21.30

$$MAD = \frac{|166 - 173| + |179 - 186| + |195 - 192| + |214 - 211| + |220 - 223|}{5}$$

$$= \frac{7 + 7 + 3 + 3 + 3}{5} = \frac{23}{5} = 4.60$$

$$= (166 - 173)^2 + (179 - 186)^2 + (195 - 192)^2 + (214 - 211)^2 + (220 - 223)^2$$

$$= 49 + 49 + 9 + 9 + 9 = 125$$

21.32

$$MAD = \frac{|57 - 63| + |60 - 72| + |70 - 86| + |75 - 71| + |70 - 60|}{5}$$

$$= \frac{6 + 12 + 16 + 4 + 10}{5} = \frac{48}{5} = 9.6$$

$$SSE = (57 - 63)^2 + (60 - 72)^2 + (70 - 86)^2 + (75 - 71)^2 + (70-60)^2$$

$$= 36 + 144 + 256 + 16 + 100 = 552$$

21.34

Quarter	t	$\hat{y} = 150 + 3t$	SI	Forecast
1	41	273	.7	191.1
2	42	276	1.2	331.2
3	43	279	1.5	418.5
4	44	282	.6	169.2

21.36 $\hat{y}_t = 625 - 1.3 y_{t-1} = 625 - 1.3(65) = 540.5$

21.38 $F_{17} = F_{18} = F_{19} = F_{20} = S_{16} = 43.08$

21.40

Quarter	t	$\hat{y} = 47.7 - 1.06t$	SI	Forecast
1	21	25.44	1.207	30.71
2	22	24.38	.959	23.38
3	23	23.32	.972	22.67
4	24	22.26	.863	19.21

21.42a $\hat{y}_{1999} = 3717 + .760y_{1998} = 3717 + .760(15{,}546) = 15{,}532$

b $F_{1999} = S_{1998} = 15{,}359$

21.44

Quarter	t	$\hat{y} = 143 + 7.42t$	SI	Forecast
1	25	328.50	1.063	349.20
2	26	335.92	.962	323.16
3	27	343.34	.927	318.28
4	28	350.76	1.048	367.60

21.46

Day	t	$\hat{y} = 90.4 + 2.02t$	SI	Forecast
1	17	124.74	1.094	136.47
2	18	126.76	0.958	121.44
3	19	128.78	0.688	88.60
4	20	130.80	1.260	164.81

21.48 The only component appears to be seasonality.

21.50

Seasonal Indexes	
Season	**Index**
1	0.6464
2	1.0450
3	1.4050
4	0.9037

Chapter 22

2.4a Chance variation represents the variation in student achievement caused by differences in preparation, motivation, and ability.

b Special variation represents variation due to unprepared instructors and poor facilities.

22.6 ARL = $\dfrac{1}{.0124}$ = 81

22.8 ARL = $\dfrac{1}{.0456}$ = 22

22.10a From Beta-mean spreadsheet, $\beta = .6604$

b Probability = $.6604^8 = .0362$

2.12 Number of units = Production × ARL = 50(385) = 19,250

22.14 P = 1 - β = 1 - .8133 = .1867; ARL = $\dfrac{1}{P} = \dfrac{1}{.1867}$ = 5.36

22.16 Number of units = Production × ARL = 2000(385) = 770,000

22.18 P = 1 - β = 1 - .7389 = .2611; ARL = $\dfrac{1}{P} = \dfrac{1}{.2611}$ = 3.83

22.20a From Beta-mean spreadsheet, $\beta = .3660$

b Probability = $.3660^4 = .0179$

22.22 Sampling 10 units per half hour means that on average we will produce 770,000 units before erroneously concluding that the process is out of control when it isn't. Sampling 20 units per hour doubles this figure. Sampling 10 units per half hour means that when the process goes out of control, the probability of not detecting a shift of .75 standard deviations is .7389 and we will produce on average 3.83 × 2000 = 7660 units until the chart indicates a problem. Sampling 20 units per hour decreases the probability of not detecting the shift to .3660 and decreases the average number of units produced when the process is out of control to $4000 \times 1.58 = 6320$.

22.24 Centerline = $\bar{\bar{x}}$ = 181.1

Lower control limit = $\bar{\bar{x}} - \dfrac{3S}{\sqrt{n}} = 181.1 - 3\left(\dfrac{11.0}{\sqrt{9}}\right) = 170.1$

Upper control limit = $\bar{\bar{x}} + \dfrac{3S}{\sqrt{n}} = 181.1 + 3\left(\dfrac{11.0}{\sqrt{9}}\right) = 192.1$

Zone boundaries: 170.10, 173.77, 177.73, 181.10, 184.77, 188.43, 192.10

22.26a

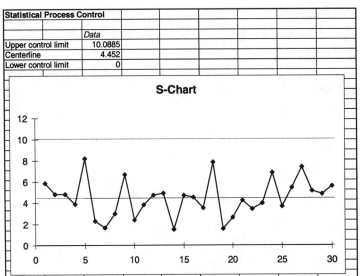

Statistical Process Control								
	Data							
Upper control limit	10.0885							
Centerline	4.452							
Lower control limit	0							

S-Chart

d

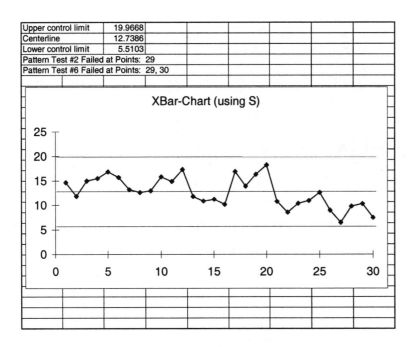

Upper control limit	19.9668					
Centerline	12.7386					
Lower control limit	5.5103					
Pattern Test #2 Failed at Points:	29					
Pattern Test #6 Failed at Points:	29, 30					

c The process is out of control at samples 29 and 30.

d A level shift occurred.

22.28

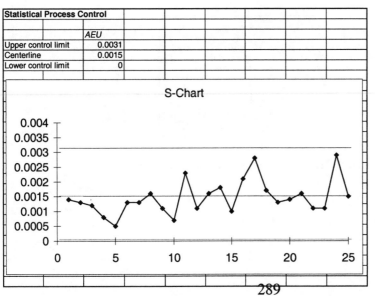

Statistical Process Control						
	AEU					
Upper control limit	0.0031					
Centerline	0.0015					
Lower control limit	0					

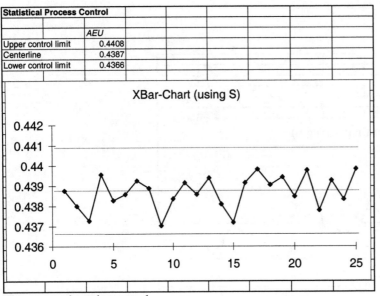

Statistical Process Control							
	AEU						
Upper control limit	0.4408						
Centerline	0.4387						
Lower control limit	0.4366						

The process is under control.

22.30

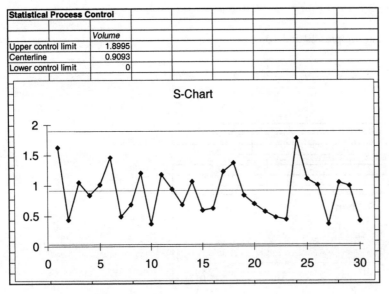

Statistical Process Control							
	Volume						
Upper control limit	1.8995						
Centerline	0.9093						
Lower control limit	0						

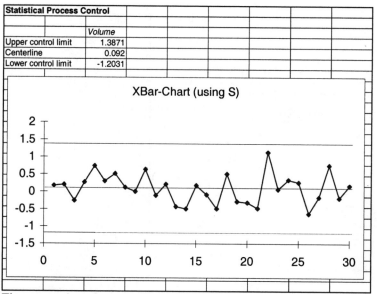

Statistical Process Control								
	Volume							
Upper control limit	1.3871							
Centerline	0.092							
Lower control limit	-1.2031							

The process is under control.

22.32

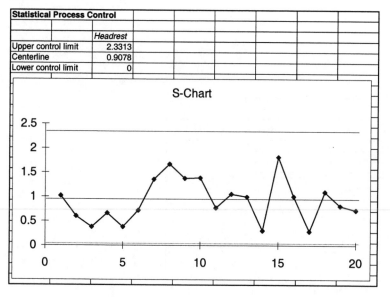

Statistical Process Control								
	Headrest							
Upper control limit	2.3313							
Centerline	0.9078							
Lower control limit	0							

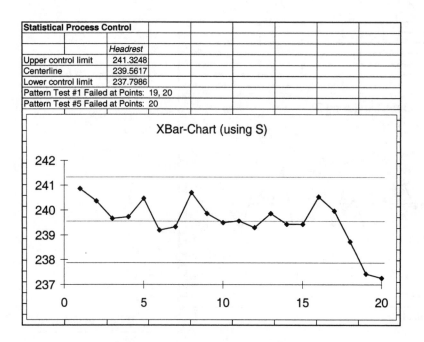

Statistical Process Control									
		Headrest							
Upper control limit		241.3248							
Centerline		239.5617							
Lower control limit		237.7986							
Pattern Test #1 Failed at Points: 19, 20									
Pattern Test #5 Failed at Points: 20									

a The process is out of control.

b The process is out of control at sample 19.

c The width became too small.

22.34

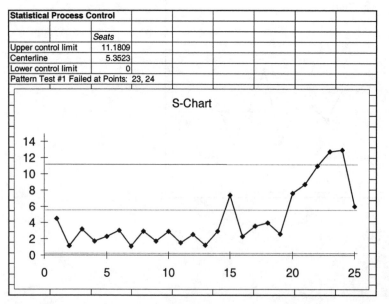

Statistical Process Control									
		Seats							
Upper control limit		11.1809							
Centerline		5.3523							
Lower control limit		0							
Pattern Test #1 Failed at Points: 23, 24									

The process is out of control at sample 23. It is not necessary to draw the $\bar{x}$ chart.

$$22.36\ S = \frac{Upper\ control\ limit - Centerline}{3} = \frac{4.9873 - 4.9841}{3} = .00107$$

$$CPL = \frac{\bar{\bar{x}} - LSL}{3S} = \frac{4.9841 - 4.981}{3(.00107)} = .97$$

$$CPU = \frac{USL - \bar{\bar{x}}}{3S} = \frac{4.987 - 4.9841}{3(.00107)} = .90$$

$$C_{pk} = Min(CPL, CPU) = .90$$

22.38

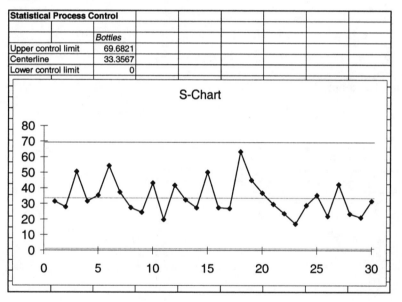

Statistical Process Control								
		Bottles						
Upper control limit		69.6821						
Centerline		33.3567						
Lower control limit		0						

Statistical Process Control								
		Bottles						
Upper control limit		803.9376						
Centerline		756.4267						
Lower control limit		708.9157						
Pattern Test #1 Failed at Points: 30								
Pattern Test #5 Failed at Points: 29, 30								
Pattern Test #6 Failed at Points: 30								

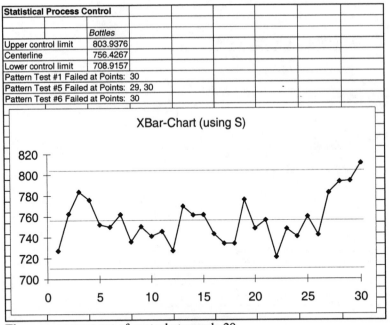

The process went out of control at sample 29.

22.40

Statistical Process Control								
		Pipes						
Upper control limit		0.0956						
Centerline		0.0372						
Lower control limit		0						

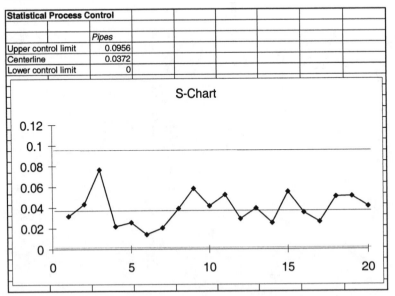

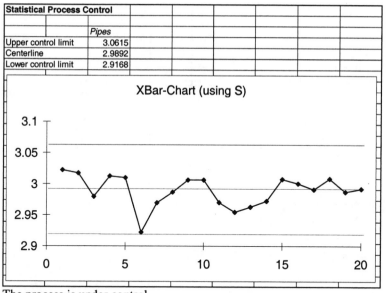

Statistical Process Control							
	Pipes						
Upper control limit	3.0615						
Centerline	2.9892						
Lower control limit	2.9168						

The process is under control.

$$22.42 \ S = \frac{Upper\ control\ limit - Centerline}{3} = \frac{1504.572 - 1496.952}{3} = 2.54$$

$$CPL = \frac{\bar{\bar{x}} - LSL}{3S} = \frac{1496.952 - 1494.5}{3(2.54)} = .32$$

$$CPU = \frac{USL - \bar{\bar{x}}}{3S} = \frac{1497.5 - 1496.952}{3(2.54)} = .07$$

$$C_{pk} = Min(CPL, CPU) = .07$$

The value of the index is low because the statistics used to calculate the control limits and centerline were taken when the process was out of control.

22.44 Centerline = $\bar{p}$ = .0324

Lower control limit = $\bar{p} - 3\sqrt{\dfrac{\bar{p}(1 - \bar{p})}{n}} = .0324 - 3\sqrt{\dfrac{(.0324)(1 - .0324)}{200}} = -.00516 \ (= 0)$

Upper control limit = $\bar{p} + 3\sqrt{\dfrac{\bar{p}(1 - \bar{p})}{n}} = .0324 + 3\sqrt{\dfrac{(.0324)(1 - .0324)}{200}} = .06996$

Statistical Process Control								
	Copiers							
Upper control limit	0.07							
Centerline	0.0324							
Lower control limit	0							
Pattern Test #1 Failed at Points: 25								

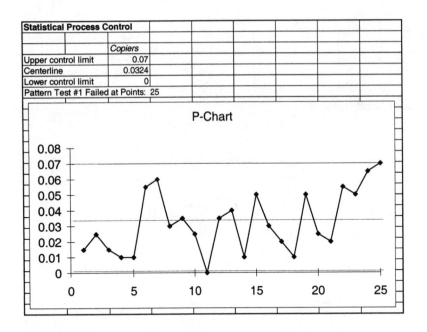

The process is out of control at sample 25.

The process is under control.

22.46 Centerline = $\bar{p} = .0383$

Lower control limit = $\bar{p} - 3\sqrt{\dfrac{\bar{p}(1-\bar{p})}{n}} = .0383 - 3\sqrt{\dfrac{(.0383)(1-.0383)}{100}} = -.0193 \ (= 0)$

Upper control limit = $\bar{p} + 3\sqrt{\dfrac{\bar{p}(1-\bar{p})}{n}} = .0383 + 3\sqrt{\dfrac{(.0383)(1-.0383)}{100}} = .0959$

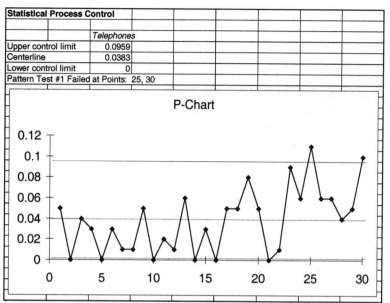

Statistical Process Control								
		Telephones						
Upper control limit	0.0959							
Centerline	0.0383							
Lower control limit	0							
Pattern Test #1 Failed at Points: 25, 30								

The process is out of control at samples 25 and 30.

22.48

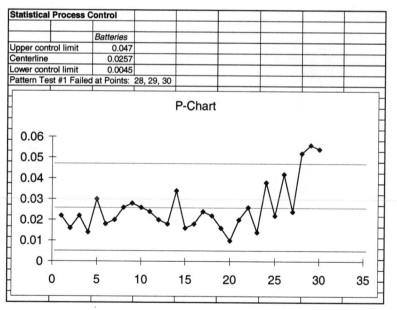

Statistical Process Control								
		Batteries						
Upper control limit	0.047							
Centerline	0.0257							
Lower control limit	0.0045							
Pattern Test #1 Failed at Points: 28, 29, 30								

The process is out of control at sample 28.

22.50

Statistical Process Control									
		Scanners							
Upper control limit		0.0275							
Centerline		0.0126							
Lower control limit		0					-		
Pattern Test #1 Failed at Points:		24							

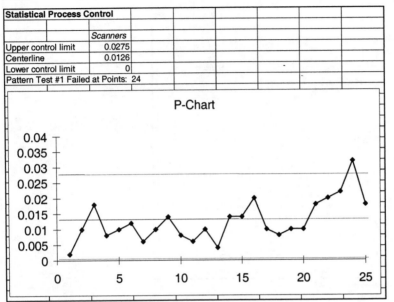

The process is out of control at sample 24.

Chapter 23

23.2

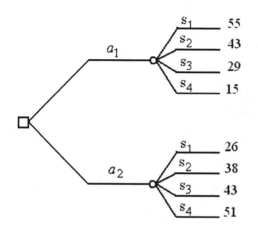

23.4

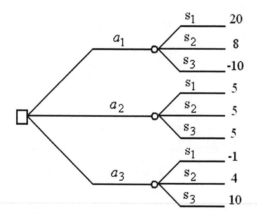

23.6 $\text{EOL}(a_1) = .2(0) + .6(0) + .2(20) = 4.0$

$\text{EOL}(a_2) = .2(15) + .6(3) + .2(5) = 5.8$

$\text{EOL}(a_3) = .2(21) + .6(4) + .2(0) = 6.6$

The EOL decision is a_1.

23.8a $EMV(a_0) = 0$

$EMV(a_1) = .25(-3.00) + .25(5.00) + .25(5.00) + .25(5.00) = 3.00$

$EMV(a_2) = .25(-6.00) + .25(2.00) + .25(10.00) + .25(10.00) = 4.00$

$EMV(a_3) = .25(-9.00) + .25(-1.00) + .25(7.00) + .25(15.00) = 3.00$

EMV decision is a_2 (bake 2 cakes)

b $EOL(a_0) = .25(0) + .25(5.00) + .25(10.00) + .25(15.00) = 7.50$

$EOL(a_1) = .25(3.00) + .25(0) + .25(5.00) + .25(10.00) = 4.50$

$EOL(a_2) = .25(6.00) + .25(3.00) + .25(0) + .25(5.00) = 3.50$

$EOL(a_2) = .25(9.00) + .25(6.00) + .25(3.00) + .25(0) = 4.50$

EOL decision is a_2 (bake 2 cakes)

23.10 $EMV(a_1) = -40,000$

$EMV(a_2) = .05(0) + .15(-18,000) + .30(-36,000) + .40(-54,000) + .10(-72,000) = -42,300$

EMV decision is a_1

23.12

$EMV(a_{100}) = 200$

$EMV(a_{200}) = .20(0) + .25(300) + .40(600) + .15(600) = 405$

$EMV(a_{300}) = .20(-150) + .25(150) + .40(450) + .15(750) = 300$

EMV decision is order 200 shirts.

23.14a $EMV(Small) = .15(-220) + .55(-330) + .30(-440) = -346.5$

$EMV(Medium) = .15(-300) + .55(-320) + .30(-390) = -338.0$

$EMV(Large) = .15(-350) + .55(-350) + .30(-350) = -350.0$

EMV decision: build a medium size plant; $EMV* = -338.0$

b   Opportunity Loss Table

	Small	Medium	Large
Low	0	80	130
Moderate	10	0	30
High	90	40	0

c EOL(Small) = .15(0) + .55(10) + .30(90) = 32.5

EOL(Medium) = .15(80) + .55(0) + .30(40) = 24.0

EOL(Large) = .15(130) + .55(30) + .30(0) = 36.0

EOL decision: build a medium size plant

23.16   Payoff Table

	Produce	Don't produce
Market share		
5%	-28 million	0
10%	2 million	0
15%	8 million	0

EMV(produce) = .15(-28 million) + .45(2 million) + .40 (8 million) = -.1 million

EMV (don't produce) = 0

EMV decision: don't produce

23.18   Opportunity Loss Table

	a_1	a_2	a_3
s_1	50	0	35
s_2	110	40	0
s_3	0	100	135
s_4	0	130	120

EOL(a_1) = .10(50) + .25(110) + .50(0) + .15(0) = 32.5

EOL(a_2) = .10(0) + .25(40) + .50(100) + .15(130) = 79.5

EOL(a_3) = .10(35) + .25(0) + .50(135) + .15(120) = 89

EOL* = 32.5

23.20 a EPPI = .75(65) + .25(110) = 76.25

$EMV(a_1) = .75(65) + .25(70) = 66.25$

$EMV(a_2) = .75(20) + .25(110) = 42.5$

$EMV(a_3) = .75(45) + .25(80) = 53.75$

$EMV(a_4) = .75(30) + .25(95) = 46.25$

EVPI = EPPI − EMV* = 76.25 − 66.25 = 10

b EPPI = .95(65) + .05(110) = 67.25

$EMV(a_1) = .95(65) + .05(70) = 65.25$

$EMV(a_2) = .95(20) + .05(110) = 24.5$

$EMV(a_3) = .95(45) + .05(80) = 46.75$

$EMV(a_4) = .95(30) + .05(95) = 33.25$

EVPI = EPPI − EMV* = 67.25 − 65.25 = 2

23.22 Posterior Probabilities for I_1

s_j	$P(s_j)$	$P(I_1|s_j)$	$P(s_j \text{ and } I_1)$	$P(s_j|I_1)$
s_1	.25	.40	(.25)(.40) = .10	.12/.20 = .500
s_2	.40	.25	(.40)(.25) = .10	.10/.20 = .500
s_3	.35	0	(.35)(0) = .0	0/.20 = 0
			$P(I_1) = .20$	

Posterior Probabilities for I_2

s_j	$P(s_j)$	$P(I_2|s_j)$	$P(s_j \text{ and } I_2)$	$P(s_j|I_2)$
s_1	.25	.30	(.25)(.30) = .075	.075/.28 = .268
s_2	.40	.25	(.40)(.25) = .10	.10/.28 = .357
s_3	.35	30	(.35)(.30) = .105	.105/.28 = .375
			$P(I_2) = .28$	

Posterior Probabilities for I_3

s_j	$P(s_j)$	$P(I_3|s_j)$	$P(s_j \text{ and } I_3)$	$P(s_j|I_3)$
s_1	.25	.20	$(.25)(.20) = .05$	$.05/.29 = .172$
s_2	.40	.25	$(.40)(.25) = .10$	$.10/.29 = .345$
s_3	.35	.40	$\underline{(.35)(.40) = .14}$	$.14/.29 = .483$
			$P(I_3) = .29$	

Posterior Probabilities for I_4

s_j	$P(s_j)$	$P(I_4|s_j)$	$P(s_j \text{ and } I_4)$	$P(s_j|I_4)$
s_1	.25	.10	$(.25)(.10) = .025$	$.025/.23 = .109$
s_2	.40	.25	$(.40)(.25) = .10$	$.10/.23 = .435$
s_3	.35	.30	$\underline{(.35)(.30) = .105}$	$.105/.23 = .456$
			$P(I_4) = .23$	

23.24a Prior probabilities: $EMV(a_1) = .5(10) + .5(22) = 16$

$EMV(a_2) = .5(18) + .5(19) = 18.5$

$EMV(a_3) = .5(23) + .5(15) = 19$

$EMV^* = 19$

I_1: $EMV(a_1) = .951(10) + .049(22) = 10.588$

$EMV(a_2) = .951(18) + .049(19) = 18.049$

$EMV(a_3) = .951(23) + .049(15) = 22.608$

Optimal act: a_3

I_2: $EMV(a_1) = .021(10) + .979(22) = 21.748$

$EMV(a_2) = .021(18) + .979(19) = 18.979$

$EMV(a_3) = .021(23) + .979(15) = 15.168$

Optimal act: a_1

b $EMV` = .515(22.608) + .485(21.748) = 22.191$

$EVSI = EMV` - EMV^* = 22.191 - 19 = 3.191$

23.26 Prior probabilities: $EMV(a_1) = .5(60) + .4(90) + .1(150) = 81$

$EMV(a_2) = 90$

$EMV* = 90$

Posterior Probabilities for I_1

s_j	$P(s_j)$	$P(I_1|s_j)$	$P(s_j \text{ and } I_1)$	$P(s_j|I_1)$
s_1	.5	.7	$(.5)(.7) = .35$	$.35/.57 = .614$
s_2	.4	.5	$(.4)(.5) = .20$	$.20/.57 = .351$
s_3	.1	.2	$\underline{(.1)(.2) = .02}$	$.02/.57 = .035$
			$P(I_1) = .57$	

Posterior Probabilities for I_2

s_j	$P(s_j)$	$P(I_2|s_j)$	$P(s_j \text{ and } I_2)$	$P(s_j|I_2)$
s_1	.5	.3	$(.5)(.3) = .15$	$.15/.43 = .349$
s_2	.4	.5	$(.4)(.5) = .20$	$.20/.43 = .465$
s_3	.1	.8	$\underline{(.1)(.8) = .08}$	$.08/.43 = .186$
			$P(I_1) = .43$	

I_1: $EMV(a_1) = .614(60) + .351(90) + .035(150) = 73.68$

$EMV(a_2) = 90$

I_1: $EMV(a_1) = .349(60) + .465(90) + .186(150) = 90.69$

$EMV(a_2) = 90$

$EMV` = .57(90) + .43(90.69) = 90.30$

$EVSI = EMV` - EMV* = 90.30 - 90 = .30$

23.28 As the prior probabilities become more diverse EVSI decreases.

23.30 $EMV* = 0$

$EPPI = .15(0) + .45(2 \text{ million}) + .40(8 \text{ million}) = 4.1 \text{ million}$

$EVPI = EPPI - EMV* = 4.1 \text{ million} - 0 = 4.1 \text{ million}$

23.32a   Payoff Table

Market share	Switch	Don't switch
5%	5(100,000) − 700,000 = -200,000	285,000
10%	10(100,000) − 700,000 = 300,000	285,000
20%	20(100,000)-700,000 = 1,300,000	285,000

b EMV(switch) = .4(-200,000) + .4(300,000) + .2(1,300,000) = 300,000

EMV(don't switch) = 285,000

Optimal act: switch (EMV* = 300,000)

c EPPI = .4(285,000) + .4(300,000) + .2(1,300,000) = 494,000

EVPI = EPPI − EMV* = 494,000 − 300,000= 194,000

23.34 Likelihood probabilities (binomial probabilities)

$P(I \mid s_1) = P(x = 12, n= 100 \mid p = .05) = .0028$

$P(I \mid s_2) = P(x = 12, n= 100 \mid p = .10) = .0988$

$P(I \mid s_3) = P(x = 12, n= 100 \mid p = .20) = .0128$

$P(I \mid s_4) = P(x = 12, n= 100 \mid p = .30) = .000013$

Posterior Probabilities

s_j	$P(s_j)$	$P(I \mid s_j)$	$P(s_j$ and $I)$	$P(s_j \mid I)$
s_1	.5	.0028	(.5)(.0028) = .0014	.0014/.0323 = .0433
s_2	.3	.0988	(.3)(.0988) = .0296	.0296/.0323 = .9164
s_3	.1	.0128	(.1)(.0128) = .0013	.0013/.0323 = .0402
s_4	.1	.000013	(.1)(.000013) = .000001	.000001/.0323 = .000031
			P(I) = .0323	

EMV(proceed) = .0433(-30,000) + .9164(-5,000) + .0402(45,000) + .000031(95,000) = -4,069

EMV (don't proceed = 0

EMV decision: don't proceed

23.36

I_0 = neither person supports format change

I_1 = one person supports format change

I_2 = both people support format change

Likelihood probabilities P($I_i | s_j$)

	I_0	I_1	I_2
5%	.9025	.0950	.0025
10%	.81	.18	.01
20%	.64	.32	.04

Posterior Probabilities for I_0

s_j	P(s_j)	P($I_0 | s_j$)	P(s_j and I_0)	P($s_j | I_0$)
s_1	.4	.9025	(.4)(.9025) = .361	.361/.813 = .444
s_2	.4	.81	(.4)(.81) = .324	.324/.813 = .399
s_3	.2	.64	(.2)(.64) = .128	.128/.813 = .157
			P(I_0) = .813	

Posterior Probabilities for I_1

s_j	P(s_j)	P($I_1 | s_j$)	P(s_j and I_1)	P($s_j | I_1$)
s_1	.4	.0950	(.4)(.0950) = .038	.038/.174 = .218
s_2	.4	.18	(.4)(.18) = .072	.072/.174 = .414
s_3	.2	.32	(.2)(.32) = .064	.064/.174 = .368
			P(I_1) = .174	

Posterior Probabilities for I_3

s_j	P(s_j)	P($I_2 | s_j$)	P(s_j and I_2)	P($s_j | I_2$)
s_1	.4	.0025	(.4)(.0025) = .001	.001/.013 = .077
s_2	.4	.01	(.4)(.01) = .004	.004/.013 = .308
s_3	.2	.04	(.2)(.04) = .008	.008/.013 = .615
			P(I_2) = .013	

I_1: EMV(switch) = .444(-200,000) + .399(300,000) + .157(1,300,000) = 235,000

EMV(don't switch) = 285,000

Optimal act: don't switch

I_2 : EMV(switch) = .218(-200,000) + .414(300,000) + .368(1,300,000) = 559,000

EMV(don't switch) = 285,000

Optimal act: switch

I_3 : EMV(switch) = .077(-200,000) + .308(300,000) + .615(1,300,000) = 876,500

EMV(don't switch) = 285,000

Optimal act: switch

EMV` = .813(285,000) + .174(546,000) + .013(876,500) = 338,104

EVSI = EMV` - EMV* = 338,104 – 300,000 = 38,104

23.38a

Payoff Table

Demand	Battery 1	Battery 2	Battery 3
50,000	20(50,000)-900,000 = 100,000	23(50,000)-1,150,000 0	25(50,000)-1,400,000 -150,000
100,000	20(100,000)-900,000 =1,100,000	23(100,000)-1,150,000 1,150,000	25(100,000)-1,400,000 1,100,000
150,000	20(150,000)-900,000 =2,100,000	23(150,000)-1,150,000 2,300,000	25(150,000)-1,400,000 2,350,000

b Opportunity Loss table

Demand	Battery 1	Battery 2	Batter3
50,000	0	100,000	250,000
100,000	50,000	0	50,000
150,000	250,000	50,000	9

c EMV(Battery 1) = .3(100,000) + .3(1,100,000) + .4(2,100,000) = 1,200,000

EMV(Battery 2) = .3(0) + .3(1,150,000) + .4(2,300,000) = 1,265,000

EMV(Battery 3) = .3(-150,000) + .3(1,100,000) + .4(2,350,000) = 1,225,000

EMV decision: Battery 2

d EOL(Battery 2) = .3(100,000) + .3(0) + .4(50,000) = 50,000

EVPI = EOL* = 50,000

23.40

I_0 = person does not believe the ad

I_1 = person believes the ad

Likelihood probabilities $P(I_i \mid s_j)$

	I_0	I_1
30%	.70	.30
31%	.69	.31
32%	.68	.32
33%	.67	.33
34%	.66	.34

Posterior Probabilities for I_0

s_j	$P(s_j)$	$P(I_0 \mid s_j)$	$P(s_j \text{ and } I_0)$	$P(s_j \mid I_0)$
s_1	.1	.70	(.1)(.70) = .070	.070/.674 = .104
s_2	.1	.69	(.1)(.69) = .069	.069/.674 = .102
s_3	.2	.68	(.2)(.68) = .136	.136/.674 = .202
s_4	.3	.67	(.3)(.67) = .201	.201/.674 = .298
s_5	.3	.66	(.3)(.66) = .198	.198/.674 = .294
			$P(I_0) = .674$	

Posterior Probabilities for I_1

s_j	$P(s_j)$	$P(I_1 \mid s_j)$	$P(s_j \text{ and } I_1)$	$P(s_j \mid I_1)$
s_1	.1	.30	(.1)(.30) = .030	.030/.326 = .092
s_2	.1	.31	(.1)(.31) = .031	.031/.326 = .095
s_3	.2	.32	(.2)(.32) = .064	.064/.326 = .196
s_4	.3	.33	(.3)(.33) = .099	.099/.326 = .304
s_5	.3	.34	(.3)(.34) = .102	.102/.326 = .313
			$P(I_1) = .326$	

I_0: EMV(Change ad) = .104(-258,000) + .102(-158,000) + .202(-58,000) + .298(42,000) +

.294(142,000) = -400

EMV (don't change) = 0.

Optimal decision: don't change ad

I_1 : EMV(Change ad) = .092(-258,000) + .095(-158,000) + .196(-58,000) + .304(42,000) +

.313(142,000) = 7,100

EMV (don't change) = 0.

Optimal decision: change ad

EMV` = .674(0) + .326(7,100) = 2,315

EVSI = EMV` - EMV* = 2,315 – 2,000 = 315

23.42

EMV(25 telephones) = 50,000

EMV(50 telephones) = .50(30,000) + .25(60,000) + .25(60,000) = 45,000

EMV(100 telephones) = .50(20,000) + .25(40,000) + .25(80,000) = 40,000

Optimal decision: 25 telephones (EMV* = 50,000)

I_1 = small number of calls

I_2 = medium number of calls

I_3 = large number of calls

Likelihood probabilities (Poisson distribution)

	I_1	I_2	I_3
$\mu = 5$	$P(X < 8 \mid \mu = 5)$	$P(8 \leq X < 17 \mid \mu = 5)$	$P(X \geq 17 \mid \mu = 5)$
	= .8667	= .1334	= 0
$\mu = 10$	$P(X < 8 \mid \mu = 10)$	$P(8 \leq X < 17 \mid \mu = 10)$	$P(X \geq 17 \mid \mu = 10)$
	= .2202	= .7527	= .0270
$\mu = 15$	$P(X < 8 \mid \mu = 15)$	$P(8 \leq X < 17 \mid \mu = 15)$	$P(X \geq 17 \mid \mu = 15)$
	= .0180	= .6461	= .3359

Posterior Probabilities for I_1

s_j	$P(s_j)$	$P(I_1 \vert s_j)$	$P(s_j \text{ and } I_1)$	$P(s_j \vert I_1)$
s_1	.50	.8667	$(.50)(.8667) = .4333$	$.4333/.4929 = .8792$
s_2	.25	.2202	$(.25)(.2202) = .0551$	$.0551/.4929 = .1117$
s_3	.25	.0180	$\underline{(.25)(.0180) = .0045}$	$.0045/.4929 = .0091$
			$P(I_1) = .4929$	

Posterior Probabilities for I_2

s_j	$P(s_j)$	$P(I_2 \vert s_j)$	$P(s_j \text{ and } I_2)$	$P(s_j \vert I_2)$
s_1	.50	.1334	$(.50)(.1334) = .0667$	$.0667/.4164 = .1601$
s_2	.25	.7527	$(.25)(.7527) = .1882$	$.1882/.4164 = .4519$
s_3	.25	.6461	$\underline{(.25)(.6461) = .1615}$	$.1615/.4164 = .3879$
			$P(I_2) = .4164$	

Posterior Probabilities for I_3

s_j	$P(s_j)$	$P(I_3 \vert s_j)$	$P(s_j \text{ and } I_3)$	$P(s_j \vert I_3)$
s_1	.50	.0	$(.50)(0) = 0$	$0/.0907 = 0$
s_2	.25	.0270	$(.25)(.0270) = .0068$	$.0068/.0907 = .0745$
s_3	.25	.3359	$\underline{(.25)(.3359) = .0840}$	$.0840/.0907 = .9254$
			$P(I_3) = .0907$	

I_1: EMV(25 telephones) = 50,000

EMV(50 telephones) = .8792(30,000) + .1117(60,000) + .0091(60,000) = 33,624

EMV(100 telephones) = .8792(20,000) + .1117(40,000) + .0091(80,000) = 22,780

Optimal act: 25 telephones

I_2: EMV(25 telephones) = 50,000

EMV(50 telephones) = .1601(30,000) + .4519(60,000) + .3879(60,000) = 55,191

EMV(100 telephones) = .1601(20,000) + .4519(40,000) + .38791(80,000) = 52,310

Optimal act: 50 telephones

I_3 : EMV(25 telephones) = 50,000

EMV(50 telephones) = 0(30,000) + .0745(60,000) + .9254(60,000) = 60,000

EMV(100 telephones) = 0(20,000) + .0745(40,000) + .9254(80,000) = 77,012

Optimal act: 100 telephones

EMV` = .4929(50,000) + .4164(55,191) + .0907(77,012) = 54,612

EVSI = EMV` - EMV* = 54,612 – 50,000 = 4,612

Because the value is greater than the cost ($4,000) Max should not sample. If he sees a small number of calls install 25 telephones. If there is a medium number install 50 telephones. If there is a large number of calls, install 100 telephones.

23.44 EMV(Release in North America) = .5(33 million) + .3(12 million) + .2(-15 million) = 17.1 million

EMV(European distributor) = 12 million

Optimal decision: Release in North America

Posterior Probabilities for I_1 (Rave review)

s_j	$P(s_j)$	$P(I_1|s_j)$	$P(s_j \text{ and } I_1)$	$P(s_j|I_1)$
s_1	.5	.8	(.5)(.8) = .40	.40/.63 = .635
s_2	.3	.5	(.3)(.5) = .15	.15/.63 = .238
s_3	.2	.4	(.2)(.4) = .08	.08/.63 = .127
			$P(I_1) = .63$	

EMV(Release in North America) = .635(33 million) + .238(12 million) + .127(-15 million) =21.9 million

EMV(European distributor) = 12 million

Optimal decision: Release in North America

Posterior Probabilities for I_2 (lukewarm response)

s_j	$P(s_j)$	$P(I_2 \mid s_j)$	$P(s_j \text{ and } I_2)$	$P(s_j \mid I_2)$
s_1	.5	.1	$(.5)(.1) = .05$	$.05/.20 = .25$
s_2	.3	.3	$(.3)(.3) = .09$	$.09/.20 = .45$
s_3	.2	.3	$\underline{(.2)(.3) = .06}$	$.06/.20 = .30$
			$P(I_2) = .20$	

EMV(Release in North America) = .25(33 million) + .45(12 million) + .30(-15 million) = 9.2 million

EMV(European distributor) = 12 million

Optimal decision: Sell to European distributor

Posterior Probabilities for I_3 (poor response)

s_j	$P(s_j)$	$P(I_3 \mid s_j)$	$P(s_j \text{ and } I_3)$	$P(s_j \mid I_3)$
s_1	.5	.1	$(.5)(.1) = .05$	$.05/.17 = .294$
s_2	.3	.2	$(.3)(.2) = .06$	$.06/.17 = .353$
s_3	.2	.3	$\underline{(.2)(.3) = .06}$	$.06/.17 = .353$
			$(I_3) = .17$	

EMV(Release in North America) = .294(33 million) + .353(12 million) + .353(-15 million) = 8.6 million

EMV(European distributor) = 12 million

Optimal decision: Sell to European distributor.

EMV` = .63(21.9 million) + .20(12 million) + .17(12 million) = 18.2 million

EVSI = EMV` - EMV* = 18.2 million – 17.1 million = 1.1 million

Because EVSI is greater than the sampling cost (100,000) the studio executives should show the movie to a random sample of North Americans. If the response is a rave review release the movie in North America. If not sell it to Europe.

Chapter 24

24.2 z-test of p

$$H_0 : p = .5$$

$$H_1 : p \neq .5$$

$$z = \frac{\hat{p} - p}{\sqrt{\dfrac{p(1-p)}{n}}}$$

z-Test of a Proportion			
Sample proportion	0.88	z Stat	3.15
Sample size	17	P(Z<=z) one-tail	0.0008
Hypothesized proportion	0.5	z Critical one-tail	1.6449
Alpha	0.05	P(Z<=z) two-tail	0.0016
		z Critical two-tail	1.9600

$z = 3.15$, p-value = .0016. There is overwhelming evidence to conclude that the new technology affects the sex of the baby.

24.4 t-test of μ_D

$$H_0 : \mu_D = 0$$

$$H_1 : \mu_D < 0$$

$$t = \frac{\bar{x}_D - \mu_D}{s_D / \sqrt{n_D}}$$

t-Test: Paired Two Sample for Means		
	Prior	After
Mean	24.91	26.24
Variance	48.65	87.88
Observations	100	100
Pearson Correlation	0.7859	-
Hypothesized Mean Difference	0	
df	99	
t Stat	-2.29	
P(T<=t) one-tail	0.0121	
t Critical one-tail	1.6604	
P(T<=t) two-tail	0.0242	
t Critical two-tail	1.9842	

$t = -2.29$, p-value $= .0121$. There is enough evidence to conclude that company should proceed to stage 2.

24.6 a t-estimator of μ

$$\bar{x} \pm t_{\alpha/2} \frac{s}{\sqrt{n}}$$

t-Estimate: Mean		
		Overdue
Mean		7.0875
Standard Deviation		6.9682
LCL		6.4026
UCL		7.7724

b LCL $= 50,000(\$.25)(6.4026) = \$80,033$

UCL $= 50,000(\$.25)(7.7724) = \$97,155$

It does appear that not all fines are collected.

24.8 Chi-squared test of a contingency table

H_0 : The two variables are independent

H_1 : The two variables are dependent

$$\chi^2 = \sum_{i=1}^{6} \frac{(f_i - e_i)^2}{e_i}$$

Contingency Table				
	Age Category			
Alcohol		1	2	TOTAL
	1	87	325	412
	2	44	297	341
	3	87	214	301
	TOTAL	218	836	1054
	chi-squared Stat			25.0273
	df			2
	p-value			0
	chi-squared Critical			5.9915

$\chi^2 = 25.0273$, p-value = 0. There is overwhelming evidence to infer that differences exist among the age categories with respect to alcohol use.

24.10 z-test of $p_1 - p_2$ (case 2)

$$H_0 : p_1 - p_2 = -.15$$

$$H_1 : p_1 - p_2 < -.15$$

$$z = \frac{(\hat{p}_1 - \hat{p}_2) - (p_1 - p_2)}{\sqrt{\frac{\hat{p}_1(1 - \hat{p}_1)}{n_1} + \frac{\hat{p}_2(1 - \hat{p}_2)}{n_2}}}$$

z-Test: Two Proportions			
		Comm 1	Comm 2
Sample Proportions		0.268	0.486
Observations		500	500
Hypothesized Difference		-0.15	
z Stat		-2.28	
P(Z<=z) one tail		0.0114	
z Critical one-tail		1.6449	
P(Z<=z) two-tail		0.0228	
z Critical two-tail		1.96	

z = -2.28, p-value = .0114. There is evidence to indicate that the second commercial is viable.

315

24.12 One-way analysis of variance

$H_0 : \mu_1 = \mu_2 = \mu_3 = \mu_4$

H_1 : At least two means differ

F = MST/MSE

ANOVA						
Source of Variation	SS	df	MS	F	P-value	F crit
Between Groups	717.3	3	239.1	1.37	0.2543	2.6507
Within Groups	34294.5	196	175.0			
Total	35011.8	199				

F = 1.37, p-value = .2543. There is no evidence to infer that the type of meal affects test scores.

24.14 Multiple regression, test of coefficients

$$t = \frac{b_i - \beta_i}{s_{b_i}}$$

The ordinary multiple regression model fit quite well. The coefficient of determination is .7042 and the p-value of the F-test is 0. However, no independent variable is linearly related to salary. This is a clear sign of multicollinearity. Stepwise regression was used with the outcome shown below.

The only independent variables that are linearly related to salary are assists in 1992-93 and goals in 1992-93. It appears that players' salaries are most strongly related to the number of goals and the number of assists in the previous season.

Results of stepwise regression					
Step 1 - Entering variable: Ast92_93					
Summary measures					
Multiple R	0.7725				
R-Square	0.5967				
Adj R-Square	0.5883				
StErr of Est	380046				
ANOVA Table					
Source	df	SS	MS	F	p-value
Explained	1	10258242603399	10258242603399	71.0232	0.0000
Unexplained	48	6932882522112	144435052544		
Regression coefficients					
	Coefficient	Std Err	t-value	p-value	
Constant	38326	82113	0.4667	0.6428	
Ast92_93	25747	3055	8.4275	0.0000	
Step 2 - Entering variable: Goal92_93					
Summary measures		Change	% Change		
Multiple R	0.8086	0.0361	%4.7		
R-Square	0.6538	0.0571	%9.6		
Adj R-Square	0.6390	0.0507	%8.6		
StErr of Est	355860	-24186	-%6.4		
ANOVA Table					
Source	df	SS	MS	F	p-value
Explained	2	11239219530119	5619609765060	44.3760	0.0000
Unexplained	47	5951905595392	126636289264		
Regression coefficients					
	Coefficient	Std Err	t-value	p-value	
Constant	65924	77524	0.8504	0.3994	
Ast92_93	14124	5062	2.7904	0.0076	
Goal92_93	18523	6655	2.7832	0.0077	

24.16 One-way analysis of variance

$$H_0 : \mu_1 = \mu_2 = \mu_3$$

$$H_1 : \text{At least two means differ}$$

$$F = MST/MSE$$

ANOVA						
Source of Variation	*SS*	*df*	*MS*	*F*	*P-value*	*F crit*
Between Groups	91.43	2	45.72	1.09	0.3441	3.1588
Within Groups	2397.50	57	42.06			
Total	2488.93	59				

F = 1.09, p-value = .3441. There is no evidence to infer that sales of cigarettes differ according to placement.

24.18 t-test of μ

$$H_0 : \mu = 480$$

$$H_1 : \mu < 480$$

$$t = \frac{\bar{x} - \mu}{s / \sqrt{n}}$$

t-Test: Mean			
			Complaints
Mean			460.53
Standard Deviation			81.10
Hypothesized Mean			480
df			29
t Stat			-1.31
P(T<=t) one-tail			0.0994
t Critical one-tail			1.6991
P(T<=t) two-tail			0.1988
t Critical two-tail			2.0452

t = -1.31, p-value = .0994. There is little evidence to conclude that the seminars should be instituted.

24.20 t-tests of μ_D

a $$H_0 : \mu_D = 40$$

$$H_1 : \mu_D > 40$$

$$t = \frac{\bar{x}_D - \mu_D}{s_D / \sqrt{n_D}}$$

t-Test: Paired Two Sample for Means		
	SAT after	*SAT before*
Mean	1235	1162
Variance	37970	28844
Observations	40	40
Pearson Correlation	0.9366	
Hypothesized Mean Difference	40	
df	39	
t Stat	2.98	
P(T<=t) one-tail	0.0024	
t Critical one-tail	1.6849	
P(T<=t) two-tail	0.0049	
t Critical two-tail	2.0227	

$t = 2.98$, p-value = .0024. There is enough evidence to conclude that the ETS claim is false.

b $\qquad H_0 : \mu_D = 110$

$\qquad H_1 : \mu_D < 110$

$$t = \frac{\bar{x}_D - \mu_D}{s_D / \sqrt{n_D}}$$

t-Test: Paired Two Sample for Means		
	SAT after	*SAT before*
Mean	1235	1162
Variance	37970	28844
Observations	40	40
Pearson Correlation	0.9366	
Hypothesized Mean Difference	110	
df	39	
t Stat	-3.39	
P(T<=t) one-tail	0.0008	
t Critical one-tail	1.6849	
P(T<=t) two-tail	0.0016	
t Critical two-tail	2.0227	

$t = -3.39$, p-value = .0008. There is enough evidence to conclude that the Kaplan claim is also false.

319

24.22 a t-test of μ

$$H_0 : \mu = 0$$

$$H_1 : \mu > 0$$

$$t = \frac{\bar{x} - \mu}{s / \sqrt{n}}$$

t-Test: Mean			
			Decrease
Mean			24.73
Standard Deviation			17.92
Hypothesized Mean			0
df			222
t Stat			20.61
P(T<=t) one-tail			0
t Critical one-tail			1.6517
P(T<=t) two-tail			0
t Critical two-tail			1.9707

t = 20.61, p-value = 0. There is overwhelming evidence to infer that there is a decreases in metabolism when children watch television.

b Wilcoxon rank sum test

H_0 : The two population locations are the same.

H_1 : The location of population 1 is to the right of the location of population 2.

$$z = \frac{T - E(T)}{\sigma_T}$$

Wilcoxon Rank Sum Test			
		Rank Sum	Observations
Obese		5750	41
Nonobese		19226	182
z Stat		3.10	
P(Z<=z) one-tail		0.001	
z Critical one-tail		1.6449	
P(Z<=z) two-tail		0.002	
z Critical two-tail		1.96	

z = 3.10, p-value = .0010. There is enough evidence to conclude that the decrease in metabolism is greater among obese children.

24.24 Two-factor analysis of variance

$$F = MS(AB)/MSE$$

$$F = MS(A)/MSE$$

$$F = MS(B)/MSE$$

ANOVA						
Source of Variation	SS	df	MS	F	P-value	F crit
Sample	427.61	2	213.81	39.97	0.0000	3.0589
Columns	20.17	1	20.17	3.77	0.0541	3.9068
Interaction	17.77	2	8.89	1.66	0.1935	3.0589
Within	770.32	144	5.35			
Total	1235.87	149				

Test for gender: F = 3.77, p-value = .0541. There is not enough evidence of a difference between men and women.

Test for fitness: F = 39.97, p-value = 0. There is overwhelming evidence of differences among the three levels of fitness.

Test for interaction: F = 1.66, p-value = .1935. There is no evidence of interaction.

24.26 Multiple regression t-tests of the coefficients

$$H_0 : \beta_i = 0$$

$$H_1 : \beta_i \neq 0$$

$$t = \frac{b_i - \beta_i}{s_{b_i}}$$

	Coefficients	Standard Error	t Stat	P-value
Intercept	1.01	1.39	0.72	0.4704
Dexterity	-0.059	0.150	-0.39	0.6953
Detail	-0.177	0.159	-1.11	0.2708
Teamwork	0.182	0.157	1.16	0.2485
Math	0.065	0.162	0.40	0.6874
ProbSolve	1.00	0.160	6.27	0.0000
Tech	1.78	0.159	11.24	0.0000

Only problem-solving skill (p-value = 0) and technical knowledge (p-value = 0) are linearly related to quality.

24.28 a Equal-variances t-test of $\mu_1 - \mu_2$

$$H_0 : (\mu_1 - \mu_2) = 0$$

$$H_1 : (\mu_1 - \mu_2) < 0$$

$$t = \frac{(\bar{x}_1 - \bar{x}_2) - (\mu_1 - \mu_2)}{\sqrt{s_p^2\left(\dfrac{1}{n_1} + \dfrac{1}{n_2}\right)}}$$

t-Test: Two-Sample Assuming Equal Variances		
	Four or more	Less
Mean	6.00	7.40
Variance	5.62	8.61
Observations	100	100
Pooled Variance	7.11	
Hypothesized Mean Difference	0	
df	198	
t Stat	-3.71	
P(T<=t) one-tail	0.0001	
t Critical one-tail	1.6526	
P(T<=t) two-tail	0.0003	
t Critical two-tail	1.9720	

t = -3.71, p-value = .0001. There is enough evidence to infer that children who wash their hands four or more times per day have less sick days due to cold and flu.

b Wilcoxon rank sum test

H_0 : The two population locations are the same.

H_1 : The location of population 1 is to the left of the location of population 2.

$$z = \frac{T - E(T)}{\sigma_T}$$

Wilcoxon Rank Sum Test			
		Rank Sum	Observations
Four or more		7584	100
Less		12516	100
z Stat		-6.03	
P(Z<=z) one-tail		0	
z Critical one-tail		1.6449	
P(Z<=z) two-tail		0	
z Critical two-tail		1.96	

z = -6.03, p-value = 0. There is enough evidence to infer that children who wash their hands four or more times per day have less sick days due to stomach illness.

24.30 Multiple regression t-tests of the coefficients

$$H_0 : \beta_i = 0$$

$$H_1 : \beta_i \neq 0$$

$$t = \frac{b_i - \beta_i}{s_{b_i}}$$

	Coefficients	Standard Error	t Stat	P-value
Intercept	-778.7	1290.2	-0.60	0.5483
P Evap	2.70	1.98	1.36	0.1772
Precip	0.30	0.31	0.98	0.3295

Neither variable appears to be related to flow.

22.32 Wilcoxon rank sum tests

H_0 : The two population locations are the same.

H_1 : The location of population 1 is to the left of the location of population 2.

$$z = \frac{T - E(T)}{\sigma_T}$$

Question 1

Wilcoxon Rank Sum Test			
		Rank Sum	Observations
No		875.5	26
Yes		8169.5	108
z Stat		-4.95	
P(Z<=z) one-tail		0	
z Critical one-tail		1.6449	
P(Z<=z) two-tail		0	
z Critical two-tail		1.96	

z = -4.95, p-value = 0. There is overwhelming evidence to infer that customers who say they will return assess quality of work higher than customers who do not plan to return.

Question 2

Wilcoxon Rank Sum Test			
		Rank Sum	Observations
No		1477	26
Yes		7568	108
z Stat		-1.56	
P(Z<=z) one-tail		0.0589	
z Critical one-tail		1.6449	
P(Z<=z) two-tail		0.1178	
z Critical two-tail		1.96	

$z = -1.56$, p-value = .0589. There is not enough evidence to infer that customers who say they will return assess fairness of price higher than customers who do not plan to return.

Question 3

Wilcoxon Rank Sum Test			
		Rank Sum	Observations
No		1656	26
Yes		7389	108
z Stat		-0.56	
P(Z<=z) one-tail		0.2888	
z Critical one-tail		1.6449	
P(Z<=z) two-tail		0.5776	
z Critical two-tail		1.96	

$z = -.56$, p-value = .2888. There is no evidence to infer that customers who say they will return assess explanation of work and guarantee higher than customers who do not plan to return.

Question 4

Wilcoxon Rank Sum Test			
		Rank Sum	Observations
No		1461	26
Yes		7584	108
z Stat		-1.65	
P(Z<=z) one-tail		0.049	
z Critical one-tail		1.6449	
P(Z<=z) two-tail		0.098	
z Critical two-tail		1.96	

z = -1.65, p-value = .0490. There is evidence to infer that customers who say they will return assess the checkout process higher than customers who do not plan to return.

24.34 Questions 1 to 4: Kruskal Wallis tests

H_0: The location of all 3 populations is the same

H_1: At least two population locations differ

$$H = \left[\frac{12}{n(n+1)} \sum \frac{T_j^2}{n_j} \right] - 3(n+1)$$

Question 1

Kruskal-Wallis Test		
Group	Rank Sum	Observations
Store 1	15555	100
Store 2	15692	100
Store 3	13903	100
H Stat		2.6349
df		2
p-value		0.2678
chi-squared Critical		5.9915

H = 2.6349, p-value = .2678. There is no evidence to conclude that there are differences in the assessment of quality of work performed among the three stores.

Question 2

Kruskal-Wallis Test		
Group	Rank Sum	Observations
Store 1	16613	100
Store 2	14648	100
Store 3	13889	100
H Stat		5.2525
df		2
p-value		0.0723
chi-squared Critical		5.9915

H = 5.2525, p-value = .0723. There is no evidence to conclude that there are differences in the assessment of fairness of price among the three stores

325

Question 3

Kruskal-Wallis Test		
Group	Rank Sum	Observations
Store 1	14996	100
Store 2	15448	100
Store 3	14706	100
H Stat		0.3716
df		2
p-value		0.8304
chi-squared Critical		5.9915

H = .3716, p-value = .8304. There is no evidence to conclude that there are differences in the assessment of explanation of work and guarantee among the three stores

Question 4

Kruskal-Wallis Test		
Group	Rank Sum	Observations
Store 1	15270	100
Store 2	15600	100
Store 3	14280	100
H Stat		1.2542
df		2
p-value		0.5341
chi-squared Critical		5.9915

H = 1.2542, p-value = .5341. There is no evidence to conclude that there are differences in the assessment of the checkout process among the three stores

Question 5 and comments: Chi-squared test of a contingency table

H_0 : The two variables are independent

H_1 : The two variables are dependent

$$\chi^2 = \sum \frac{(f_i - e_i)^2}{e_i}$$

326

Question 5

Contingency Table

Store	Return	1	2	3	TOTAL
	1	28	24	34	86
	2	72	76	66	214
	TOTAL	100	100	100	300

chi-squared Stat			2.4777
df			2
p-value			0.2897
chi-squared Critical			5.9915

$\chi^2 = 2.4777$, p-value = .2897. There is no evidence to conclude that differences exist among the three stores with respect to whether the customer will return in the future.

Comments

Contingency Table

Store	Comment	1	2	3	TOTAL
	1	34	20	34	88
	2	12	7	28	47
	3	54	73	38	165
	TOTAL	100	100	100	300

chi-squared Stat			30.9799
df			4
p-value			0
chi-squared Critical			9.4877

$\chi^2 = 30.9799$, p-value = 0. There is overwhelming evidence to conclude that differences exist among the three stores with respect to customer comments.

22.36a Chi-squared goodness-of-fit test

$H_0 : p_2 = 1/36, \ p_3 = 2/36, \ldots, \ p_{12} = 1/36$

H_1 : At least one p_i is not equal to its specified value

$$\chi^2 = \sum \frac{(f_i - e_i)^2}{e_i}$$

Total	Actual	Probability	Expected
2	37	0.028	27.78
3	59	0.056	55.56
4	77	0.083	83.33
5	120	0.111	111.11
6	134	0.139	138.89
7	161	0.167	166.67
8	144	0.139	138.89
9	117	0.111	111.11
10	67	0.083	83.33
11	52	0.056	55.56
12	32	0.028	27.78
		p-value	0.4943

p-value = .4943. There is no evidence to indicate that the dice are not fairly balanced.

b z-test of p

$H_0 : p = 1/6$

$H_1 : p < 1/6$

$$z = \frac{\hat{p} - p}{\sqrt{\dfrac{p(1-p)}{n}}}$$

z-Test: Proportion			
			2 Dice
Sample Proportion			0.161
Observations			1000
Hypothesized Proportion			0.1667
z Stat			-0.48
P(Z<=z) one-tail			0.3143
z Critical one-tail			1.2816
P(Z<=z) two-tail			0.6286
z Critical two-tail			1.6449

z = -.48, p-value = .3143. There is no evidence to infer that the dice are set up so that the probability of 7 is less than 6/36.

24.38 Question 1: Equal-variances t-test of $\mu_1 - \mu_2$

$$H_0 : (\mu_1 - \mu_2) = 0$$

$$H_1 : (\mu_1 - \mu_2) < 0$$

$$t = \frac{(\bar{x}_1 - \bar{x}_2) - (\mu_1 - \mu_2)}{\sqrt{s_p^2 \left(\dfrac{1}{n_1} + \dfrac{1}{n_2} \right)}}$$

t-Test: Two-Sample Assuming Equal Variances		
	U.S.	Canada
Mean	26.98	29.44
Variance	55.90	56.82
Observations	300	300
Pooled Variance	56.36	
Hypothesized Mean Difference	0	
df	598	
t Stat	-4.00	
P(T<=t) one-tail	0.0000	
t Critical one-tail	1.6474	
P(T<=t) two-tail	0.0001	
t Critical two-tail	1.9639	

t = -4.00, p-value = 0. There is enough evidence to indicate that recovery is faster in the United States.

Question 2: z-tests of $p_1 - p_2$ (case 1)

$$H_0 : (p_1 - p_2) = 0$$

$$H_1 : (p_1 - p_2) < 0$$

$$z = \frac{(\hat{p}_1 - \hat{p}_2)}{\sqrt{\hat{p}(1 - \hat{p}) \left(\dfrac{1}{n_1} + \dfrac{1}{n_2} \right)}}$$

z-Test: Two Proportions			
		U.S.	Canada
Sample Proportions		0.6267	0.6867
Observations		300	300
Hypothesized Difference		0	
z Stat		-1.55	
P(Z<=z) one tail		0.0609	
z Critical one-tail		1.6449	
P(Z<=z) two-tail		0.1218	
z Critical two-tail		1.96	

z = -1.55, p-value = .0609. There is not enough evidence to infer that recovery is faster in the United States.

6 months after heart attack:

z-Test: Two Proportions			.
		U.S.	Canada
Sample Proportions		0.1867	0.1733
Observations		300	300
Hypothesized Difference		0	
z Stat		0.43	
P(Z<=z) one tail		0.3354	
z Critical one-tail		1.6449	
P(Z<=z) two-tail		0.6708	
z Critical two-tail		1.96	

z = .43, p-value = 1 - .3354 = .6646. There is no evidence to infer that recovery is faster in the United States.

12 months after heart attack

z-Test: Two Proportions			
		U.S.	Canada
Sample Proportions		0.1167	0.11
Observations		300	300
Hypothesized Difference		0	
z Stat		0.26	
P(Z<=z) one tail		0.3984	
z Critical one-tail		1.6449	
P(Z<=z) two-tail		0.7968	
z Critical two-tail		1.96	

z = .26, p-value = 1 - .3984 = .6016. There is no evidence to infer that recovery is faster in the United States.

24.40 b Two-factor analysis of variance

$F = MS(AB)/MSE$

$F = MS(A)/MSE$

$F = MS(B)/MSE$

Product C

ANOVA						
Source of Variation	SS	df	MS	F	P-value	F crit
Sample	425.07	1	425.07	14.06	0.0004	4.0195
Columns	223.05	2	111.53	3.69	0.0315	3.1682
Interaction	62.48	2	31.24	1.03	0.3628	3.1682
Within	1632.93	54	30.24			
Total	2343.54	59				

Test for flow: F = 3.69, p-value = .0315. There is evidence to infer that there are differences in yield among the three flows.

Test for temperature: F = 14.06, p-value = .0004. There is evidence to infer that there are differences in yield between the two temperatures

Test for interaction: F = 1.03, p-value = .3628. There is no evidence of interaction.

Product Y

ANOVA						
Source of Variation	SS	df	MS	F	P-value	F crit
Sample	405.08	1	405.08	32.05	0.0000	4.0195
Columns	1714.94	2	857.47	67.85	0.0000	3.1682
Interaction	354.63	2	177.32	14.03	0.0000	3.1682
Within	682.48	54	12.64			
Total	3157.14	59				

Test for flow: F = 67.85, p-value = 0. There is evidence to infer that there are differences in yield among the three flows.

Test for temperature: F = 32.05, p-value = 0. There is evidence to infer that there are differences in yield between the two temperatures

Test for interaction: F = 14.03, p-value = 0. There is enough evidence to conclude that temperature and flow interact to affect product yield.

24.42 One way analysis of variance

$$H_0 : \mu_1 = \mu_2 = \mu_3$$

H_1 : At least two means differ

F = MST/MSE

ANOVA						
Source of Variation	*SS*	*df*	*MS*	*F*	*P-value*	*F crit*
Between Groups	595.6	2	297.81	34.35	0.0000	3.0648
Within Groups	1144.5	132	8.67			
Total	1740.1	134				

$F = 34.35$, p-value = 0. There is enough evidence to conclude that the type of music affects test results.

24.44 The data are observational. There may be a link between arthritis and Alzheimer's disease that explains the statistical result.

24.46 a One-way analysis of variance

$$H_0 : \mu_1 = \mu_2 = \mu_3 = \mu_4 = \mu_5 = \mu_6$$

H_1 : At least two means differ

$F = MST/MSE$

ANOVA						
Source of Variation	*SS*	*df*	*MS*	*F*	*P-value*	*F crit*
Between Groups	527465	5	105493	4.43	0.0015	2.35
Within Groups	1571667	66	23813			
Total	2099132	71				

$F = 4.43$, p-value = .0015. There is overwhelming evidence that the six groups differ.

b Two-factor analysis of variance

$F = MS(AB)/MSE$

$F = MS(A)/MSE$

$F = MS(B)/MSE$

ANOVA						
Source of Variation	SS	df	MS	F	P-value	F crit
Sample	303247	2	151623	6.37	0.0030	3.1359
Columns	190139	1	190139	7.98	0.0062	3.9863
Interaction	34080	2	17040	0.72	0.4927	3.1359
Within	1571667	66	23813			
Total	2099132	71				

Test for age: $F = 6.37$, p-value = .0030. There is enough evidence to conclude that age affects offers.

Test for gender: $F = 7.98$, p-value = .0062. There is enough evidence to conclude that gender affects offers.

Test for interaction: $F = .72$, p-value = .4927. There is no evidence of interaction.